MW00963498

LAYOUT MENU

Layout	Tools	Font
Line		Shift+F9 ▶
Paragraph		▶
Page		Alt+F9 ▶
Columns		Alt+3hift+F9 ▶
Tables		Ctrl+F9 ▶
Document		Ctrl+Shift+F9 ▶
Footnote		▶
Endnote		▶
Advance...		
Typesetting...		
Justification		▶
Margins...		Ctrl+F8
Styles...		Alt+F8

Line submenu

Tab Set...	
Spacing...	
Height...	
Numbering...	
Hyphenation...	
Center	Shift+F7
Flush Right	Alt+F7
Special Codes...	

Paragraph submenu

Indent	F7
Double Indent	Ctrl+Shift+F7
Hanging Indent	Ctrl+F7
Margin Release	Shift+Tab

Page submenu

Page Break	Ctrl+Enter
Center Page	
Headers...	
Footers...	
Numbering...	
Suppress...	
Paper Size...	
Widow/Orphan	
Block Protect	
Conditional End of Page...	

Columns submenu

Columns On
Columns Off
Define...

Tables submenu

Create...
Options...
Join
Split...
Insert...
Delete...
Cell...
Column...
Row...
Lines...
Formula...
Calculate

Document submenu

Summary...
Initial Font...
Initial Codes...
Redline Method...
Display Pitch...

Footnote submenu

Create...
Edit...
New Number...
Options...

Endnote submenu

Create...
Edit...
New Number...
Options...
Placement...

Justification submenu

√ Left	Ctrl+L
Right	Ctrl+R
Center	Ctrl+J
Full	Ctrl+F

Computer users are not all alike.
Neither are SYBEX books.

We know our customers have a variety of needs. They've told us so. And because we've listened, we've developed several distinct types of books to meet the needs of each of our customers. What are you looking for in computer help?

If you're looking for the basics, try the **ABC's** series. You'll find short, unintimidating tutorials and helpful illustrations. For a more visual approach, select **Teach Yourself**, featuring screen-by-screen illustrations of how to use your latest software purchase.

Mastering and **Understanding** titles offer you a step-by-step introduction, plus an in-depth examination of intermediate-level features, to use as you progress.

Our **Up & Running** series is designed for computer-literate consumers who want a no-nonsense overview of new programs. Just 20 basic lessons, and you're on your way.

We also publish two types of reference books. Our **Instant References** provide quick access to each of a program's commands and functions. SYBEX **Encyclopedias** and **Desktop References** provide a *comprehensive reference* and explanation of all of the commands, features and functions of the subject software.

Sometimes a subject requires a special treatment that our standard series don't provide. So you'll find we have titles like **Advanced Techniques, Handbooks, Tips & Tricks,** and others that are specifically tailored to satisfy a unique need.

We carefully select our authors for their in-depth understanding of the software they're writing about, as well as their ability to write clearly and communicate effectively. Each manuscript is thoroughly reviewed by our technical staff to ensure its complete accuracy. Our production department makes sure it's easy to use. All of this adds up to the highest quality books available, consistently appearing on best-seller charts worldwide.

You'll find SYBEX publishes a variety of books on every popular software package. Looking for computer help? Help Yourself to SYBEX.

For a complete catalog of our publications:

SYBEX Inc.
2021 Challenger Drive, Alameda, CA 94501
Tel: (510) 523-8233/(800) 227-2346 Telex: 336311
Fax: (510) 523-2373

SYBEX is committed to using natural resources wisely to preserve and improve our environment. As a leader in the computer book publishing industry, we are aware that over 40% of America's solid waste is paper. This is why we have been printing the text of books like this one on recycled paper since 1982.

This year our use of recycled paper will result in the saving of more than 15,300 trees. We will lower air pollution effluents by 54,000 pounds, save 6,300,000 gallons of water, and reduce landfill by 2,700 cubic yards.

In choosing a SYBEX book you are not only making a choice for the best in skills and information, you are also choosing to enhance the quality of life for all of us.

WORDPERFECT 5.1 FOR WINDOWS TIPS AND TRICKS

WORDPERFECT® 5.1 FOR WINDOWS™ TIPS AND TRICKS

Alan R. Neibauer

SYBEX

San Francisco • Paris • Düsseldorf • Soest

Acquisitions Editor: Dianne King
Developmental Editor: Christian Crumlish
Copy Editor: Marilyn Smith
Project Editor: Brendan Fletcher
Technical Editor: Maryann Brown
Word Processors: Ann Dunn, Susan Trybull
Book Designer: Amparo del Rio
Chapter Art: Lucie Živny
Screen Graphics: Aldo Bermudez
Typesetter: Dina F Quan
Proofreader: David Silva
Indexer: Ted Laux
Cover Designer: Ingalls + Associates
Cover Photographer: Michael Lamotte
Screen reproductions produced with Collage Plus.

Collage Plus is a trademark of Inner Media Inc.

SYBEX is a registered trademark of SYBEX Inc.

TRADEMARKS: SYBEX has attempted throughout this book to distinguish proprietary trademarks from descriptive terms by following the capitalization style used by the manufacturer.

SYBEX is not affiliated with any manufacturer.

Every effort has been made to supply complete and accurate information. However, SYBEX assumes no responsibility for its use, nor for any infringement of the intellectual property rights of third parties which would result from such use.

Library of Congress Card Number: 92-81033
ISBN: 0-89588-831-9

Manufactured in the United States of America
10 9 8 7 6 5 4 3 2 1

To Esther Neibauer, for having enough faith not to believe my fifth grade teacher

ACKNOWLEDGMENTS

ehind every author is a team of professionals whose work often goes unheralded. Those at SYBEX, whose efforts made this book a reality, deserve to be acknowledged and thanked.

My appreciation goes to Christian Crumlish, who served as developmental editor, and to copy editor Marilyn Smith. Christian helped to develop the overall concept and scope of this book. Marilyn showed me once again what an editor can do to make an author looked polished and organized.

My special thanks to Brendan Fletcher, who helped coordinate our efforts, to managing editor Barbara Gordon, and to technical reviewer Maryann Brown. Among other tasks, the technical reviewer is responsible for checking the accuracy of every step presented and for painstakingly testing each macro and merge program.

A sincere thank you to Dianne King and Dr. Rudolph S. Langer.

This book would not have been possible without Barbara Neibauer—scientist, artist, musician, chef, and Tae Kwon Do black belt. She is a talented, accomplished, and charming woman who honors me by being my wife.

CONTENTS AT A GLANCE

TABLE OF

CONTENTS

Chapter 10
CONVERTING WORDPERFECT FOR DOS MACROS   215

INTRODUCTION

Typing and printing documents is one level—the entry level—of word processing. Becoming a productive word processor is the next level. To be productive, you need to be able to produce the widest range of high-quality documents with the least amount of effort and time.

There is still another level of word processing, however, that few users achieve. That level is information processing, which involves more than the typed and printed word. An information processor uses word processing skills to automate office operations and enhance decision-making processes.

This book will show you how to reach the top level with WordPerfect for Windows. Because it is designed for the WordPerfect user who wants to go beyond word processing, this book is quite unlike any other you will find. The skills you will learn here will vastly increase your personal productivity. If you work in an office, your new-found skills will enhance your value to your employer, along with your career potential.

WHAT THIS BOOK CONTAINS

This book assumes that you already know how to use WordPerfect for Windows to create documents. It does not explain how to enter or format routine text. Instead, it begins with some information about the Windows environment, and then continues with effective techniques for sophisticated tasks.

Chapter 1 explains some fundamentals of WordPerfect in the Windows environment. It includes a discussion of WordPerfect printer drivers and page forms that will help you decide whether you want to use your Windows printer drivers or those supplied by WordPerfect.

Chapter 2 describes a frequently overlooked and underused resource: WordPerfect styles and stylesheets. You will learn how styles can provide consistent formatting even when different people prepare documents.

Chapter 3 covers formatting and printing envelopes and labels. In addition, you will learn how to use labels for special documents, including business cards, tickets, brochures, folders, greeting cards, and place cards.

Desktop publishing techniques are discussed in Chapters 4 through 6. In Chapter 4, you will learn how to add graphic rules and boxes. Chapter 5 describes how to work with graphic images. The projects covered in these chapters include brochures with both portrait- and landscape-oriented text (even if your printer cannot rotate text), page borders, and numbered raffle tickets.

Graphic characters and equations are discussed in Chapter 6. It describes how to map characters to the keyboard to create a custom graphics or foreign-language keyboard layout. In addition, you will learn how to create logos and graphic headlines, even on printers without built-in fonts.

Chapter 7 is about columns and tables. Not only will you learn how to create spreadsheets, you will also discover how to create extra-wide tables, invoices that automatically compute sales tax and totals, questionnaires, graphics, and charts.

The next three chapters are devoted to macros. Chapter 8 covers the fundamentals of macros and Button Bars, including how to record, edit, and write macros. Chapter 9 covers advanced macro programming, such as input, conditional, and repetition commands. Converting WordPerfect for DOS macros to work in WordPerfect for Windows is covered in Chapter 10. You will learn how to use the Macro Facility to convert and compile macros, and how to edit macros that do not convert properly.

Chapter 11 covers merging files to create form documents and database reports. You will also learn how to create interactive merges, so you can add information and select records as documents are created.

Chapters 12, 13, and 14 describe how to use macros and merge files to create applications. In Chapter 12, you will learn how to use macros and merge files to manage mailing lists and databases. Chapter 13 describes an advanced document-assembly application. This application is completed in Chapter 14, which explains how to automate a receivables system and organize the application with menus.

Chapter 15 covers document-management techniques for the busy office. It describes a file-management system for automatically naming and saving documents in multiple directories. In addition, you will learn how to use Windows macros to perform operations that WordPerfect macros cannot.

Appendix A is designed for legal professionals, but it can be invaluable for consultants and other professionals as well. It shows how to automate standard forms, such as pleadings and legal notices, and how to maintain a log of computer time for client billing.

Appendix B includes tips and tricks for creating academic documents. It covers using templates to standardize report and dissertation formats, including the layout of footnotes.

CONVENTIONS USED IN THIS BOOK

Although a mouse is not absolutely necessary for using WordPerfect for Windows or other Windows applications, it is highly recommended. The instructions in this book assume that you have a mouse, or are already familiar with using the keyboard to access menu bar options and work with dialog boxes.

In the book, the ➤ symbol is used to separate items that you must select, as in

Select Layout ➤ Document (Ctrl-Shift-F9) ➤ Initial Codes.

This instruction means "Select the Layout menu, then select the Document option from the menu, and then select the Initial Codes option." The key combination shown in parentheses is the shortcut key that performs the previous selections. For example, pressing Ctrl-Shift-F9 (all three keys at the same time) performs the same function as selecting Layout ➤ Document. So you can press Ctrl-Shift-F9, then select the Initial Codes option from the menu that appears.

USING THE INTERIM RELEASE

WordPerfect Corporation issued an interim release of WordPerfect for Windows in April 1992. In addition to correcting some errors in the original version, the new release includes several features that make the program easier to use and even more powerful.

Where a feature has been added, you'll see a note in the margin of this book, referring you to Appendix C if you are using a version of the program dated after April 1992. There you will find a description of the new feature that relates to the discussion in the chapter.

With one exception, the new features add to rather than change the WordPerfect interface. So even if you have the new release, the tips, tricks, and techniques explained in this book still apply. The one exception is the way WordPerfect automatically creates an envelope, described in Chapter 3. If you have the new release, see Appendix C for a description of the method used in the interim release.

A NOTE FROM THE AUTHOR

On a personal note, I hope you enjoy the advanced techniques and macros covered in this book as much as I enjoyed writing them. In addition to applying the techniques directly to your own work, I hope they stimulate you to go beyond them—to modify and expand them to solve even the most complex problem you encounter while using WordPerfect for Windows. Design your own macros and merge files to automate your work and perform information-processing tasks.

When you've completed this book, you will be able to harness the power of WordPerfect for Windows. I hope you will share your efforts with me. You can write to me in care of SYBEX.

CHAPTER 1

WordPerfect in the Windows Environment

ordPerfect's many capabilities have made it one of the most popular word processing programs. Using the tips and techniques presented in this book, you will be able to take your work with the software far beyond basic text entry and printing. But before getting into specifics of how to take advantage of WordPerfect's features, we will review the effects of the Windows environment on the program's operations.

CONTROLLING THE SCREEN DISPLAY

 If you are using a version of Word- Perfect 5.1 for Windows dated after April 1992, refer to Appendix C for more information on this feature.

WordPerfect uses the graphic environment of Windows. In most cases, the screen display in WordPerfect's Normal view will closely match the appearance of the printed document. However, some large fonts (more than 36 points) will not be displayed in a high-resolution screen font. The characters will appear rough and jagged on the screen, although they will print correctly.

Also, some lines of text will not wrap correctly on the screen. This will usually occur with fonts and font attributes that take up more space on the screen then they do when printed. WordPerfect will display the line to show how it will wrap when printed, so the text may appear past the right edge of the screen.

You can change the display from Normal mode to Draft or Print Preview mode. Draft mode is useful when you are entering or editing text, not formatting it. Print Preview mode shows exactly how the page will appear when printed. Switch to this mode when you want to check the layout of a document or to ensure that it will print correctly before issuing a Print command.

If you are not satisfied with the appearance of the screen display, you can change it to some extent. WordPerfect provides options for changing screen colors and removing or adding items to the display.

WORKING IN DRAFT MODE

If you have a slower computer, you may notice some delay when scrolling or editing long documents, particularly those with several fonts, sizes, and other graphic elements. When the delay is distracting, you can turn on Draft mode by selecting View ➤ Draft Mode.

WordPerfect works faster in Draft mode than it does in other display modes. In this mode, all characters appear the same on the screen, no matter which fonts or sizes have been selected. The mode affects only the screen display; printed characters will be formatted in the selected fonts and sizes. To turn off Draft mode, select it again from the View menu.

PREVIEWING DOCUMENTS

To display a detailed facsimile of the printed document, select File ➤ Print Preview (Shift-F5). The display will change to a graphic representation of the printed document, including character formats (such as underlines and italics), graphic images, and special characters. The resolution of your preview image will depend on your computer system.

The Button Bar along the left side of the Print Preview mode screen contains buttons for working with the preview image. You can also use the options on the View menu to magnify the preview image:

◆ **100:** Displays the image in the actual printed size.

◆ **200:** Displays the image in twice the printed size.

◆ **Zoom In:** Magnifies the displayed page. Each time it is selected, the view is enlarged so a smaller portion can be displayed at one time.

◆ **Zoom Out:** Reduces the size of the display. Each time it is selected, the view is reduced to show a larger portion of the page. You can continue to zoom out until the full page is displayed.

◆ **Zoom Area:** Allows you to select an area to be magnified.

◆ **Zoom to Full Width:** Enlarges the display so the image fills the width of the screen.

◆ **Reset:** Displays the document in the same view as when you entered Print Preview mode.

◆ **Button Bar:** Turns the Button Bar on and off.

◆ **Button Bar Setup:** Allows you to change the Button Bar's contents or display options.

Use the options in the Page menu to control the display of pages in Print Preview mode:

◆ **Full Page:** Displays the entire page (the default setting).

◆ **Facing Pages:** Displays pages that face each other (for documents that will be printed on both sides of the page).

◆ **Go to Page:** Allows you to select a page to display.

◆ **Previous Page:** Displays the previous page in the document.

◆ **Next Page**: Displays the next page in the document.

CUSTOMIZING THE SCREEN DISPLAY

If you are using a version of Word-Perfect 5.1 for Windows dated after April 1992, refer to Appendix C for more information on this feature.

You might want to change certain display settings to customize the appearance of a document window. Select File ➤ Preferences ➤ Display to see which settings can be adjusted.

In the Display Settings dialog box, shown in Figure 1.1, you can set the colors used for Draft and Reveal Codes modes, choose which elements appear on the screen, turn on and off the vertical and horizontal scroll bars, and set the units of measurement displayed by the status-bar indicators.

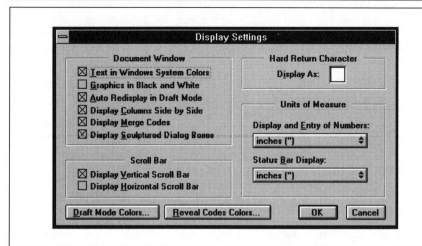

FIGURE 1.1:

Display Settings dialog box

SETTING UP FOR PRINTING

The printing management features of Windows can affect your production of WordPerfect documents. You can use either the Windows or WordPerfect printer drivers.

The Windows drivers are those that you selected when you installed Windows on your system. Windows drivers can take advantage of any installed scalable font packages, such as Adobe Type Manager or Intellifont for Windows. The printer drivers supplied with WordPerfect for Windows provide greater layout flexibility than the Windows drivers, but they do not take advantage of your Windows setup.

When you installed WordPerfect, you were given the opportunity to install WordPerfect drivers. Even if you have already customized your Windows environment to work with your printer, you should consider installing a WordPerfect driver as well. Then you will be able to switch between Windows and WordPerfect drivers to take advantage of the best features of both.

Before printing for the first time, you should make sure that the correct printer is selected. Select File ➤ Select Printer. In the Printers dialog box, select the WordPerfect or Windows button to display a list of available printer drivers. If you are using a WordPerfect printer driver, highlight the name of the printer that is connected to your system, and then select Info. If WordPerfect has any information about the driver for your printer, it will appear in the dialog box. Read it and then select Close. Finally, choose the Select command button to select the printer and return to the document window.

ADDING NEW PRINTER DRIVERS

When you want to use a new printer for your documents, you must add its driver to those available to WordPerfect. To add the printer to a Windows printer driver, use the Windows Control Panel (see the *Microsoft Windows User Manual* for details).

If you selected a WordPerfect printer driver when you installed Word-Perfect for Windows, you have a driver file with an .ALL extension in the WPC directory of your hard disk. This file contains a set of drivers for similar printers. For example, the file WPHP1.ALL contains the drivers for Hewlett-Packard and compatible laser printers. You can select any printer whose driver is in the .ALL file directly from within WordPerfect. If the driver is not in the file, you must run the WordPerfect Install program and select the printer to add its .ALL file to the disk.

Follow these steps to add a new printer whose driver is in the .ALL file on disk:

1. Display the Select Printer dialog box by selecting File ➤ Select Printer.

2. Make sure the WordPerfect button is selected and choose Add to display the Add Printer dialog box, as shown in Figure 1.2.

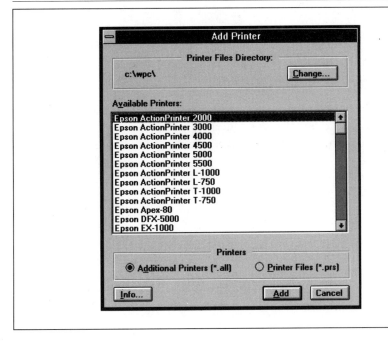

3. Highlight your printer and select Add. The printer will be added to the list in the Select Printer dialog box.

4. If necessary, select Setup and configure the driver.

5. Highlight the printer and choose the Select button.

ADDING A PRINTER DRIVER CUSTOMIZED FOR WORDPERFECT FOR DOS

If you customized a WordPerfect 5.1 for DOS printer driver to use down-loadable fonts or other features, you can probably use that driver with Word-Perfect for Windows. You will not be able to use the following drivers:

◆ Drivers customized with font-scaling programs that require you to start the DOS version with a special command (such as Glyphix and Fonts on the Fly)

◆ Some WordPerfect 5.1 printer drivers supplied by manufacturers other than WordPerfect for use with printer emulators and other special hardware or software

To add a driver from WordPerfect 5.1, select Change in the Add Printer dialog box (see steps 1 and 2 in the previous section). In the dialog box that appears, enter the path where the WordPerfect printer drivers are located (such as C:\WP51).

USING WORDPERFECT PRINTER DRIVER FEATURES FOR THE LASERJET III

The WordPerfect printer driver for the LaserJet III printer allows you to control the density of printed text (the dot patterns) by the color selected for the text. The colors and corresponding density percentages are as follows:

Blue	90%
Brown	70%
Red	40%
Green	30%
Gray	20%

Yellow   10%

Orange   2%

For example, if you format text as red, it will print in a 40-percent density.

Another special feature of the LaserJet III driver is that you can print in reverse (with white characters on a black background). To set up the driver for reverse printing, follow these steps:

1. From the DOS prompt, change to the WPC directory.

2. Type **PTR HPLASIII.PRS** and press ↵.

3. Press ↵ when the program window opens.

4. Select Attribute Methods and press ↵.

5. Select Strikeout and press ↵.

6. Select Auto Strikeout on Same Pass, and then press the asterisk key (*).

7. Press Alt-F7, then Y, then ↵ to save the file.

8. Press Y to exit the PTR program.

Then, whenever you want to print in reverse, select the Strikeout attribute in the WordPerfect Font menu or dialog box.

SOLVING WORDPERFECT PRINTER DRIVER PROBLEMS

In most cases, the WordPerfect printer driver will automatically be configured properly for your hardware, and you will be able print your documents without difficulty. If you do have a printing problem, first make sure the correct printer driver is selected.

When the printer driver selection is correct but a document still does not print, check the printer port assignment within WordPerfect. For example, WordPerfect will assume a LaserJet printer is connected to the parallel printer port. If your printer is connected to the serial port, you must change the printer driver from within WordPerfect.

To see which port your printer is assigned to and change it if necessary, select File ➤ Select Printer ➤ Setup. The Port box shows the currently selected port for the printer. For example, the Printer Setup dialog box shown in

Figure 1.3 indicates a LaserJet III printer is connected to the LPT 1 port. If the port shown is incorrect, scroll through the Port box until the correct one is displayed. Press ⏎ twice to return to the document window.

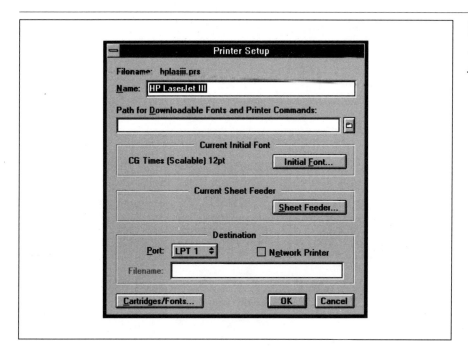

FIGURE 1.3:

Printer Setup dialog box for LaserJet III

SETTING PAGE SIZE AND ORIENTATION

The method you use to change the paper size and orientation depends on whether you are using a Windows or WordPerfect printer driver. With a Windows driver, you modify the page size through the Select Printer function. If you are using a WordPerfect printer driver, you can select a page size through the Layout Page function, which provides greater flexibility.

CHOOSING ANOTHER PAPER SIZE

To change the page size when you are using a Windows printer driver, select File ➤ Select Printer ➤ Setup. Your Setup dialog box may contain a drop-down list box of paper sizes, as in Figure 1.4, or separate list boxes for the page width and height. You can select any of the sizes listed in the dialog box. To set the page orientation, select the Portrait or Landscape button. Select

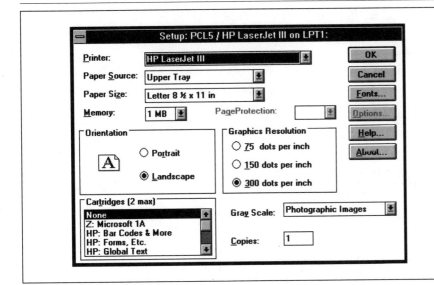

FIGURE 1.4:

Setup dialog box for LaserJet III with Windows printer driver

OK to return to the Select Printer dialog box, and then choose the Select button to return to WordPerfect.

To change the page size when you are using a WordPerfect printer driver, select Layout ➤ Page (Alt-F9) ➤ Paper Size. The Paper Size dialog box shows paper types that have been established for your printer, as in the example in Figure 1.5. You may see more than one form that has the same Paper Type name, but the size of each form is different. Highlight the page size you want to use and choose the Select button.

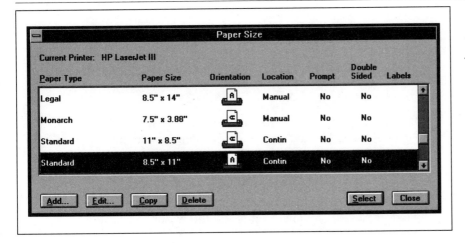

FIGURE 1.5:

Paper Size dialog box for WordPerfect printer drivers

ADDING A PAPER SIZE

If you are using a WordPerfect printer driver and the page size you want to use is not listed in the Page Size dialog box, you can create a form for a new page size and add it to your printer driver. Select Add in the Paper Size dialog box (Layout ➤ Page ➤ Paper Size ➤ Add) to display the dialog box shown in Figure 1.6.

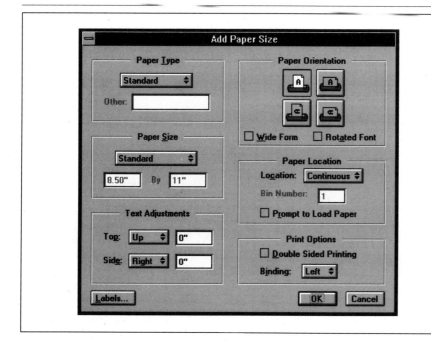

FIGURE 1.6:

Add Paper Size dialog box

Define the paper size by setting the options in the dialog box:

◆ **Paper Type:** Select a type name from the drop-down list. To give the paper type another name, select Other and enter the name in the Other text box.

◆ **Paper Size:** Select a size from the drop-down list. To set up another size, select Other and enter the measurements, from the printer's point of view. For example, a 5-by-7 envelope feeds into a dot-matrix or daisy-wheel printer lengthwise, so the 7-inch dimension is the width (7 by 5). An envelope feeds through a laser printer with the narrow dimension in toward the printer, but with landscape orientation the 7-inch dimension is still the width (7 by 5).

◆ **Paper Orientation:** Select one of the four icons to set the orientation. The top two icons choose either narrow or wide-form portrait. The bottom icons select narrow or wide-form landscape. Selecting the Wide Form check box is the same as selecting a wide-form icon; selecting Rotated Text is the same as selecting a landscape icon.

◆ **Paper Location:** Select from three locations. Choose Continuous for a laser or ink-jet printer with a paper cassette (or another printer with continuous paper). Select Manual if you are feeding individual sheets of paper or envelopes. When you are using a printer with multiple paper sources, choose Bin and enter the bin number. If you want WordPerfect to pause before printing to let you insert paper into your printer, select Prompt to Load Paper.

◆ **Print Options:** If your printer has duplex-printing capabilities, you can set double-sided printing. Select Double Sided Printing, then the type of binding. Use Left if the pages will be bound along the left side, as in a book. Use Top when the pages will be bound along the top, as in a calendar.

◆ **Text Adjustments:** Change these settings if the first line of the page does not print at the top and left margins. (The default margins place the first line of text 1 inch from the top and 1 inch from the left side.) Select Up or Down from the Top list box to move the first line toward the top or bottom of the page. Select Right or Left from the Side list box to move the text toward the right or left margin. Enter the distances to move the line, using positive measurements regardless of the direction. Note that these text adjustments will not be reflected in Print Preview mode.

◆ **Labels:** Select this button to see a dialog box for creating and printing labels. Label forms and their special uses are discussed in Chapter 3.

The size and orientation settings work together. When the measurement in the Paper Size text box on the left is larger than the size in the right box and portrait orientation is set, WordPerfect automatically selects the wide-form option. Similarly, if you create a form that is 3 by 5, then select wide-form portrait or narrow landscape orientation, the size boxes change to 5 by 3.

You cannot have two paper-size definitions with the same type and size, even if they have different orientations or locations. If you want to create a definition that is the same except for one item, give it a new type name.

Do not use the Text Adjustments options in the Add Paper Size dialog box to change the top or left margins, or you will lose some of the text on the page. For example, if you set the Top option down 2 inches and print a full page on a laser printer, the first line of text will begin 3 inches from the top of the page (the standard 1 inch plus the 2-inch adjustment), but Word-Perfect will still transmit the entire page to the printer. The printer will print as much of the text as it can and discard the rest.

If you need to adjust the left margin for duplex printing, select File ➤ Print ➤ Binding Offset. This adds extra space on the right side of odd-numbered pages and on the left side of even-numbered pages.

After adding a paper size, select OK to return to the Paper Size dialog box. Select the form you want to use, and then choose the Select button. Before printing the document, select File ➤ Print Preview (Shift-F5) to see if the shape of the page matches the paper in the printer.

DEFINING FILE LOCATIONS

WordPerfect for Windows is stored in the WPWIN and WPC directories. The WPC directory contains printer, spelling, thesaurus, and hyphenation files. All other parts of WordPerfect are in WPWIN, which has two subdirectories: GRAPHICS and MACROS.

WordPerfect is set to find certain files in specific directories, such as macros and keyboard definitions in \WPWIN\MACROS, and WPG graphic files in \WPWIN\GRAPHICS. Also by default, WordPerfect will save your document files in the WPWIN directory. If you want to save a document in some other location, enter the complete path when saving the file or select a directory in the Save As dialog box.

You can change the default directories by selecting File ➤ Preferences ➤ Location of Files to display the dialog box shown in Figure 1.7. Enter the directories you want to use in the appropriate text box. Alternatively, you can click on the button to the right of the text box (or press Alt-↓) and choose directories from the Select Directory dialog box.

Your changes will take effect as soon as you close the dialog box. Any changes to the Styles Directory or Filename options do not affect documents that have already been assigned a stylesheet.

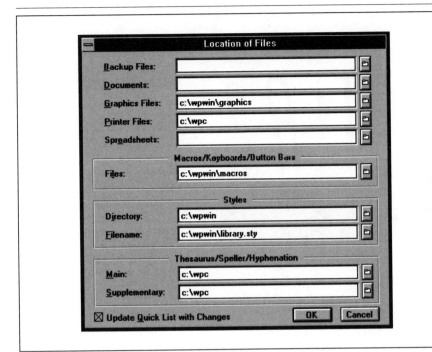

*Location of Files
dialog box*

CHAPTER 2

Defining and using custom styles
Solving printing problems with styles
Creating document templates

Instant Formatting with Styles

WordPerfect *style* is a collection of formatting codes and, optionally, text. You can create and save any number of styles in a special file called a *stylesheet*.

Styles provide consistency and flexibility. You can standardize formats for similar documents, such as memos, or repeated elements, such as headings. After formatting a document with styles, you can easily change the format by applying different styles. This chapter describes how styles can streamline your work and solve some common word processing problems.

USING WORDPERFECT 5.1 STYLESHEETS

WordPerfect for Windows can use stylesheets created with WordPerfect 5.1 for DOS. In fact, the same sample stylesheet is provided in both versions. If you created styles using WordPerfect 5.1 for DOS, copy them to the WPWIN directory of your hard disk so they will be easily accessible from WordPerfect for Windows.

WordPerfect for Windows will recognize most but not all of the format codes from the DOS version. For example, it does not recognize the border option code. When there is no equivalent code in the Windows version, it will appear in the style as *[unknown]*.

WordPerfect for DOS styles that contain graphic images may not display the image when they are applied in the Windows version. WordPerfect automatically uses the Graphic on Disk option when you include a graphic image in a style. If you did not copy the graphic file to the WPWIN\GRAPHICS subdirectory, WordPerfect for Windows will not be able to locate and print the graphic image.

Note that in the Windows version you will see only open and paired styles in the Styles dialog box displayed from the Layout menu. You access outline styles through the Tools menu.

STYLES AND FILE SIZE

You work with styles by selecting Styles from the Layout menu to access the Styles dialog box. After you display this dialog box, all the styles listed (including any that you create) are automatically stored as part of the document. Using the default stylesheet, this adds about 6000 bytes to the size of the document's file. This overhead is added when you open the Styles dialog box, even if you don't actually use any of the styles.

Deleting the four default styles from the stylesheet won't save much disk space. WordPerfect will still add about 5950 bytes of overhead to the file. If you are not using styles and want the smallest possible file size, *do not* select Styles from the Layout menu.

CREATING CUSTOM STYLES

The Styles dialog box, shown in Figure 2.1, contains five options:

◆ **Create:** Adds a style to the stylesheet.

◆ **Edit:** Changes the codes or text in an existing style.

◆ **Delete:** Deletes a style from the stylesheet.

◆ **Retrieve:** Opens a stylesheet, making its styles available to your document.

◆ **Save As:** Saves the current styles in a stylesheet.

 If you are using a version of Word-Perfect 5.1 for Windows dated after April 1992, refer to Appendix C for more information on this feature.

The four styles listed in the dialog box have been provided by WordPerfect for use with its workbook lessons. They are part of the LIBRARY.STY file, which is the default style library that WordPerfect uses for every new document.

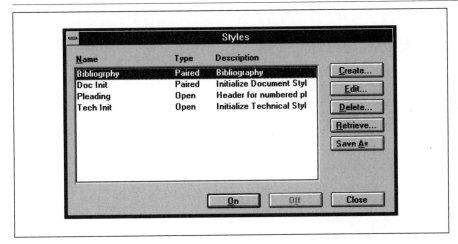

Styles dialog box

Styles that you create are automatically saved with the document. Changes you make to the styles in the dialog box are not automatically saved in the stylesheet file on the disk. If you want to use your new or edited styles with another document, you must select to save the stylesheet itself. This allows you to create styles for a specific document without affecting the default style library. It also means that a document's styles will be available even if you delete the stylesheet from the disk.

REMOVING STYLES

We will begin working with styles by creating a style to automatically print your letterhead and two heading styles. We will change the LIBRARY.STY stylesheet by removing the default styles so it contains only the three new ones, which will be available for every new document. But before deleting the default styles, we will save them in a different file so you can still use them.

1. Start WordPerfect and select Layout ➤ Styles (Alt-F8).

2. In the Styles dialog box, select Save As to display the dialog box shown in Figure 2.2.

3. Type **STANDARD.STY**, and then select Save.

4. The Bibliography style is already highlighted. Select Delete to remove it.

The dialog box that appears contains three options. Leave Format Codes deletes the style but leaves any format codes inserted by the styles in the document. Delete Format Codes removes the style and any format codes it inserted

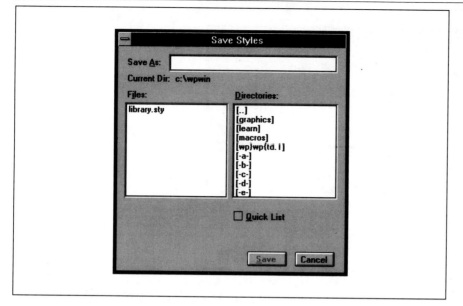

FIGURE 2.2:

Save Styles dialog box

in the document. Delete Definition Only deletes the definition of the style but leaves the style codes and name in the document. Since we haven't used the styles in a document, it doesn't matter which option you select.

5. Select OK.

6. In the same manner, delete the rest of the styles listed.

DEFINING A LETTERHEAD STYLE

The first style we will create will print your letterhead and the date in one font, and then change to another font for the remainder of the letter.

1. In the Styles dialog box, select Create to create a style. You will see the Style Properties dialog box shown in Figure 2.3.

2. In the Name text box, type **Letter**. The style name can be up to 20 characters. It is used to retrieve the styles from the stylesheet. Use a name that identifies the purpose of the style, such as Legal for legal-sized paper.

3. In the Description text box, type **Inside address and date**. The description can be up to 53 characters. It is used to explain the purpose and use of the style.

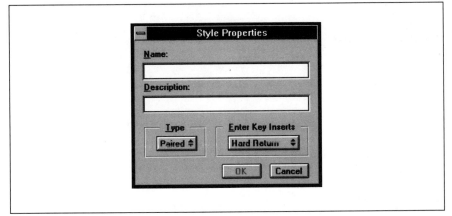

FIGURE 2.3:
*Style Properties
dialog box*

4. Pull down the Type list box and select Open. Open styles are used for the entire document. The Enter Key Inserts option dims because it pertains to paired styles.

5. Select OK, and the Style Editor window will appear. It contains an Edit pane and a Reveal Codes pane, as shown in Figure 2.4.

As you select the codes of the style, they will appear in the Reveal Codes pane. You can use the Properties command button to return to the Style Properties dialog box and change any of the settings.

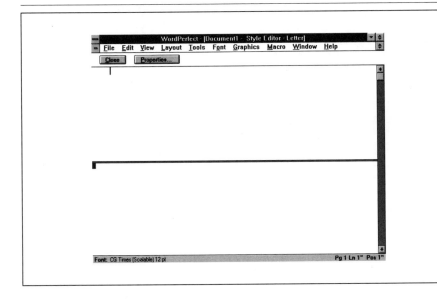

FIGURE 2.4:
*Style Editor window
for adding style codes
and text*

To ensure that the correct page size for standard-size letterhead paper is used, the style will begin with the codes to select 8½-by-11-inch paper. These instructions assume you are using a WordPerfect printer driver. For more information about printer drivers, see Chapter 1.

6. Select Layout ➤ Page (Alt-F9) ➤ Paper Size.

7. Select the standard 8½ × 11 (portrait) form.

8. Choose the Select button. The [Paper Sz/Typ;8.5" × 11",Standard] code will appear on the screen.

9. Use the Font menu to select a font and size for the address and date.

10. Press Ctrl-J to center the insertion point, type your name, and press ↵.

11. Type your street address and press ↵.

12. Type your city, state, and zip code.

13. Press ↵ twice to double-space after the address.

14. Select Tools ➤ Date ➤ Code (Ctrl-Shift-F5) to insert the date code into the style.

15. Press ↵ twice, and then press Ctrl-L to return to left alignment.

16. Use the Font menu to select the font and size you want to use for the remainder of the letter. Figure 2.5 shows the codes for this style.

17. Select Close to return to the Styles dialog box (do not close the dialog box).

CREATING HEADING STYLES

Reports or other long documents may contain several levels of headings, and you can create a style for each one. We will define a major subject heading style, in an extra large, bold font, and a subtopic heading style, in a large font.

For these styles, we will use the default paired type, which includes codes to turn the style on and off. This style type is for formats that will not be used for an entire document, much like the [BOLD] and [bold] codes to turn on and off boldface.

1. In the Styles dialog box, select Create.

2. Type **Heading 1** as the style name.

3. Type **Heading for main topics** as the style description.

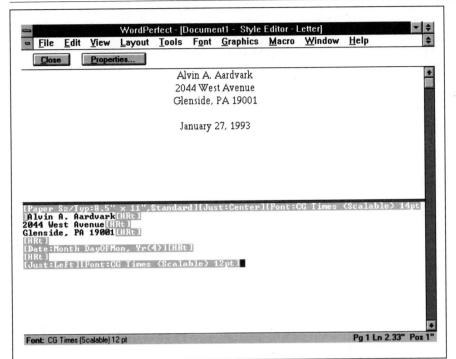

Because we are using the default paired type, the Enter Key Inserts options are available. You can select Hard Return to have the ↵ key perform a carriage return and line feed as normal, Style Off to have the ↵ key turn the style off, or Off/On to have the ↵ key turn the style off then on again. For our heading styles, we want to use the ↵ key to turn off the style.

4. In the Enter Key Inserts list box, select Style Off, and then select OK. The Style Editor will appear with a comment box displayed in the Editing pane and a comment code in the Reveal Codes pane. The codes that turn the function on are entered on the left side of the comment; the codes that turn it off go on the right side.

5. Select Font ➤ Bold (Ctrl-B).

6. Select Font ➤ Size (Ctrl-S) ➤ Extra Large.

7. Press the → key to move the insertion point after the comment.

8. Press Ctrl-N for normal text. This inserts the end bold and end large codes, [Large Off] [Bold Off].

9. Select Close to return to the Styles dialog box.

10. To begin defining the second heading style, select Create.

11. Type **Heading 2** as the style name.

12. Type **Subhead** as the style description.

13. In the Enter Key Inserts list box, select Style Off, and then select OK.

14. Select Font ➤ Size (Ctrl-S) ➤ Large.

15. Press the → key to move the insertion point after the comment.

16. Press Ctrl-N for normal text.

17. Select Close to return to the Styles dialog box.

SAVING STYLES

When you save your document, your styles will be saved along with it. But in order to use the styles with another document, you must save them onto the disk in a separate style file. We will save our styles in the LIBRARY.STY file.

1. In the Styles dialog box, select Save As.

2. Select LIBRARY.STY in the list box, and then select Save.

3. Select Yes to replace the file.

4. Select Close to exit the Styles dialog box and return to the document window.

5. Select File ➤ Close (Ctrl-F4), then No to clear the document window.

USING CUSTOM STYLES

When you are working with a new document, pulling down the Styles box on the ruler adds the stylesheet to the document.

We will use our letterhead and heading styles to create a sample will.

1. If the ruler is not displayed, select View ➤ Ruler (Alt-Shift-F3).

2. Pull down the Styles box on the ruler. The names of your styles (and any others in the default style file) will be listed, as shown in Figure 2.6.

3. Drag the pointer to highlight the Letter style and release the mouse button.

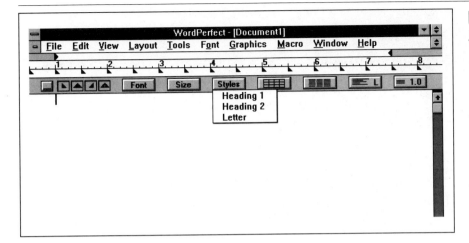

4. Press Ctrl-Home to refresh the screen. The document will appear, with your address centered at the top.

Because this is an open style, you don't have to turn it off after using it. If you revealed codes, you would see [Open Style:LETTER] in the lower pane.

5. Select the style Heading 1 from the ruler's Style box.

6. Type the main heading: **Last Will and Testament**.

7. Press ↵ to turn off the style. The insertion point will not go to the next line.

8. Press ↵ again. Now that the style is off, the insertion point will move down.

9. Type the following sentence, and then press ↵ twice.

   Being of sound mind and body, I hereby make this my Last Will and Testament and revoke any and all prior Wills and/or Codicils.

10. To insert the second-level heading, select Heading 2 from the Styles box.

11. Type the heading **Bequeaths**.

12. Press ↵ twice: once to turn off the style and another time to insert a carriage return.

13. Type the following sentence, and then press ↵ twice.

    I give and bequeath my estate as specified below.

14. Select Heading 2 from the Styles box, and then type **To My Cat**.

15. Press ↵ twice, and then type the following sentences.

> **For her years of love and loyalty, I give and bequeath my cat, Lovejoy, my entire estate with the exception of the following bequest.**

16. Press ↵ twice, select Heading 2, and type **To My Wife**.

17. Press ↵ twice and type the following sentence.

> **For her years of love and loyalty, I give and bequeath my wife, Gertrude, $500.**

EDITING STYLES

All the codes and text in a style are inserted into the document as a group. You cannot delete or edit individual elements of the group from within the document. If you delete the style-on or style-off code, all the elements within the style will be deleted. To modify the parts of a style, you must edit the style through the Styles dialog box.

We will change the Heading 2 style to an italic, extra-large font and see how it affects our document.

1. Select Layout ➤ Styles (Alt-F8).

2. Highlight the style named Heading 2, and then select Edit.

3. Select Font ➤ Italic (Ctrl-I).

4. Select Font ➤ Size (Ctrl-S) ➤ Extra Large.

5. Press End to move the insertion point to the right of the comment, and then press Ctrl-N.

6. Delete the Large Off code.

7. Select Close to return to the Styles dialog box, then Close again to return to the document window. Notice that each heading in the Heading 2 style has automatically changed to the new format.

8. Select File ➤ Exit (Alt-F4), then No to exit WordPerfect.

If you saved the document, the edited styles would be saved along with it. If you want to also save the changes to be used for other documents, you must save the stylesheet again by choosing Save As in the Styles dialog box.

To change the style name, description, type, or the function of the ↵ key, select the Properties command button in the Styles dialog box. If you change the name of a style in the Properties box, you will see the message

Rename styles in document?

Select Yes to rename each instance of the style in the document.

RETRIEVING STYLES

When you open an existing document, its styles will be immediately available. To access styles other than those saved with the document, or to use a stylesheet other than LIBRARY.STY with a new document, you must retrieve the stylesheet from the disk.

To use other styles, select Retrieve from the Styles dialog box, select the stylesheet from the list box, and then choose Retrieve. WordPerfect will merge the styles in the retrieved stylesheet with those already in the dialog box. For example, if you open a document that contains four styles, then retrieve a stylesheet with five custom styles, nine styles will be listed in the Styles dialog box.

If you try to retrieve styles that have the same names as ones already listed in the dialog box, you will be asked if you want to replace the existing styles. Select No to bring in only the styles without matching names, or select Yes to replace the existing ones with those from the disk.

CHANGING THE DEFAULT STYLESHEET

Store the styles that you apply often in the LIBRARY.STY file, which contains the default style library. You can create and save other stylesheets in files with the .STY extension and retrieve a specific library when you want to use the styles it contains. But suppose that you have created a number of stylesheets and you are about to write a series of documents that use styles in a file other than LIBRARY.STY. Rather than manually retrieving the stylesheet with each new document, you can use it as the default instead of LIBRARY.STY.

To change the default stylesheet, select File ➤ Preferences ➤ Location of Files. In the Directory box, type the name of the directory that contains the stylesheet. In the Filename box, type the stylesheet name, including the .STY extension. If you prefer, you can type the complete file path without making an entry in the Directory box.

After you have typed the documents using the new default stylesheet, you can reinstate LIBRARY.STY. In the Location of Files dialog box, enter C:\WPWIN in the Directory box and LIBRARY.STY in the Filename box.

If WordPerfect cannot find the stylesheet when you pull down the Styles box or select Styles from the Layout menu, it will display the message

File not found C:\WPWIN\LIBRARY.STY

USING STYLES TO SOLVE COMMON WORD PROCESSING PROBLEMS

Stylesheets and the style library can be powerful editing and formatting tools. They also provide a means of solving some common word processing problems. You can use styles to adjust fonts for different printers, print on paper in different printer bins, and print characters in a precise position.

SUBSTITUTING FONTS FOR MULTIPLE PRINTERS

Suppose that you want to print a draft copy of documents designed for a laser printer on your dot-matrix printer at home. When you select the new printer, WordPerfect will automatically adjust the document to use the default dot-matrix font for all text formatted with the laser printer's default font.

For example, text formatted for a LaserJet printer's Courier font will print in Pica on an Epson FX-286. For other fonts, WordPerfect will try to make the best adjustment, such as substituting Pica Condensed for Line Printer. However, these substitutions may not be appropriate for your documents.

To solve this problem, you can assign elements in the document that have font changes to styles. Include a style called Body Text if you do not want WordPerfect to substitute the default font for the regular text.

With the laser printer selected, create a stylesheet called Laser that contains open styles for each element, such as the following:

STYLE NAME	LASER PRINTER FONT
Body Text	10-point CG Times
Heading 1	18-point CG Times Bold
Heading 2	14-point CG Times
Quotation	8-point Univers

With the dot-matrix printer selected, create a second stylesheet called Matrix with open styles that have the same names as in the Laser stylesheet but with appropriate fonts and paragraph formats:

STYLE NAME	DOT-MATRIX FONT
Body Text	Elite
Heading 1	Double-width Elite
Heading 2	Italic Elite
Quotation	Condensed Elite

Use the styles to format all the text. Before starting the document, select the style Body Text. When you want to type a heading or quotation, select the appropriate style.

To print the document with either printer, make sure the correct printer is the selected one, and then retrieve the Laser stylesheet for the laser printer or the Matrix stylesheet for the dot-matrix printer. The appropriate fonts will be substituted automatically.

You can use this same technique to control font substitutions when changing to any printer. Just create a stylesheet for each printer you plan to use. If you use more than one printer, you should always create styles for font changes.

USING MULTIBIN PAPER SOURCES

Suppose that you have a laser printer and you want to print a series of documents using letterhead paper in bin 1 and plain paper in bin 2. You can accomplish this by creating two page-size forms using standard 8½-by-11-inch paper.

Add a new paper size to create a form for the letterhead paper. In the Add Paper Size dialog box (Layout ➤ Page ➤ Paper Size ➤ Add), select Other for Paper Type and enter Letterhead as the type name. For Location, select Bin (the first bin is the default).

Add another paper size to create a form for the plain paper. Select Other for Paper Type and enter Plain as the type name. Select Bin for Location and enter 2 in the Bin Number text box.

Then create the open Letterhead style with the following commands:

◆ Select Layout ➤ Margins (Ctrl-F8), and then set the top margin to position the first line of text below the preprinted letterhead.

◆ Select Layout ➤ Page (Alt-F9) ➤ Paper Size.

◆ Select the Letterhead page-size form, then choose the Select button.

Create the Plain style with the following commands:

◆ Press Ctrl-⏎ to enter a page break.

◆ Select Layout ➤ Page (Alt-F9) ➤ Paper Size.

◆ Select the Plain paper size, then choose the Select button.

◆ Select Layout ➤ Margins (Ctrl-F8) and set the top margin to 1 inch.

Save the stylesheet. When you want to use different printer bins, select the Letterhead style. It will change the margins and choose bin 1. Type the text of the first page. At the end of the page, select the Plain style. It will insert the page break, change the margin to 1 inch, and select bin 2.

REPEATING COMPLEX FORMATTING

You might use advance up and advance down codes to precisely place graphic characters in relation to the text. For example, you may include a mathematical symbol to represent pi, or a trademark symbol next to a product name. The amount of the advance depends on the size of the font being used.

Instead of entering the advance codes and the character itself each time you change font, you can use styles. For each font, create a style that includes the appropriate up and down advance codes as well as the graphic character. This will require some trial-and-error testing with each font, but after you determine the correct advance amounts, you can change fonts and still have the characters appear in the proper locations.

FORMATTING WITH DOCUMENT TEMPLATES

As an alternative to creating stylesheets to format a document, you can define initial codes for a file. These codes will automatically apply to the document; you do not have to apply them from a stylesheet.

Unlike styles, initial codes can contain only formatting instructions, such as line, page, and document formats and an initial font. They cannot contain any text. However, you can add text to a document that has initial formatting codes to create a template. A template is a formatted file that you can use to standardize similar documents.

CREATING TEMPLATES

A typical problem in business offices is that the format of similar documents varies depending on when and who produces them. To ensure consistency, you can create a template for each standard format or document.

Creating a template is a three-step process:

◆ Use the Document item on the Layout menu to enter initial format codes that will apply to every document that uses the template.

◆ Define any styles that you will need to provide consistent formatting within the template.

◆ Add the text that you want to print with each document that uses the template.

We will use this method to create a sample template for a memo. Start Word-Perfect, or open a new document if you are already using the program, and then follow these steps:

1. Select Layout ➤ Document (Ctrl-Shift-F9) ➤ Initial Font.

2. Select Courier or another font you want to use for the body of the memo, and then choose OK.

3. Select Layout ➤ Document (Ctrl-Shift-F9) ➤ Initial Codes. You will see the default [Just: Left] code.

4. Select Layout ➤ Page (Alt-F9) ➤ Numbering.

5. Pull down the Position list box, choose Bottom Center, and then select OK.

6. Select Layout ➤ Margins (Ctrl-F8).

7. Set all four margins to **.75**, select OK, and then select Close.

The text of the memo will appear using the template's initial font and for-matted with the margins set in the initial codes, in WordPerfect's default left justification and single spacing. Now we will continue and create headings and citation (for legal references or other citations) styles for the memo template.

8. Select Layout ➤ Styles (Alt-F8) ➤ Create.

9. Type **Headings** as the style name.

10. Choose Style Off from the Enter Key Inserts list, and then select OK.

11. Select Font ➤ Bold (Ctrl-B).

12. Select Font ➤ Font (F9) and choose one of the fonts available in various sizes, such as Times.

13. Select OK to close the Font dialog box, and then select Close to save the style.

14. Select Create and type **Citation**.

15. Select the Open type, and then choose OK.

16. Select Layout ➤ Margins (Ctrl-F8).

17. Set the left and right margins to **1.5**, and then select OK.

18. Select Font ➤ Italic (Ctrl-I).

19. Select Layout ➤ Page (Alt-F9) ➤ Conditional End of Page.

20. Type **10**, and then select OK.

21. Select Close to close the Style Editor window, then Close again to close the Styles dialog box.

Since these styles are automatically saved with the template, we do not have to save them in a separate stylesheet. The next step is to add the memorandum headings that we want to print with each document that uses this template.

22. Display the ruler (Alt-Shift-F3) and select the Headings style.

23. Select Font ➤ Size (Ctrl-S) ➤ Very Large.

24. Press Shift-F7 to center the insertion point, type **MEMORANDUM**, and press →.

Pressing the → key moves the insertion point beyond the code that turns off the Very Large font size. This accomplishes the same function as pulling down the Font menu and selecting Normal or Very Large again, but with less hand movement. You can use this same technique to turn off all character-formatting codes. For example, after typing boldface characters, press → to turn off boldface. This is faster then pressing Ctrl-B or pulling down the Font menu and selecting Bold.

25. Press ↵ four times: once to turn off the Heading style and then to insert two blank lines.

26. Select the Headings style again.

27. Type **TO:**, press ↵ to turn off the style, and then press Tab twice. The two tab spaces leave the line ready for the name of the recipient, positioned correctly.

28. Press ↵ twice and select the Heading style.

29. Type **FROM:**, press ↵, and press Tab.

30. Press ↵ twice and select the Heading style.

31. Type **SUBJECT:**, press ↵, and press Tab.

32. Press ↵ twice and select the Heading style.

33. Type **DATE:**, press ↵, and press Tab.

34. Select Tools ➤ Date ➤ Code (Ctrl-Shift-F5). The date will appear in the default Courier font.

35. Press ↵ twice.

36. Select File ➤ Save (Shift-F3), type **Memo.tmp**, and then select Save.

37. Select File ➤ Close (Ctrl-F4).

USING TEMPLATES

To use a template, open it and type the text for the document. Then print the document and save it under a different name to leave the template unchanged for the next time it is needed. We will type a sample memo using our Memo template.

1. Open the document MEMO.TMP. It will appear with the headings of the memo, as shown in Figure 2.7. The current date is inserted by the date code, which is part of the template.

2. Click the mouse at the end of the line containing the TO heading, or press ↓ to reach the TO line and press End. The insertion point will appear after the tab spaces in the correct position. Do not press ↵ to move the insertion point—it will insert additional blank lines into the document.

3. Type **Rose Savage**. Text you enter in the document will appear in the default Courier font.

4. Press ↓ twice, type **Adam Chesin**, and press ↓ twice.

5. Type **Budget** and press ↓ four times.

6. Type **Please submit your budget requests within three weeks.**

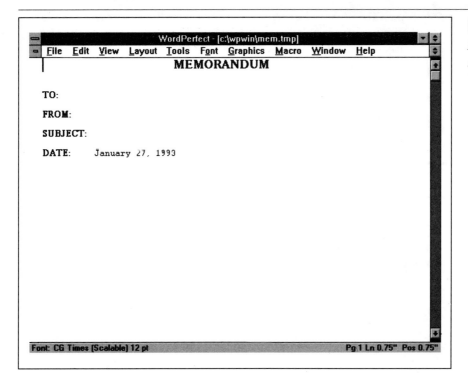

7. Select File ➤ Print (F5) ➤ Print.

8. Select File ➤ Save As (F3), type **Savage**, and select Save. Be sure to use Save As so the original template is not changed.

9. Select File ➤ Exit (Alt-F4).

To standardize document formats in an office, create a template for each type of document that your office produces. Train each word processor how to retrieve and use each template, and how to access any styles that it may contain. Your staff will quickly learn that the templates save time, as well as provide consistent formatting. Mark each template as a read-only file (as explained in Chapter 15) or stress that individual documents must be saved using the Save As option in the File menu.

CHAPTER 3

Formatting envelopes and labels
Creating tickets and ticket folders
Printing business cards and place cards
Designing greeting cards

Printing Envelopes, Labels, and Small-Size Documents

WordPerfect provides two ways of formatting envelopes and labels: manually using the Page Size dialog box and automatically through macros. The macros provide a quick way to print envelopes and create labels, but the Page Size options provide more flexibility.

You can take advantage of the label format to print small-size documents, such as business cards and invitations. Other special formats you can set up using label specifications are rotated text and booklets. This chapter describes the methods for printing standard envelopes and labels, as well as special techniques for working with label forms. Chapter 11 explains how to print envelopes and labels using merge techniques.

POSITIONING PAPER IN THE PRINTER

Certain printing tasks require you to know which side of the page your printer prints on. If you have a dot-matrix printer, you always insert paper so the side to be printed on is facing the print head. The paper position depends on how your printer handles paper. For example, if you insert the paper in the back, behind the roller, you place the printing side away from you so it will face the print head when it rolls around.

With laser printers, the position of the paper depends on the printer model and whether you are inserting it in a paper cassette or manually. Take the time to determine just how the paper feeds through your printer so you do not waste paper later:

1. Write the word *Cassette* on several pieces of paper, and the word *Manual* on some others. Then write the words *Face Up* on one end of each sheet.

2. Start WordPerfect and type **Printed Side**.

3. Insert a sheet of paper marked Cassette in the tray so the words *Face Up* are facing up and go into the printer first, and then print one copy of the document.

4. If the printed text is at the same end and side as the words *Face Up*, you know that you feed the paper with the printed side up and the top of the sheet in first. On a label (use a diskette label if you have one), write *Print side up, top in first*, and stick it somewhere visible on the paper cassette.

5. If the words are not on the same side, insert another sheet of paper into the cassette so the words *Face Up* are facing down but still going into the printer first. Print another copy of the document. If the words align now, write *Print side down, top in first* on the label and adhere it to the cassette.

6. Repeat the same procedure with the sheets marked Manual, but feed the paper into the manual input tray. When you discover how the paper feeds, write it on a label and put that label somewhere near the manual input area. The cassette and manual tray may or may not feed paper the same way.

PRINTING ENVELOPES MANUALLY

Printing an envelope manually requires four steps:

◆ Select the envelope form or create one if it is not already defined for your printer. This includes setting the envelope size and method of paper feed.

◆ Set the page margins to place the address, and optionally your return address, at the correct location.

◆ Type the address in the form.

◆ Print the envelope.

How you select the envelope form depends on the type of printer driver you are using. If you are not sure which type of printer driver you are using, select File ➤ Select Printer and see which button at the bottom of the dialog box is selected: WordPerfect or Windows.

USING A WINDOWS PRINTER DRIVER

If you are using a Windows printer driver, follow these steps to set up the page for envelopes:

1. Select File ➤ Select Printer.

2. Make sure the Windows radio button is selected and the names of your Windows printer drivers are listed in the Available Printers list box. If not, select Windows.

3. In the Available Printers list box, select the printer you want to use to print the envelopes.

4. Select Setup to display the Setup dialog box.

5. For a laser printer with an envelope feeder, select envelope as the paper source. If you have a nonlaser printer with an envelope feeder, select continuous. If your printer does not have a feeder, select manual (you must then use the Windows Print Manager to control when each page prints).

6. If you are using a laser printer, select Landscape orientation (Alt-L).

7. Select OK to return to the Select Printer dialog box, and then choose Select to return to the document window.

USING A WORDPERFECT PRINTER DRIVER

Follow these steps to determine if your WordPerfect printer driver already has an envelope form defined and then create one if necessary:

1. Select File ➤ Select Printer.

2. Make sure the WordPerfect button is selected and the names of your WordPerfect printer drivers are listed in the Available Printers list box. If not, select WordPerfect.

3. In the Available Printers list box, select the printer you want to use to print the envelopes.

4. Select the Select button to return to the document editing window.

5. Select Layout ➤ Page (Alt-F9) ➤ Paper Sizc.

6. Scroll through the list box and look for a form called Envelope.

7. If there is such a form, select it, and then click on the Select button. You can skip the remaining steps and proceed to format your envelopes.

8. If the driver does not have a envelope form defined, select Add.

9. From the Paper Type drop-down menu, select Envelope.

10. From the Paper Size drop-down menu, select Envelope.

11. If 9.50" and 4" do not appear in the text boxes, select Other and enter the measurements manually.

12. If you are using a laser printer, select Landscape orientation (the lower-left icon under Paper Orientation) or Rotated Font. For other printers, select Wide-Form Portrait orientation (the upper-right icon) or Wide Form.

13. Select OK, and then choose Select.

FORMATTING ENVELOPES FOR A WORDPERFECT PRINTER DRIVER OR NONLASER PRINTER

To format envelopes, you set the margins to print the recipient's address in the correct location. These instructions are for users of dot-matrix and daisy-wheel printers, and for those using laser printers with a WordPerfect printer driver. If you are using a laser printer with a Windows printer driver, skip to the next section.

1. Select Layout ➤ Margins (Ctrl-F8).

2. Set the left margin a **4"**, the right margin at **.5"**, the top margin at **2"**, and the bottom margin at **.5"**. Then select OK.

3. Type the following address:

Sally Kallerman
187 West Fifth Street
New York, NY 10987

Figure 3.1 shows how the envelope form will appear in Print Preview mode if you are using a WordPerfect printer driver. When you type more than one address, press Ctrl-⏎ after each one.

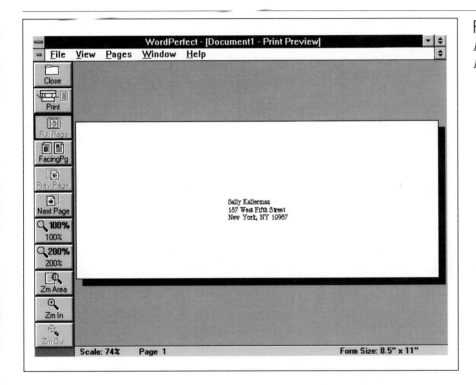

FIGURE 3.1:

Envelope in Print Preview mode

4. Select File ➤ Print (F5) ➤ Print.

The envelope will move up past the 2-inch top margin, and the address will start printing 4 inches from the left.

For laser printers, the WordPerfect printer drivers will automatically adjust for where envelopes feed in your printer. For example, the LaserJet III feeds envelopes in the center of the tray. The LaserJet Plus feeds envelopes from the side. The 2-inch top margin will place the address in the correct position on both printers; just be sure you are using the correct printer driver for your model printer.

With some other printers, you may have to adjust the position manually. For example, if the address started 1 inch too close to the left edge (looking at the envelope horizontally), add an inch to the left margin.

If the address did not appear on the envelope at all, print the envelope again using a sheet of 8½-by-11-inch paper in the manual tray. After it is printed, place an envelope on the sheet with the envelope's right edge at the top of the page, in the position where you would feed the envelope into the printer. For example, if you feed envelopes in the center of the tray, place the envelope centered between the right and left margin. Trace around the envelope, and then measure how far the printed address is from the position where it should appear.

Using Windows Laser Printer Drivers

If you are using a Windows printer driver, WordPerfect thinks it is printing on an 8½-by-11-inch sheet. You must position the address by setting the margins.

With printers that feed envelopes in the center, set the left and top margins at 4.5 inches, the right and bottom margins at .5 inch. For printers that accept envelopes at the edge of the input tray, set the left margin at 4.5 inches and the top margin at 6.5 inches. You might have to adjust these settings to suit your own envelopes and spacing requirements.

When you start to print, a code will flash on the printer's control panel. Insert an envelope into the tray, and the printer will do the rest.

COMBINING LETTERS AND ENVELOPES

Suppose that you have a laser printer and you want to print a letter and then print its envelope as one multipage document. The problem is that the letter prints using portrait orientation on letter-size paper. The envelope prints in landscape orientation using manual feed.

If you have a WordPerfect printer driver, you can create a style to handle the different orientations. The Windows printer drivers will not allow you to combine portrait and landscape pages in the same document.

Create an open style called Envelope using the following codes:

◆ Press Ctrl-↵ to enter a page break.

◆ Select Layout ➤ Page (Alt-F9) ➤ Paper Size, the Envelope form, then Select.

◆ Select Layout ➤ Margins (Ctrl-F8) and set the envelope margins as explained earlier in this chapter.

Type the text of your letter, and then select the Envelope style. The style inserts the page break and the envelope form, and places the insertion point at the correct position for the address. You can either type the address or copy it from the letter.

USING THE ENVELOPE MACRO

If you are using a version of Word-Perfect 5.1 for Windows dated after April 1992, refer to Appendix C for more information on this feature.

Instead of creating styles to format an envelope, you can use WordPerfect's Envelope macro. The macro works when you already have the address on the screen, typically as the inside address of a letter. You select the address, and the macro formats and prints the envelope.

The first time you run this macro for a selected printer, WordPerfect will guide you through the process of creating the MacroEnv form. This is the envelope form that the macro will use to print envelopes. The macro then temporarily inserts the form at the beginning of the document on the screen, copies the selected address to it, and changes the margins before printing the envelope. When completed, the macro deletes the address, returning the document to its original condition.

Unfortunately, the Envelope macro has certain limitations: it can be used only with WordPerfect printer drivers, it assumes you are using a number 10 envelope, and it sets certain default margins that may not be appropriate for your printer. However, you can edit the macro to adjust the envelope position, as described in Chapter 8.

We will use the macro to print an envelope for a short letter.

1. Start WordPerfect, make sure a WordPerfect printer driver is selected, and then type the following letter:

January 2, 1993

Miss Daisy Renaldi

3467 West Palm Avenue

Palm Court, FL 81029

Dear Miss Renaldi:

We have received your order and will ship the materials by the end of this week. Thank you for your business.

Sincerely,

Alvin A. Aardvark

2. Select Macro ➤ Play (Alt-F10), scroll through the Files list box, and double-click on envelope.wcm.

The first time you run each of WordPerfect's macros, you will see the message

Compiling Macro

as WordPerfect processes the macro instructions. If you run this macro in a blank document window, a message box will appear telling you that the macro is being canceled.

If this is the first time you are running the macro for the selected printer, the MacroEnv form will not exist, and you will see the message

Would you like to check to make sure the correct WordPerfect printer is selected?

After you complete this macro, the form will be added to your printer driver. The next time you run the macro, you will not see this message, unless you delete the form or select another printer, and you can skip ahead to step 8.

3. Select No, and a dialog box will appear with the options Continuous, Bin, and Manual.

4. Select the type of paper feed you will use for envelopes, and then choose OK.

5. If you select Continuous, the macro will continue. If you selected Bin, you will be asked to enter a bin number between 1 and 31. Enter a valid bin number, and then select OK. If you chose Manual, a dialog box will appear asking if you would like WordPerfect to prompt to load. Select Yes if you want WordPerfect to pause before printing the envelope, or choose No if you expect to have the envelope ready.

6. A dialog box will appear with the options Landscape and Portrait. Select the orientation that is appropriate for your printer, and then choose OK. WordPerfect places the insertion point at the start of the document, and displays the message

Move to the beginning of the address, press ENTER to continue

7. Select OK to remove the dialog box.

8. Move the insertion point to the start of the address and press ↵.

WordPerfect now looks for the end of the address. The macro assumes that the address will end with two hard carriage returns the end of the address and a blank line between it and the salutation. If it locates two consecutive carriage returns, it selects all the text from the position where you pressed ↵ to the first of the two carriage returns. It then formats the envelope, copies the selected text, and prints the envelope, as it will do in this case.

If the address does not print correctly on your printer, you must format and print your envelopes manually (as explained earlier in this chapter) or edit the macro (as explained in Chapter 8).

Keep in mind that the Envelope macro is not all that smart. Suppose that you run it in this incorrectly formatted letter:

Miss Daisy Renaldi
3467 West Palm Avenue
Palm Court, FL 81029
Dear Miss Renaldi:

   We have received your order and will ship the materials by the end of this week. Thank you for your business.

The macro will include the salutation as the last line of the address.

If WordPerfect cannot locate two consecutive carriage returns, it will display the message

Move to the end of the address, press ENTER to continue

Click on OK to remove the dialog box, place the insertion point at the end of the address, and press ↵ to print the envelope.

If the macro created the MacroEnv form, the form will be added to your printer driver. The next time you run this macro, WordPerfect will locate the form and you will only have to designate the start, and possibly the end, of the address.

If you selected to have WordPerfect prompt you to load paper with manual feed, you will see a dialog box containing the message

Load paper:macroenv 4" x 9.5"

Select OK to print the envelope.

PRINTING LABELS

Like envelopes, labels can be formatted manually or automatically by a Word-Perfect macro. The macro, which only works with WordPerfect printer drivers, lets you choose from a list of common label forms.

Before printing labels, print a test sheet on plain paper that is the same size as your label stock. Place the test sheet under a sheet of labels and hold them up to the light to check the positioning of the text. If the text is not aligned properly, adjust the label definition and print another test sheet.

SELECTING THE PRINTER DRIVER AND PAGE SIZE

Before you set up a label form, make sure the correct printer driver and page size are selected. Have a ruler and a sample of the label stock on hand.

1. Select File ➤ Select Printer.

2. Select either the WordPerfect or Windows button to display a list of printer drivers.

3. Select the printer driver you want to use for labels.

4. If you are using a Windows printer driver, select Setup, and then choose the paper size that corresponds to the sheet containing the labels. Most labels are supplied on letter-size $8\frac{1}{2}$-by-11-inch sheets. Select OK to return to the Select Printer dialog box.

5. Select OK, and then choose Select to return to WordPerfect.

6. Select Layout ➤ Page (Alt-F9) ➤ Paper Size ➤ Add.

7. If you are using a WordPerfect printer driver, set the page size to the dimensions of the label sheet, and then select Labels. If you are using a Windows printer driver, select OK when you see the message

Only label definitions can be added when using Windows printer drivers

You will see the dialog box shown in Figure 3.2. If you are using a Windows printer driver, the Remove Labels option is not included.

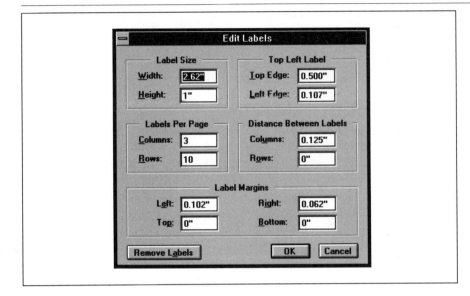

DEFINING THE LABELS

In the Edit Labels dialog box, you can enter measurements as either decimals, such as 2.25, or fractions (WordPerfect will convert the fraction to decimals). Set the options to describe the labels you are using:

◆ **Label Size:** Enter the width and height of the individual labels; do not include the spaces between labels or margins to the end of the sheet.

◆ **Labels Per Page:** Enter the number of labels across (Columns) and down (Rows).

◆ **Top Left Label:** The Top Edge and Left Edge settings tell WordPerfect the exact location of the first label on the page. Enter the distance from the top of the page to the top of the first label, and from the left side of the page to the left edge of the labels.

◆ **Distance Between Labels:** Enter the amount of spacing, if any, between labels across (Columns) and down (Rows).

◆ **Label Margins:** Enter margin settings to control where WordPerfect prints text on the label. For example, the top margin is the amount of space between the top of the label and the first line of text.

TYPING LABELS

When you are ready to type labels, follow these steps:

1. Select Layout ➤ Page (Alt-F9) ➤ Paper Size.

2. Highlight the label form, and then select the Select button.

3. Type your labels, pressing Ctrl-↵ after each one.

On the screen, each label will be separated by a page-break line, and the page counter will increment as you move from label to label. However, the labels will print in the correct number of rows and columns and will be displayed that way in Print Preview mode, as shown in Figure 3.3.

For multicolumn labels, the labels fill the sheet row by row. Using three across labels, for example, labels 1, 2, and 3 take up the first row, labels 4, 5, and 6 fill the second row, and so on.

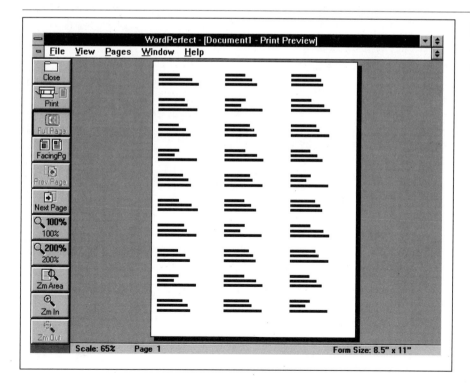

FIGURE 3.3:

Labels displayed in Print Preview mode

USING THE LABELS MACRO

After you run the Labels macro to set up a particular label form, you can print the same type of labels again by selecting the form in the Page Size dialog box. Like the Envelope macro, the Labels macro requires a WordPerfect printer driver, but you can edit it to work with Windows printer drivers, as explained in Chapter 8.

To use the Labels macro, follow these steps:

1. Select Macro ➤ Play (Alt-F10), scroll through the list box, and double-click on Labels.wcm. After the macro is compiled, you will see the message

> **A WordPerfect printer driver must be selected for this macro to run properly. Would you like to check if a WordPerfect printer is selected?**

2. Select No if you are certain the correct WordPerfect printer is selected. If you are not sure, select Yes to specify a WordPerfect driver, and then choose Select to continue the macro.

3. In the dialog box that appears, select the type of label, Page or Tractor-feed (dot matrix), to see a list of predefined forms.

4. Select the label form that you want to add to your printer driver, and then select Install.

5. In the next dialog box, select the appropriate feed: Continuous, Manual, or Bin.

If you select a label form that is not compatible with your printer, a dialog box will appear with a message similar to

Check the label defined in the Paper/Size dialog to see if margins overlap.

If you previously inserted this label into your driver, you will see a dialog box telling you that the label is already defined.

6. If you want to create labels now, select Yes in the dialog box that asks

> **Label *XXX* is now installed for your currently selected printer. Would you like to insert this label into the current document for use now?**

WordPerfect will select the form and display a dialog box informing you that the document is formatted for use with the label form and ready for you to enter data.

If you are just setting up the label form and do not want to type labels at this time, select No to complete the process. You will see a dialog box that tells you that the label format has been added to the list of available paper sizes for your currently selected printer and can be selected from the Paper Size dialog box.

You can use the macro to insert more than one label form in your printer driver at a time. When the list of labels appears, select each one that you want to insert, and then choose Insert. You will be asked to select the type of feed for each. After the label forms are added, WordPerfect will ask if you want to insert one of them into the current document. If you select Yes, you can select from a list of the label forms.

To use a label form created by a macro, select Layout ➤ Page (Alt-F9) ➤ Paper Size and select the form. If you run the label macro for a form that is already defined, the macro will report that the form exists and give you the opportunity to insert it into the document.

USING LABEL FORMS FOR SPECIAL FORMATS

Instead of wasting paper printing small documents one per page, you can format them as labels. Using this method, you can print multiple copies per page without manually measuring and spacing them. For even more efficient printing, you can merge the labels with a database, as explained in Chapter 11.

FORMATTING TICKETS

Suppose that you are creating numbered tickets for a special event and will print them on a laser printer. You can format these tickets using a label form and give them page numbers so they will print with unique numbers.

We will create sample tickets that are 2 inches by 4 inches. Although this is the size of the Avery 5163 label, we will set up the form manually to space the tickets for cutting.

1. Select Layout ➤ Page (Alt-F9) ➤ Paper Size.

2. In the dialog box, select Add. If you are using a Windows printer driver, select OK and skip to step 5.

3. From the Paper Type drop-down menu, select Other and type **Tickets** in the Other text box.

4. Select Labels.

5. For Label Size, enter **4** for Width and **2** for Height.

6. For Labels Per Page, enter **2** for Columns and **5** for Rows.

7. For Top Left Label, enter **.5** for the Top Edge and **.25** for the Left Edge.

8. For Distance Between Labels, enter **0** for both Columns and Rows.

9. For Label Margins, enter **.25** for all four margins to leave a ¼-inch border around each label.

10. Select OK twice: once to return to the Add dialog box and again to return to the Page Size dialog box.

11. Choose the Select button to insert the form into the document.

12. Select Layout ➤ Page (Alt-F9) ➤ Numbering.

13. Pull down the Position list box and select Bottom Right.

14. In the New Page Number text box, type **100**, and then select OK.

15. Press Ctrl-J to center the insertion point, type the following text for the ticket, and then press Ctrl-↵ to insert a page break.

You Are Invited To Attend
The Annual Masked Ball Presented by
Aardvark Computers
Sunday, June 3, 1993, 7 P.M.
345 West Franklin Street, Philadelphia

16. To copy the ticket to the other labels, select the text including the page break (place the mouse pointer at the start of the first line of text and drag below the page-break line), and then select Edit ➤ Copy (Ctrl-Ins).

17. Click the mouse below the page-break line to deselect the text.

18. Press Shift-Ins nine times to paste the label down the page. Figure 3.4 shows the tickets in Print Preview mode.

19. Delete the hard-page-break line that follows the last ticket (if you leave it, a blank page will be ejected after the tickets are printed).

20. Select File ➤ Print (F5) ➤ Print to print a page of the tickets.

Figure 3.5 illustrates how the tickets might appear when printed. The dotted lines represent the trim lines where you would cut the sheet to produce the individual tickets.

For your own tickets, select appropriate fonts and font sizes, but make sure that the text does not exceed the label size. You can also include graphics,

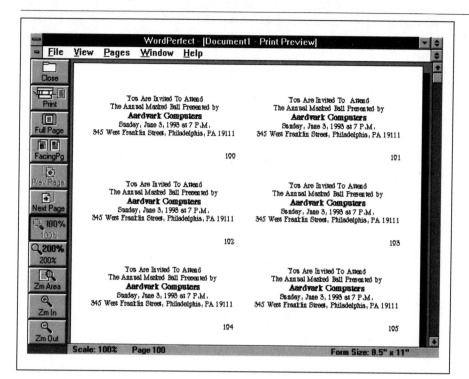

FIGURE 3.5:

*Sheet of printed tickets
showing trim lines*

rules, and boxes, as explained in Chapters 4 and 5. You can save yourself the work of copying the text onto each label form by using a header to duplicate the contents (described in Chapter 4) or by using a macro (discussed in Chapter 8).

Tickets printed on thick paper look more professional. Although most laser printers cannot handle card stock, you should be able to find a heavier weight paper that your printer can feed. If necessary, adjust your printer so the paper feeds along the straightest path possible. You might want to print one camera-ready sheet and have a commercial printer duplicate it on card stock, print numbers, and cut the individual tickets.

FORMATTING BUSINESS CARDS

You can produce business cards using a label form following the procedure described for creating tickets, but without choosing to number the pages. To print business cards, create a label form with the following specifications:

Width	3.5
Height	2
Labels Per Page	
Columns	2
Rows	5
Top Edge	.5
Left Edge	.75
Distance Between Labels	
Columns	0
Rows	0
Left Margin	.15
Right Margin	.15
Bottom Margin	.15
Top Margin	.15

Enter the text for the first card, press Ctrl-↵, and then copy the card nine times to fill the first page.

Reorienting Text for Invitations and Greeting Cards

Suppose that you want to print a folded invitation or greeting card. The programs that are designed to produce greeting cards print the text for the outside of the card in one orientation and the inside text in another orientation. When the printed page is folded properly, it forms the card. Rather than using this type of software, which limits your choices of fonts and graphics, you can set up a WordPerfect label form to produce greeting cards.

Create a label form with a top margin set large enough to properly place the text on the page. Print the text in one orientation, flip the paper around, and print the other text. This technique allows you to take full advantage of your fonts and WordPerfect's graphics features.

To create a form for a greeting card or invitation, set up an 8½-inch-by-11-inch label form with the following specifications:

Width	4.25
Height	11
Labels Per Page	
Columns	2
Rows	1
Top Edge	0
Left Edge	0
Distance Between Labels	
Columns	0
Rows	0
Left Margin	.5
Right Margin	.5
Bottom Margin	.5
Top Margin	6

It may be necessary to adjust the settings to accommodate your printer's minimum margin areas.

If you are using a WordPerfect driver, display the Add Paper Size dialog box and set the Location to Manual and select Prompt to Load Paper. For a

Windows printer driver, display the Setup dialog box for your printer, select Manual Feed for Paper Source, then OK, then Select.

The greeting card form consists of four labels, two on each page. To create a card, select the form and enter the text and graphics in the following order. Press Ctrl-↵ to insert a page break after each side. The design for each side of the card cannot be larger than will fit on one-quarter of the sheet (one "label").

◆ Back of the card. Press Ctrl-↵ to insert a page break even if you do not want anything to appear on the back of the card.

◆ Front of the card. You may want to center the text and graphics inserted on this side.

◆ Inside left page. Again, press Ctrl-↵ even if you want this side to be blank.

◆ Inside right page. This is the usual location for a greeting or the invitation information.

To print the card on a printer that cannot rotate fonts, insert the appropriate paper, and select File ➤ Print (F5) ➤ Print. The 6-inch top margin will cause the front and back covers to print on the bottom section of the page. Because the form is set for manual feed, the printer will pause. Remove the printed sheet and feed it into the printer so the blank section of the page will be printed. Do not turn the page over but turn it so the opposite edge enters the printer first. If your printer accepts the top of the sheet in first, insert the printed side in first. The inside pages will also print on the bottom section of the page.

Figure 3.6 shows an example of a printed, unfolded greeting card. Fold the sheet into quarters, with the blank side facing in.

If you have a laser printer that can rotate fonts, you can print the entire card at one time, as explained in Chapter 4.

CREATING TICKET FOLDERS

Another type of folded document is a ticket holder. A small section of the page is folded up from the bottom, then the page is folded in half like a booklet. The small folded section serves as a pocket to hold a ticket or other material, as illustrated in Figure 3.7.

You can format text or graphics to appear on the front and back covers, as well as on the flap of the pockets on the inside. As with a greeting card

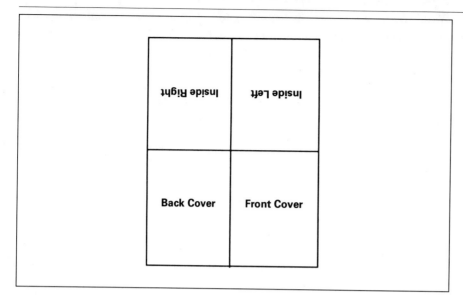

FIGURE 3.6:
Unfolded greeting card

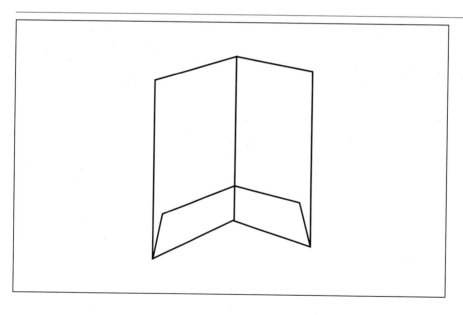

FIGURE 3.7:
Ticket holder or pocket folder

form, all the text for the folder is printed on the same side of the sheet, is rotated on one end so it appears in the correct position when the pa. folded.

You need to set up two different label forms for this format: one fo. the cover and one for the flap. To create a packet that can hold a ticket up to 4 inches by 10 inches, start with an 8½-inch-by-11-inch form with these specifications for the cover:

Width	4.25
Height	11
Labels Per Page	
Columns	2
Rows	1
Distance Between Labels	
Columns	0
Rows	0
Top Edge	0
Left Edge	0
Left Margin	.5
Right Margin	.5
Bottom Margin	2.5
Top Margin	.5

Type the text for the back cover in the first label on the page, type the text for the front cover on the second page, and then print the document. The bottom section of the page is blank because of the 2½-inch margin. It will be used to store the text for the flap.

Next set up the form for the flap using these specifications:

Width	4.25
Height	11
Labels Per Page	
Columns	2
Rows	1

Distance Between Labels

Columns	0
Rows	0
Top Edge	0
Left Edge	0
Left Margin	.5
Right Margin	.5
Bottom Margin	8.5
Top Margin	.5

Type the text of the left-hand flap in the first label on the page, the text of the right-hand cover on the second. Remove the printed sheet and reinsert it in the printer. Make sure the side that is already printed will be printed on again but rotate the page end to end. That is, what was the top edge of the page previously must now be the bottom. Print the page. Finally, fold the flaps in first, then fold the page in half.

FORMATTING PLACE CARDS

Folded place cards do not require rotated text or rotating the page, but they do use a large top margin to position text properly. Figure 3.8 illustrates a printed, folded place card.

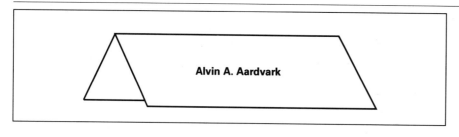

Alvin A. Aardvark

FIGURE 3.8:
Place card

To create place cards that are 4 inches wide and 1½ inches high after being folded, use an 8½-by-11-inch label form with the following settings:

Width	4
Height	3

Labels Per Page

Columns	2
Rows	3
Top Edge	1
Left Edge	.25

Distance Between Labels

Columns	0
Rows	0
Left Margin	.167
Right Margin	.167
Bottom Margin	.167
Top Margin	2.37

Press Ctrl-J to center the text and type the names, pressing Ctrl-↵ between each one. Print the page, and then cut it into place cards, as shown by the trim lines in Figure 3.9. Fold each place card so it can stand on its edge (see Figure 3.8).

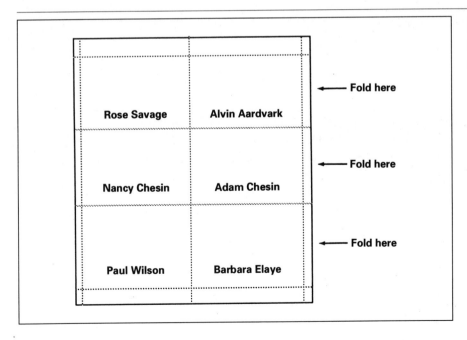

FIGURE 3.9:

Place card trim lines and fold locations

Printing Booklets

An easy way to create booklets is to use standard 8½-inch-by-11-inch paper folded in half. The final booklet will be 5½ inches by 8 inches. Set up the form to print in landscape orientation and choose manual feed.

To format a booklet, create an 8½-by-11-inch label form with the following specifications:

Width	5.5
Height	8.5
Labels Per Page	
Columns	2
Rows	1
Top Edge	0
Left Edge	0
Distance Between Labels	
Columns	0
Rows	0
Left Margin	.5
Right Margin	.5
Bottom Margin	.5
Top Margin	.5

These specifications will leave a ½-inch margin around each page, with a 1-inch gutter (space between the text on facing pages).

To create a booklet, select the form and enter the text and graphics. When the document is completely edited, change each soft page break into a hard page break.

Next create a dummy (a sample layout) by folding full pages in half. Write the page number of each page, and then unfold the sheet to see which pages are actually next to each other on the paper, as illustrated in Figure 3.10. For example, if you are creating a four-page booklet on a sheet folded in half, your pages will be in the order 4, 1 on one side and 2, 3 on the other.

Copy the last page to the beginning of the document, and insert a hard page break between it and the following page. The pages will now appear in the order 4, 1, 2, 3.

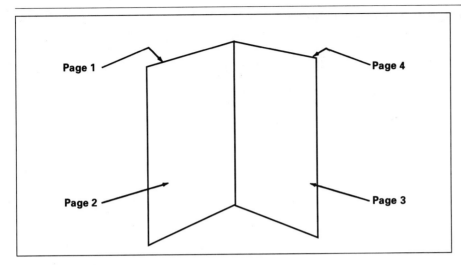

FIGURE 3.10:

Layout for a four-page brochure

If you want to print numbers on the pages, make sure you change the page numbers to match the folded order. Select Layout ➤ Page (Alt-F9) ➤ Numbering to set the page number of what is now the first document page to 4. Change the number of the next page to 1; the remaining pages will be correctly numbered 2 and 3.

When you print the document, the first page will print with page 4 on the left and page 1 on the right. Turn the paper around, reinsert it in the printer, and then print the next page; pages 2 and 3 will print in the correct order.

If you want to print multiple copies, rather than use manual feed, select continuous. Before printing the booklet, however, experiment so you know the direction to insert the paper. In the Print dialog box, set the number of copies. Then select Multiple Pages, then Print to print just the pages that will appear on the side of one sheet. If you did not number the pages, enter 1,2 in the Print Range text box, then select Print. The first side of all the copies will print. Turn all the pages around, and then repeat the process but enter 3,4 in the Print Range text box. If you numbered your pages, enter 4,1 when printing the first side, and 2,3 when printing the second.

You can save time by printing multiple pages rather than rearranging them physically in the document only in certain instances. Page combinations in which the page on the left is a lower number than that on the right can be printed without rearranging their order. For example, suppose your pages are entered in consecutive order: 1, 2, 3, 4. Select Multiple Pages from the Print dialog box and enter the page range as 2,3. Page 2 will print on the left side, page 3 on the right. If you are printing an eight-page booklet, you would have two such combinations: 2, 7; 4, 5.

Unfortunately, you cannot use this technique for page combinations where the page on the left has a number higher than that on the right. If you enter 4,1 as the page range, WordPerfect will print only page 4. The solution is to physically rearrange the pages, as we did in this chapter.

CHAPTER 4

Adding line-draw and graphic rules
Creating and formatting boxes
Printing a brochure with an
address panel
Designing page borders

Enhancing Documents with Rules and Boxes

ordPerfect's desktop publishing features include the capability to include horizontal and vertical rules (lines) and boxes on a page. This chapter describes how to create and manipulate these graphic elements.

You can create simple free-hand line drawings and graphs directly in WordPerfect. However, keep in mind that Windows comes with Paintbrush, a drawing program. Paintbrush drawings can be merged into your document using the graphics techniques discussed in Chapter 5. To create ruled forms, use WordPerfect's table features, as described in Chapter 7.

ADDING RULES TO YOUR DOCUMENTS

You can add two types of rules (lines) to your documents: a line-draw rule or a graphic rule. WordPerfect's line-drawing function lets you draw horizontal and vertical rules on the screen using the arrow keys. You cannot use the mouse to draw rules and you cannot draw diagonal lines. Line drawing is a character-based function; a rule consists of a series of individual line segments, each a separate and distinct character from the WordPerfect character set.

When you create a graphic rule, WordPerfect inserts a line code into the document rather than individual line segments. Deleting the code deletes the entire rule.

In deciding whether to use line-draw or graphic rules, keep these points in mind:

◆ You can export a document that contains line-draw rules to text-based word processors or other applications that can produce line drawing characters. You may not be able to export a document that contains graphic rules (or boxes).

◆ With the line-drawing function, you can use any of WordPerfect's 1500 special characters as the drawing character. This lets you create some special effects that may not be possible with graphic rules, such as a line of arrows or bullets.

◆ You can move and change the size of graphic rules using a mouse. You can also control the thickness of graphic rules and their color and shading. Line-draw rules cannot be manipulated in these ways.

◆ When you add or delete text within a box or near a vertical line created with the line-drawing function, you must be in Typeover mode. In Insert mode, editing can change the location of line segments, destroying the arrangement of your rules and boxes.

Creating Line-Draw Rules

Before adding rules with the line-drawing function, make sure you are using a fixed-width font. Line-draw rules may not align properly when a proportionally spaced font is selected.

To create a rule, select Tools ➤ Line Draw (Ctrl-D). WordPerfect changes to Draft mode and displays the Line Draw dialog box at the bottom of the screen, as shown in Figure 4.1. For line drawing, WordPerfect automatically switches to Typeover mode, although there will be no indicator in the status bar.

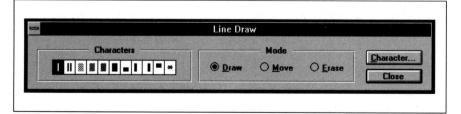

FIGURE 4.1:

Line Draw dialog box

If the dialog box is covering the area where you want to draw, drag it by its title bar to move it out of the way. With the keyboard, press Alt-spacebar and select Move to position the dialog box with the arrow keys.

Use the default single-line character, or select another drawing character from those displayed in the dialog box. If none of the options are suitable, select Character to display the dialog box shown in Figure 4.2, and then enter the character you want to use.

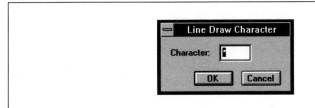

FIGURE 4.2:

Dialog box for selecting the line-drawing character

You can also choose one of WordPerfect's special characters. While the Character dialog box is on the screen, press Ctrl-W to display the WordPerfect Characters dialog box. Select the set and character you want, then Insert, then Close. (Special characters are discussed in Chapter 6.) The character you select will replace the asterisk (*) under Characters. Some graphic characters will appear as small boxes in the Line Draw dialog box and in Draft mode, but they will appear correctly in Normal mode and when printed.

Draw the rule by moving the insertion point with the arrow keys. You can also use the following keystrokes to draw rules:

Home or Ctrl-←	Draws a rule from the insertion point to the left margin.
End or Ctrl-→	Draws a rule from the insertion point to the right margin.
Ctrl-↑	Draws a rule to the top of the page.
Ctrl-↓	Draws a rule to the bottom of the page. If no other pages exist, WordPerfect will insert a page break and extend the rule into the next page.

While you are adding rules with the line-drawing function, select Move in the Line Draw dialog box to move the insertion point without drawing a line on the screen. For example, to draw two separate rules, draw the first one, select Move, and then move the insertion point to the starting position of the next rule. Select Draw to continue drawing.

Use Erase in the Line Draw dialog box to remove lines. Select Erase, and then move the insertion point back over the rules you want to remove. Use the → and ← keys to delete horizontal rules; use ↑ and ↓ to delete vertical rules. Do not use the Del or Backspace key to erase individual line-draw characters. Instead, make sure you are in Typeover mode and use the spacebar to type a blank space over the character that you want to delete. If you use Del by mistake, turn off Typeover mode by pressing the Ins key, and then press the spacebar until the lines are realigned.

When you are finished drawing, select Close to remove the Line Draw dialog box and return to Normal mode

After drawing a line, make sure you are in Typeover mode before entering text. If you enter text in Insert mode, the rules will move as you add new characters.

Boxes created with the line-drawing function will have different proportions on the screen than when printed. To draw a box that will print as a square, try using a 5 to 3 ratio. Draw the horizontal lines by pressing the → or ← key five times; draw the vertical lines by pressing the ↑ or ↓ key three times. The box will look like a rectangle on the screen but print as a square.

INSERTING GRAPHIC RULES

When you choose to add a horizontal or vertical graphic rule to a document, WordPerfect inserts it in the specified size and position. You can then move and resize the rule as necessary.

Placing a Rule

To create a graphic rule, place the insertion point where you want the line to appear in the document, such as between two paragraphs, and select Graphics ➤ Line. Then choose the direction of the line, Horizontal or Vertical. To bypass the menus, use the shortcut keys: Ctrl-F11 to add a horizontal rule, or Ctrl-Shift-F11 for a vertical one.

Figure 4.3 shows the dialog box displayed when you choose to create a horizontal rule. The default settings create a single, solid, horizontal line extending from the left margin to the right margin. To enter a different line length, you must first change the Horizontal Position setting to something other than Full. The horizontal rule settings can be adjusted as follows:

◆ **Length:** Sets the length of the line in inches.

◆ **Thickness**: Sets the thickness of the line in inches or points.

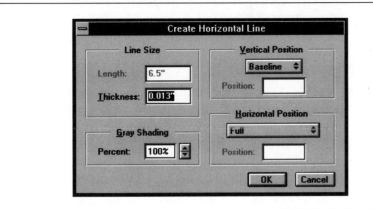

*Create Horizontal Line
dialog box*

◆ **Vertical Position:** Determines the position of the line in relation to the text line where the insertion point is located. You can have the line print on the baseline or you can specify an exact location.

◆ **Horizontal Position:** Determines the position of the line in relation to the left and right margins. Options include Left, Right, Center, Full, and Specify (which allows you to enter an exact position in the text box).

◆ **Gray Shading:** Sets the density of the line. Enter a percentage, where 100 is solid black, or click on the up- or down-pointing arrow to increase or decrease the density.

The dialog box for creating a vertical rule has similar options but with some important differences. Use the Horizontal Position setting to place the lines at the right or left margin, between columns, or at some specific position. The Vertical Position setting determines if the rule appears along the full length of the page; near the top, center, or bottom; or at the position you specify. You can enter a line length only if the Vertical Position is set to something other than Full.

Manipulating Graphic Rules

Because rules placed using the Graphics menu are graphic objects, you can change them without affecting other elements of the document. Now we will insert a short line and then manipulate it using common mouse techniques.

1. Type the numbers 1 through 5 down the page and press ↵. We will use these numbers for visual reference later.

2. Place the insertion point after the number 3 and select Graphics ➤ Line ➤ Horizontal (Ctrl-F11).

3. Pull down the Horizontal Position list box and select Center.

4. In the Length text box, type **2**.

5. Select OK, and the horizontal rule will appear on the screen, on the same baseline as the number 3.

6. Move the insertion point to the top of the page and press ↵ twice.

Each time you press ↵ to insert a blank line, the graphic rule moves down the page. The position of a rule set at the baseline (with Baseline selected for Vertical Position) is defined by the location of its code within the text. Therefore, a baseline rule will move up and down as you delete and insert blank lines and text.

7. Move the I-beam to the rule until the I-beam changes to an arrow. Now you are ready to reposition the rule.

8. To select the rule, click the left mouse button. The mouse pointer will change to a four-directional arrow, and the rule will be surrounded by six small black squares, called *handles*. A dotted line, called a *selection box*, will appear over the solid line.

9. With the mouse pointer shaped as a four-directional arrow, hold down the left mouse button and drag the pointer around the screen. As you drag the mouse, the selection box will move with it.

10. Position the rule next to the number 4 and release the mouse button.

11. Click the mouse to deselect the line, move the insertion point above the line, and press ↵ twice.

This time, the rule did not change position when you inserted blank lines. After you move a rule, its definition changes to a specific vertical and horizontal position. The rule will appear in that location no matter where its code is on the page. If you insert lines above the code, the code will move down the page but the position of the horizontal rule will remain the same. A rule that is initially inserted in a specific vertical or horizontal position will behave in the same way, except when editing moves its code to another page. In that case, the rule will also move to that page but remain in the specified position.

12. To change the size and shape of the rule, select it again and point to the handle in the lower-right corner of the selection box.

13. Move the pointer until it changes to a diagonal-pointing arrow.

14. Hold down the left mouse button and drag the handle down and to the right. As you move the mouse, the rule changes size and shape.

15. Drag the handle so the box is approximately 3 inches long and ¼ inch thick, and then release the mouse button. Now that the line is thicker, there are eight handles around the selection box: one in each corner and one on each side.

16. Point to the handle in the lower-left corner and drag it all the way to the right and down to the bottom of the screen. By dragging the handle, you created what now appears to be a vertical rule, although WordPerfect still defines it as a horizontal graphic rule.

17. Close the window without saving the document.

You can change the size of a selected rule (or any other graphic object) by dragging one of its handles:

◆ Drag the center handle on the top or bottom to change the height of the graphic.

◆ Drag the center handle on the left or right to change the width of the graphic.

◆ Drag a handle on a corner to change both the width and height at the same time.

Editing Graphic Rules

To delete a rule, select it and then press Del or select Cut from the Edit menu. To copy a rule, select it, choose Copy from the Edit menu (Ctrl-Ins), and paste (Shift-Ins) the duplicate in the desired position.

You can change a rule's size, position, and shading by using the options in the Edit Line dialog box. To display the dialog box, use one of the following methods:

◆ Double-click on the rule.

◆ Click on the rule with the right mouse button to see an editing prompt, and then select Edit.

◆ Select Graphics ➤ Line ➤ Edit Horizontal or Edit Vertical. WordPerfect will search backward from the insertion point to find the nearest line code and then display the dialog box.

The dialog box for editing graphic rules contains the same settings as the one for creating them. Make your changes in the dialog box and then select OK.

RULE-DRAWING SHORTCUTS

If you frequently add rules to your documents, you might want to use some shortcuts. When you want a rule to appear on every page of a long document, you can make the rule part of a header or footer. Select Layout ➤ Page (Alt F9) ➤ Headers or Footers ➤ Create. Then enter the text and insert the graphic rule in the header or footer window. For example, use this technique to place a vertical rule down the side of the page or a horizontal rule to separate text from page numbers. You can create headers and footers for every page or for alternating odd and even pages.

If you prefer to draw rules with the mouse rather than the line-drawing or graphics function, you can create a macro for this approach. Define a macro that inserts a horizontal line in the center of the window, .018 inch long and .05 inch thick. When you play the macro, a small rectangle (the rule) will appear in the middle of the screen. Select the rectangle and drag the appropriate handles to create a rule of any length and width. See Chapter 8 for more information about creating macros.

ADDING BOXES TO DOCUMENTS

WordPerfect lets you create five different types of boxes: figure, text, equation, table, and user. Table 4.1 summarizes the contents of each type and its default settings. The boxes with their default settings are shown in Figure 4.4. Adding graphics (in figure boxes) and creating equations and tables are covered in later chapters. Here we will discuss adding the boxes that enclose these items.

In WordPerfect 5.1 for DOS, each box type could store any type of material. For example, you could place a graphic image in a text box. With the Windows version, only table and user boxes have this capability. The other types are used only for their designated contents.

CREATING BOXES

To create a box, pull down the Graphics menu, select the type of box you want to insert, and then choose Create. The editor window you see—Text Box, Figure, or Equation—depends on the box type. In the editor window, you enter the text or equation you want, or recall a text, graphic, or equation file from the disk.

BOX TYPE	CONTENTS	DEFAULT SETTINGS
Figure	Graphic images and drawings in WPG and other popular formats	Single-line border on all sides; 0.167" outside and 0 inside border space, captions use bold figure numbers (such as **Figure 1**) below the box and outside the borders; no shading
Text	Text entered, pasted, or retrieved in the Text Box Editor	Thick top and bottom border lines; 0.167" outside and inside border space; captions use bold numbers only below the box and outside the borders; 10% shading
Equation	Equations and special characters	No borders; 0.083" outside and 0 inside border space; captions use bold numbers
Table	Graphics, text, or equations	Thick top and bottom border lines; 0.167" outside and inside border space; captions use bold table roman numerals (such as **Table I**) above the box and outside the borders; no shading
User	Graphics, text, or equations	No borders; 0.167" outside and 0 inside border space; captions use bold numbers below the box and outside the borders; no shading

TABLE 4.1:

Types of WordPerfect Boxes

Figure 4.5 shows the Text Box Editor window, which appears when you select to create a text box. In this window, you can type the text you want in the text box, paste text that you cut or copied into the clipboard, or retrieve text from a file. You can format characters, lines, and paragraphs as in any other part of the document. The right margin symbol in the ruler indicates the default size of the box.

As you enter text, the lines will wrap as indicated. The height of the box will adjust to hold the text, although a box cannot be larger than one page. If you enter more than one page, a warning dialog box will appear when you try to close the box and return to the document; you must delete some text before you close the window.

If you select to create a table or user box, a dialog box will appear in which you can select to use the Text, Figure, or Equation editor. Choose the

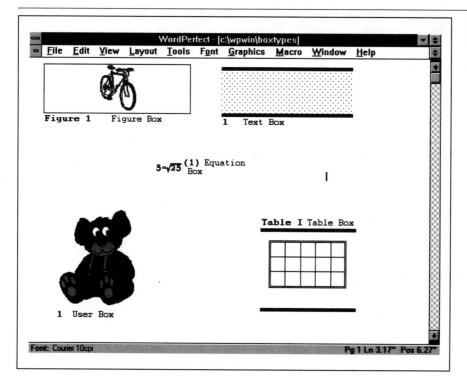

one that is most appropriate for the contents of the box. For example, if you are creating a user box that will contain a Paintbrush drawing, select the Figure Editor. This is the only editor window in which you can retrieve and manipulate a Paintbrush image.

Table and user boxes are particularly useful because they can store text, graphics, or equations. When you want two or more boxes with the same type of contents but with different borders or other features, set one type up as a table or user box. For example, when you want to insert a box with borders to contain a graphic, select to create a figure box. When you want to add a box without borders for a graphic, select to create a user box and use the Figure Editor.

ADDING BOX CAPTIONS

WordPerfect can automatically number, insert, and position box captions (see Figure 4.4). To add a caption, select the box, then select Caption from the Graphics submenu for the box type. A Caption Editor window appears with the next number for that type of box already inserted.

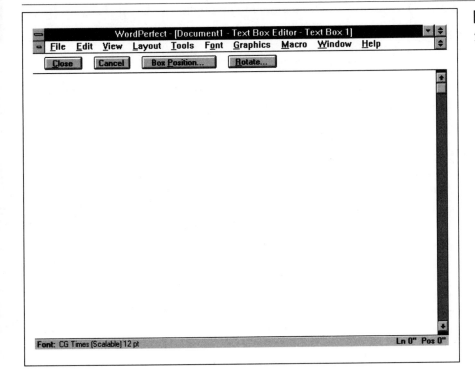

In this window, enter the text for the caption, or select New Number to change the number of the box. Select Close to save the caption and return to the document window. You can change the numbering scheme and the number format in the Box Options dialog box, as explained later in the chapter.

Note that table boxes are numbered consecutively with tables created using WordPerfect's table features. For example, suppose that a document has a table, then a graphic image in a table box (created with the Figure Editor), then another table. They will be numbered Table 1, 2, and 3, respectively, even though the table box does not contain a table. See Chapter 7 for more information about creating tables.

EDITING BOXES

After you create a box, you can edit or adjust its contents in its editor window. To display the editor window for an existing box, use one of the following techniques:

◆ Double-click on the box.

◆ Click on the box with the right mouse button and select Edit Box from the list box that appears.

◆ Select Graphics, the box type, then Edit. Enter the box number in the dialog box that appears, and then select OK.

◆ Press Shift-F11 to edit a figure box or Alt-Shift-F11 to edit a text box. Enter the box number and select OK.

POSITIONING BOXES

You can change the size and position of any type of box by selecting it and dragging it with the mouse. When you click on a graphic box, it will be surrounded by a selection box with eight handles. To move the box, position the pointer on it, and the mouse pointer will become a four-directional arrow. Drag the box to the desired position.

To change the size of a box, drag the appropriate handle, as described in the section about resizing graphic rules. You can also adjust the size and position of a box using the options in the dialog box shown in Figure 4.6. Display the dialog box using one of the following methods:

◆ Hold down the Shift key and double-click on the box with the left mouse button.

◆ Click on the box with the right mouse button and select Box Position.

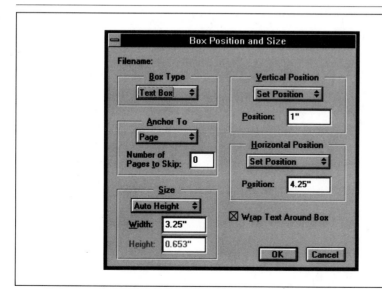

FIGURE 4.6:

Box Position and Size dialog box

◆ Select Graphics, the box type, then Position. Enter the box number in the dialog box that appears, and then select OK.

◆ Display the editor window for the box, and then select the Fig Pos, Equ Pos, or Box Position button.

The Box Position and Size dialog box contains options for controlling the type, position, and size of the box:

◆ **Box Type:** Sets one of the five types of boxes. When you select a different box type, you change the borders and other default settings determined by the type, not the contents or the editor. For example, changing a text box to a figure box will not let you insert a graphic because the Text Box Editor will still be in use.

◆ **Anchor To:** Determines whether a box is fixed to a paragraph, page, or character. Paragraph boxes align with the paragraph in which the box is defined, and they will move up and down as you insert and delete text. Page boxes can be placed anywhere on the page and will not change position as you edit text. Character boxes can be placed within lines and will change position as you enter characters.

◆ **Vertical Position:** Sets the position of the box in relation to the text or top margin.

◆ **Horizontal Position:** Sets the position of the box in relation to the right and left margins.

◆ **Number of Pages to Skip:** Allows you to place the graphic on another page.

◆ **Size:** Sets the size of the box. Auto Height adjusts the box to fit the text.

◆ **Wrap Text Around Box:** Flows text around the box rather than through the box (and its contents).

Making a box too small or too large can cause problems. If you reduce a box too much, it might disappear from the screen and not appear in Print Preview mode or when printed, although you will see the box code if you reveal codes. Use the Graphics menu to display the Box Position and Size dialog box and set the small box to a larger size.

If you have anchored a box to a page and then make it too big to fit on that page, it will move to the next page. WordPerfect will insert a page break and start a new page if necessary. You can either reduce the size of the box or delete other material on the page.

SETTING BOX OPTIONS

You can change the default settings for a box type so that each new box in that type will have those characteristics. To set new defaults, select Graphics, the type of box you want to change, then Options. You will see the Box Options dialog box for the selected type. Figure 4.7 shows the dialog box for text boxes.

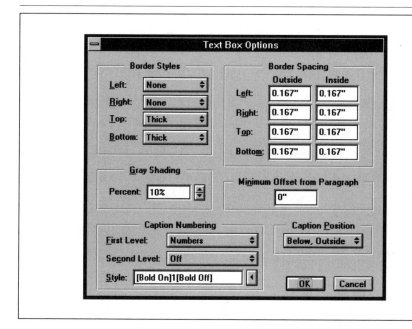

FIGURE 4.7:

Text Box Options dialog box

The text box options determine the type and position of border lines, the space between the text and the border, the numbering and style used to reference the boxes, and the shading inside the box. Notice that the default text box has only top and bottom lines. To make it a complete box, add left and right lines.

For box captions, you can set the numbering scheme for the first and second levels to numbers, letters, or roman numerals. For example, you can set up a scheme that includes 1.1, I.a, or a.1. The format for caption numbers is set in the Style text box in the Caption Numbering section of the dialog box. For example, the codes [Bold On]1[Bold Off] shows the numbers will be boldfaced. If you select to have a second level, you must indicate how you want it to appear. For example, enter [Bold On]1.1[Bold Off] to boldface both levels and separate them with a period.

Each of the five box types is controlled by separate options settings. For example, selecting Graphics ➤ Figure ➤ Options and changing the settings in the dialog box will have no effect on text or equation boxes in the document.

Changing box options inserts a code in the document at the position of the insertion point. The code will affect only the boxes that follow it. It will remain in effect until you select new options or delete the [Txt Opt] code in the text. To change the options for an existing box, place the insertion point before the code for the box before displaying the Box Options dialog box.

CREATING A BROCHURE WITH PORTRAIT AND LANDSCAPE TEXT

Suppose that you need to create a brochure that includes a mailing address, as shown in Figure 4.8. This format requires text in landscape orientation as well as one panel with text in portrait orientation.. If you are using a laser printer with a WordPerfect printer driver, you can create this type of document even if your printer cannot rotate fonts. We will define label forms for the text and use boxes to set up the mailing address panel.

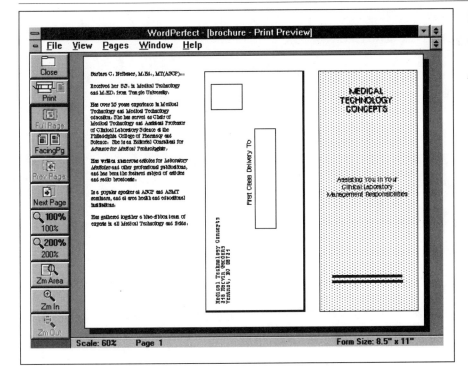

FIGURE 4.8:

Brochure with landscape and portrait text

SETTING UP A LANDSCAPE TEXT LABEL FORM

We will start by creating a label form in landscape orientation (see Chapter 3 for more information about defining label forms). If your printer can rotate fonts, this is the only form you need. For printers that cannot rotate text, you must create this form and a form for the address panel, as described in the next section.

Select Layout ➤ Page (Alt-F9) ➤ Paper Size ➤ Add. From the Paper Type drop-down menu, select Other, and type **Brochure** in the Other text box. From the Paper Size drop-down menu, select Stand Land, and then select Labels.

Create a label with the following specifications:

Width	3.67
Height	8.5
Labels Per Page	
Columns	3
Rows	1
Top Edge	.0
Left Edge	.0
Distance Between Labels	
Columns	0
Rows	0
Left Margin	.25
Right Margin	.25
Top Margin	.5
Bottom Margin	.5

SETTING UP AN ADDRESS PANEL FORM

If your laser printer cannot rotate text, create another form for printing the address panel in portrait orientation. Select Layout ➤ Page (Alt-F9) ➤ Paper Size ➤ Add. Choose Other from the Paper Type drop-down menu, and type

Address in the Other text box. Make sure that Paper Size is set to Standard and Orientation is set to Portrait, and then select Labels.

Create a label with the following specifications:

Width	8.5
Height	3.67
Labels Per Page	
Columns	1
Rows	3
Top Edge	.0
Left Edge	.0
Distance Between Labels	
Columns	0
Rows	0
Left Margin	.5
Right Margin	.5
Top Margin	.25
Bottom Margin	.25

ADDING TEXT TO THE BROCHURE PAGES

All three of the inside pages (labels) use landscape orientation. To create the inside of the brochure, follow these steps:

1. Select Layout ➤ Page (Alt-F9) ➤ Paper Size.

2. Select Brochure, then Select.

3. Type the text of the inside pages. To end one page and start another, press Ctrl-↵ or let WordPerfect insert soft page breaks for you.

4. Print the page.

The outside pages of the brochure contain both landscape and portrait orientation. Because this part of the brochure will be folded, you must consider the order in which you enter the text.

5. Select Layout ➤ Page (Alt-F9) ➤ Paper Size.

6. Select Brochure, then Select.

7. Type the text that you want to appear on the panel that will be folded inside, and then press Ctrl-⏎ to insert a page break.

8. Press Ctrl-⏎ to insert another page break, and then type the text you want to appear on the cover. The example shown in Figure 4.8 includes a text box on the cover.

Designing the Address Panel

If your printer cannot rotate the text, print the page for the outside of the brochure now, and then create the address panel using the Address label form and print it in a second pass. If you have a printer that can rotate text (such as a LaserJet III), you can print the address panel and the remainder of the outside at the same time. If your printer can rotate text, move the insertion point to the second panel, between the page-break lines, and then begin with step 5 below.

1. Insert the page that you just printed so the blank side will be printed, and then print the document now on the screen.

2. Save the document on the screen, and then close the window to start a new document.

3. Select Layout ➤ Page (Alt-F9) ➤ Paper Size, select the Address form, and choose Select.

4. Press Ctrl-⏎ to insert a page break.

5. Select Graphics ➤ Text Box ➤ Options.

6. Change the Border Styles options: Left to Single, Right to Thick, and Top to Single.

7. Set Gray Shading to 0, and then select OK to return to the document.

8. Select Graphics ➤ Text Box ➤ Create (Alt-F11) to display the Text Box Editor window.

9. If your printer can rotate fonts, select Rotate to see the options None, 90, 180, and 270. Select 90, then OK.

10. Select Box Position to display the Box Position and Size dialog box. Set the Vertical Position to Full Page and the Horizontal Position to Margins Full, and then select OK.

11. Type the text for the panel, including your return address. In Figure 4.8, the boxes that represent the position of the stamp and mailing label were created with the line-drawing function. Note that you will not see the rotated text on the screen in Normal mode; in some cases it will not appear in Print Preview mode either. However, the text will print correctly.

12. Select Close.

13. If your printer cannot rotate text, reinsert the page so the side with the two outside panels will be printed. If your printer can rotate text, insert the page so the blank side—opposite the inside pages—will be printed.

14. Print the document.

FRAMING PAGES WITH BOXES

Suppose that you want to print a border around each page in the document. Using a text box with its vertical position set to Full Page and its horizontal position set to Margins Full will not work. If you set up a box with these specifications, when you enter text into the box or retrieve a file from the disk, you will not be able to save the box because the text is longer than one page.

To place a border around each page, insert the text box in a header. In the header window, select Graphics ➤ Text Box ➤ Options and set the type of lines you want for the borders and the percent of shading. Next select Graphics ➤ Text Box ➤ Create (Alt-F11) ➤ Box Position and set the box size and position as follows:

Vertical Position	.5
Horizontal Position	.5
Size	Set Both
Width	7.5
Height	9.5
Wrap Text Around Box	Off

Turning off text wrap allows you to enter text on the page. When you return to the document, you won't see the box on the screen (except in Print Preview mode), but it will print on each page.

To edit the box, select Layout ➤ Page (Alt-F9) ➤ Headers ➤ Edit to display the header window. Then select Graphics ➤ Text Box ➤ Edit (Alt-Shift-F11) and make your changes.

PRINTING LARGE QUANTITIES OF SPECIAL-FORMAT DOCUMENTS

Suppose that you need to print several hundred raffle tickets for a fund-raising effort. The tickets are formatted with numbers and rotated text, as shown in Figure 4.9. You can quickly create the document without having to manually copy the label repeatedly.

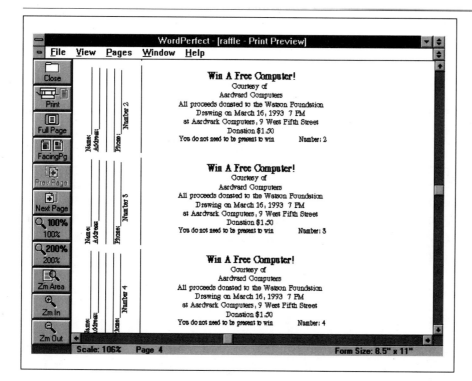

FIGURE 4.9:

Numbered raffle ticket with rotated text

You can set up this format by creating a text box for the rotated text and a header to repeat the entire label on every page. The document used to create these tickets is a little unusual because all the text is contained in the header. Start by creating a label form with the following specifications:

Width	6
Height	2
Labels Per Page	
Columns	1

Rows	5
Top Edge	.5
Left Edge	.5
Distance Between Labels	
Columns	0
Rows	.05
All Margins	0

Select Layout ➤ Page (Alt-F9) ➤ Headers ➤ Create. In the header window, select Graphics ➤ Text Box ➤ Options and set the Border Styles as None for Left, Top, and Bottom, and Single for Right. (The line on the right will serve as the border between the stub and the raffle.) Set Gray Shading to 0% and each of the Border Spacing options to 0".

Next create a text box with 90-degree rotation. In the Box Position and Size dialog box, change the settings as follows:

Vertical Position	Center
Horizontal Position	Margin Left
Size	Set Both
Width	1.25
Height	1.88
Wrap Text Around Box	Off

After you set the box size and position, enter the text for the stub using a font that is 10 points (or smaller). To add the raffle number, select Layout ➤ Page (Alt-F9) ➤ Numbering ➤ Insert Page Number to insert the ^B code. You cannot select a page-number position within a text box.

Close the Text Box Editor window (you will see just a vertical line, not the text). Do not close the header window.

Press Alt-F3 to reveal codes, and make sure the insertion point is after the options and box codes. Press ↵ and then select Layout ➤ Margins (Ctrl-F8) and set the left margin to 1.5 to move the text beyond the graphic box. Type and format the text for the raffle. To insert the raffle number, select Layout ➤ Page (Alt-F9) ➤ Numbering ➤ Insert Page Number. The numbers on the stub and on the ticket will be the same because they are on the same page.

Close the header window. If you see an error message reporting that the header contains too much text, reduce the size of a font, combine two lines of the ticket, or delete some text.

Finally, press Ctrl-↲ for each raffle ticket that you want to insert. The label on the screen will be blank, but the header, which contains the entire text of the ticket, will print on each label. To save even more time, you can create a macro to insert the page breaks, as explained in Chapter 9.

CHAPTER 5

Adding Graphics to Your Documents

ordPerfect's handling of graphic files makes it easy to add graphic images to your documents. Images are inserted in graphic boxes. You can then change the position and dimensions of the box, as well as some of the characteristics of the graphic image within the box. Chapter 4 describes how to work with WordPerfect boxes. This chapter explains techniques for inserting and manipulating graphic images.

INSERTING A GRAPHIC FILE

To insert a graphic image, select Graphics ➤ Figure ➤ Retrieve (F11). WordPerfect will display a dialog box listing .WPG files (WordPerfect graphic files) in the Graphics subdirectory. To display other graphic file types, select the directory in the Directories list box and enter an asterisk followed by the extension in the Filename text box, such as *.PCX or *.PIC.

If you want to see what a file contains before retrieving it, click on it and then click on the View button. To bring the image into the document, double-click on its file name. The image appears in the document in a figure box. The dimensions of the box are based on the size of the graphic image.

EDITING GRAPHIC IMAGES

After you insert a graphic image into a document, you can change its size, shape, and position. To edit an image, double-click on it. WordPerfect will display the image in the Figure Editor window, as shown in Figure 5.1.

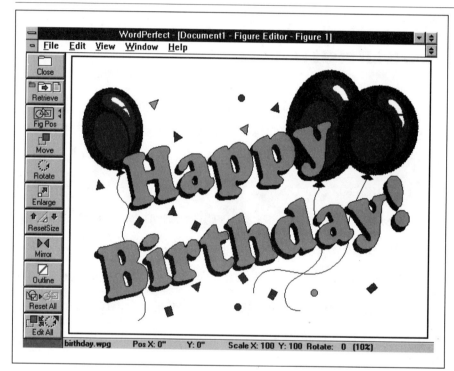

FIGURE 5.1:

Figure Editor window with a WPG file

USING THE FIGURE EDITOR BUTTONS

The button bar along the left side of the window contains tools for editing the image:

◆ **Close:** Closes the Figure Editor window and inserts the graphic image into the document. To cancel your changes, select File ➤ Cancel.

◆ **Retrieve:** Loads a graphic image into the Figure Editor window, replacing any image on the screen.

◆ **Fig Pos:** Displays the Box Position and Size dialog box, which contains settings for changing the position and size of the figure box within the document. (You can also move the box by dragging it with the mouse.)

◆ **Move:** Moves the image within the figure box, not the box within the document.

◆ **Rotate:** Rotates the graphic image within the box; it does not rotate the box itself.

◆ **Enlarge:** Enlarges, or zooms in on, a section of the image; it does not enlarge the box. To change the size of the box, use the mouse or Box Position and Size dialog box.

◆ **Reset Size:** Returns the image to its original size.

◆ **Mirror:** Flips the image from left to right.

◆ **Outline:** Converts a color image to black and white by converting all colors to white.

◆ **Reset All:** Returns the image to all its original settings.

◆ **Edit All:** Displays a dialog box for making multiple changes and changing the scale of the image.

You can perform the same tasks by selecting options from the menus. Use the File menu to change the box size and position, close the Figure Editor, and retrieve and save an image. Use the Edit menu to select formatting options.

Now we will retrieve the WPG file shown in Figure 5.1 and change it to look like the image shown in Figure 5.2. We will convert the original to a black-and-white line drawing, rotate it so the words are straight on the page, and then crop it to remove the word *Birthday*.

1. Select Graphics ➤ Figure ➤ Retrieve (F11) and double-click on Birthday.wpg to recall it from the disk.

2. Double-click on the graphic to display the Figure Editor window.

FIGURE 5.2:

Edited graphic image

3. Select the Outline button in the button bar. All the colors in the image will be converted to white, but the black areas and lines will remain unchanged.

4. Select the Rotate button and move the mouse pointer into the graphic area. A large crosshairs will appear on the screen.

5. Point to the right end of the X-axis and drag the mouse slightly down. As you move the mouse, the crosshairs will rotate along with it, and the number next to the Rotate prompt in the status bar will change.

6. Drag the mouse down until the status line reads Rotate: 347, and then release the mouse button. The image will rotate so the text is straight.

You can quickly rotate the crosshairs by clicking anywhere in the image. The crosshairs will rotate so that the right end of the axis is pointing to where your clicked. For instance, clicking at the left of the image will rotate it 180 degrees. You can also press Ctrl-→ to rotate the graphic clockwise, and Ctrl-← to rotate it counterclockwise. Each time you press the key, the image rotates by the percentage shown in the status bar. To change the percentage, press Ins to cycle between 25%, 10%, 5%, and 1%.

7. Select the Enlarge button and move the mouse pointer onto the image. A large, dotted crosshairs will appear, with the mouse pointer at the intersection of the X and Y axes.

8. Move the mouse pointer to the upper-left corner of the window, hold down the mouse button, and drag the pointer to the right and just above the word *Birthday*. As you move the mouse, a dotted selection box will appear. You can select any rectangular portion of the graphic image.

The starting position of the pointer (where you pressed the mouse button) serves as an anchor. The diagonal corner of the box follows the pointer as you move the mouse. Notice that the Pos (Position) and Scale prompts in the status bar change to reflect the position of the pointer and the scale of the enlargement.

9. Move the pointer and release the mouse button when the status bar shows

POS X: .0"   Y: -1.4"   Scale X: 189   Y: 189

(If you cannot get the position exactly as shown, get as close as possible, making sure that the box surrounds the word *Happy*.)

10. Select Close to insert the edited image into the document.

When you enlarge an image, the size of its box will remain the same; it will not be wider or taller than the size set in the Box Position and Size dialog box.

To enlarge or reduce the graphic within the box but maintain the image's original proportions, press Ctrl-↑ or Ctrl-↓. Each time you press one of these keys, the image will change by the percentage shown in the status bar. To change the proportions, use the Edit All dialog box, as described shortly.

The position indicators in the status bar help you precisely position the image. When you press the mouse button to set one corner of the selection box as the anchor, the position indicators show the relative distance you have to move the mouse for both corners of the selection box to be the same distance from their corresponding corner of the figure box. For example, if you place the pointer ¼ inch from the left of the box and ½ inch from the top and press the mouse button, the position indicators will read

Pos X: 1.95   Y: 2.46

This means that you could move the pointer 1.95 inches to the right to be ¼ inch from the right of the box, and 2.46 inches down to be ½ inch from the bottom of the box. A negative X dimension means that you would have to move the mouse pointer to the left; a positive Y dimension indicates that you have to move the pointer up.

SCALING AND MAKING MULTIPLE CHANGES

When you want to make a number of changes to a graphic image at the same time, select the Edit All button in the Figure Editor window. You will see the Edit All dialog box, shown in Figure 5.3. This dialog box includes scaling options, which you can set to control the proportions of the image. Adjust the settings in the dialog box, and then select Apply to see how the changes affect the image. You can then close the box to accept the new settings or select Cancel to leave the image unchanged.

In addition to Mirror, Outline, and Rotate, which are also in the Button Bar, the dialog box contains the following items:

◆ **Move:** Moves the position of the image in the box. Enter positive measurements to move the image up (horizontal) and to the right (vertical); enter negative measurements to move the image down and to the left.

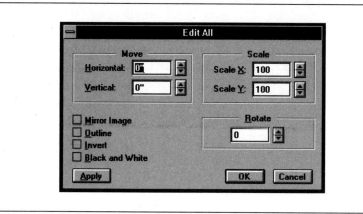

◆ **Scale:** Changes the size, shape, and proportions of the image (not the box). Setting X larger than Y creates a compressed image; setting Y larger than X creates a taller, thinner image. Setting either scale larger than 100 will make the graphic larger than the box so not all of it will appear. To change the size of the box and the graphic at one time, use the size options in the Box Position and Size dialog box.

◆ **Black and White:** Converts all color areas to black.

◆ **Invert:** Converts each pixel to its complementary color, creating a negative or reverse image.

WRAPPING TEXT AROUND AN IMAGE

When you want the text on a page to wrap around the contour of the graphic rather than the rectangular figure box, turn off Wrap Text Around Box in the Box Position and Size dialog box. This allows you to manually adjust lines of text so they follow the contour of the image, as in the example in Figure 5.4.

Note that when Wrap Text Around Box is turned off, you cannot select the image by clicking on it with the left mouse button. Instead, click on it with the right mouse button and then select from the list of four options: Select Box, Edit Figure, Box Position, and Edit Caption. To deselect the box, click the right mouse button again. The first option in the list will change to Unselect Box.

One way to move the lines of text to the proper position is to insert spaces at the beginning of the sentence, moving the text over until you are satisfied with its appearance. However, if you are using a proportionally spaced font, the spaces on the screen may not be the same as the printed spaces, and the text will not wrap correctly.

Another way to wrap the text is to use tab stops. Since tabs are set at definite locations on the page, the text will print exactly as it appears. For example, to create Figure 5.4, you could use this general procedure:

1. Retrieve the image, display the Box Position and Size dialog box, and turn Wrap Text Around Box off.

2. For each line of text, press Tab until the insertion point is at the tab stop closest to the desired position, type the text, and then press ↵.

3. Place the insertion point in the first line of text.

4. In the ruler, point to the tab stop that represents the starting position of the line and hold down the mouse button. A line will appear down the screen to indicate the tab-stop position.

5. Drag the tab stop so the line is at the desired position on the contour of the graphic.

6. Repeat steps 3 through 5 for each of the lines, working from the first line down.

7. Check the appearance of the page in Print Preview mode. Continue to make adjustments as necessary.

SPECIAL GRAPHIC APPLICATIONS

You can take advantage of WordPerfect's desktop publishing features to add graphics in a variety of ways. Using label forms and graphic options, you can produce documents completely filled with an image. You can also print in-line graphics, link files for the most up-to-date graphics, and insert captured screen images into a document.

ENLARGING IMAGES TO FIT

Suppose that you want to print invitations using a label form and the graphic border BORD-2.WPG supplied by WordPerfect, as shown in the example in Figure 5.5. The main steps in producing this type of document are to create the label form and to enlarge the graphic image so it fills the label space.

FIGURE 5.5:

Labels using a border

Create a label form in landscape format with the following specifications:

Width	5.5
Height	4.25
Labels Per Page	
Columns	2
Rows	2
Top Edge	0

Left Edge	0
Distance Between Labels	
Columns	0
Rows	0
All Margins	.25

With some laser printers, WordPerfect will adjust the bottom margin to .29 to accommodate for the nonprintable area around the edge of the paper.

Create a user box, choose the Figure Editor, and retrieve the BORD-2.WPG graphic file. To enlarge the image to fill the label form, select the following settings in the Box Position and Size dialog box:

Anchor To	Page
Size	Auto Both
Vertical Position	Full Page
Horizontal Position	Margin Full
Wrap Text Around Box	Off

When you are ready to type the text for the invitation, select the form and then press ↵ to move the insertion point to the correct position. After you complete the invitation, press Ctrl-↵ to insert a page break.

PRINTING IN-LINE GRAPHICS

You may want to print a graphic image as part of a line of text. Figure 5.6 shows an example of an in-line logo.

To set up this format, type the text you want to appear before the graphic image. Then create a user box, choose the Figure Editor, and retrieve the

The ABC'S of **WP** 5.1 for Windows

FIGURE 5.6:

Text with in-line graphic image

graphic file. In the Box Position and Size dialog box, select these settings:

Anchor To	Character
Size	Auto Width
Height	Point size of text
Vertical Position	Center
Wrap Text Around Box	On

LINKING FILES FOR DYNAMIC GRAPHICS

Suppose that you want to print a graphic image in a document, but there is a chance that the image will later be changed in some way. You can ensure that the most recent version of a graphic file prints with the document by linking the file instead of storing the image with the document.

To link a graphic file, create its box, select File ➤ Graphic on Disk, and then retrieve the file. This inserts a link to the graphic file on your disk. If you edit the graphic image and save it to a file with the same name, the edited version will be retrieved automatically when you open the document in WordPerfect.

If you select Graphic on Disk *after* retrieving the image into the Figure Editor, a Save As dialog box will appear. You can select to save the graphic image as a WPG file separate from the document; however, if you do, the link will be with the WPG file, not the original graphic file. To maintain the original link, select Cancel in the Save As dialog box.

You can also use this technique to separate a graphic that has already been inserted into a document. For example, suppose you have a document file containing a drawing created with GEM Draw. To use the graphic in another document, display it in the Figure Editor window and select File ➤ Graphic on Disk. Then enter a file name with the WPG extension. The image will be saved on the disk as a separate WordPerfect graphic file, which you can retrieve into any document.

INSERTING SCREEN CAPTURES

You can easily capture an image of the screen display and insert it into a document as a graphic figure. Display the window or screen that you want to capture, and then press Print Screen to capture the entire screen or Alt-Print Screen to capture just the active window. Switch to WordPerfect and select Edit ➤ Paste (Shift-Ins) to insert the image in a figure box.

After the screen image is added to your document, you can manipulate the image or its box as necessary. Move, scale, or edit it using the techniques described in this chapter.

CHAPTER 6

Inserting symbols and graphic
characters
Remapping the keyboard
Formatting equations
Creating graphic headlines and logos

Working with Special Characters, Equations, and Typesetting Features

long with text and graphic files, WordPerfect can print special characters and symbols, such as foreign-language characters and typographic symbols. For equations, it provides mathematical and scientific characters. You can also use the Equation Editor to create equations that print as graphics. You can take advantage of these capabilities to produce special text effects and graphic images.

WordPerfect also provides many typesetting options that allow you to precisely control the appearance of your document. For example, you can adjust the letter spacing, word spacing, and line height for your text.

PRINTING SPECIAL CHARACTERS

WordPerfect includes more than 1500 special characters that it can print on a graphics printer. The characters are grouped into 12 sets, plus a user-defined set for users who require their own set of special characters. Table 6.1 lists the WordPerfect character sets and the types of characters they contain. Each character is identified by its set number and its number within the set.

NAME	NUMBER	CONTENTS
ASCII	0	The same characters on the regular keyboard
Multinational 1	1	Common international characters
Multinational 2	2	Less common international characters
Box Drawing	3	Graphics, single lines, double lines, and box segments
Typographic Symbols	4	Common typographical symbols
Iconic Symbols	5	Picture symbols
Math/Scientific	6	Regular-size math and scientific characters
Math/Scientific Extension	7	Large-size and less commonly used math and scientific characters
Greek	8	Greek characters (ancient and modern)
Hebrew	9	Hebrew characters, vowel signs, and punctuation
Cyrillic	10	Cyrillic characters (ancient and modern)
Japanese Kana	11	Hiragana and Katakana characters
User Defined	12	Reserved for a user-created set of special characters.

TABLE 6.1:

WordPerfect Character Sets

The appearance of the printed characters depends on two settings in the Print dialog box: Graphics Quality and Text Quality. When either option is set to Do Not Print, the special characters will not print. If Text Quality is set to High, special characters will print in high quality, even if Graphics Quality is set to Medium or Draft. If Text Quality is set at either Medium or Draft, special characters will print in the mode selected for Graphics Quality.

For a reference list of all the special characters, print either CHAR-MAP.TXT or CHARACTR.DOC, two files supplied by WordPerfect in the WPC directory. But before you print them, set both Graphics Quality and Text Quality (in the Print dialog box) to either Medium or High. If you print one of these files with its default setting of Do Not Print for Graphics Quality, only those characters available in your printer's fonts will appear.

A laser printer may not have enough memory to print an entire set on one page. If you get an out-of-memory error, divide the set into several sections and print each section separately.

INSERTING SPECIAL CHARACTERS

To insert a special character in a document, position the insertion point where the character should appear and select Font ➤ WP Characters (Ctrl-W). In the WordPerfect Characters dialog box, shown in Figure 6.1, pull down the Set list box and select the set that contains the character. With the keyboard, press Alt-S, then press ↓ to cycle through the sets until the one you want to use appears.

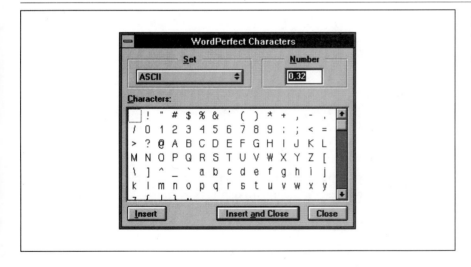

FIGURE 6.1:

WordPerfect Characters dialog box

The characters in the selected set are displayed in the Characters box. A dotted selection box will appear around the first character in the box, and the character's set and number will appear in the Number text box. To select a character in the set, click on it with the mouse (or press Alt-C, then select the character by using the arrow keys).

You can also display and select special characters by typing set and character numbers in the Number text box. As soon as you enter the set number, a comma, and a character number, the set appears in the Characters box, with the specified character selected.

Select Insert and Close to add the character and to return to the document. If you want to select several characters at one time, choose Insert. This adds the character to the document at the position of the insertion point, but leaves the dialog box active. Click in the document with the mouse and place the insertion point where you want the next special character to be inserted. Then click in the dialog box to return to it so that you can select another character.

SPECIAL CHARACTER FONTS AND SIZES

Special characters are inserted in the same size as the text. If you are using an 18-point font, for example, WordPerfect will scale the special characters to match that size. You can change the size of special characters by selecting them in the document and choosing another relative size from the Font ➤ Size (Ctrl-S) submenu.

If you insert special characters that include letters, such as ©, WordPerfect will try to match the typeface of the current font. WordPerfect can simulate Times, Helvetica, and Courier fonts. If you are using any other font, it will select the best alternative.

ADDING SPECIAL CHARACTERS TO THE KEYBOARD

If you use certain special characters often, you might want to assign them to keys on the keyboard. Then you will be able to type the character rather than selecting it from the dialog box.

To create or modify a keyboard definition, select File ➤ Preferences ➤ Keyboard. You will see the Keyboard dialog box, shown in Figure 6.2. Choose

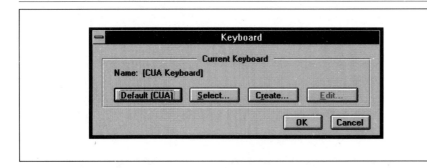

FIGURE 6.2:

Keyboard dialog box

Create to select items to add to a new keyboard definition. To change an existing keyboard definition, choose the keyboard name and then select Edit. Note that you cannot edit the default (CUA) keyboard.

We will now create a keyboard definition for Japanese Kana characters. You can use the same procedure to insert any characters from the WordPerfect character sets.

1. Select File ➤ Preference ➤ Keyboard ➤ Create. WordPerfect will display the Keyboard Editor dialog box, as shown in Figure 6.3.

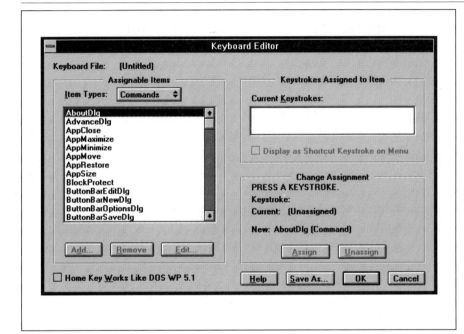

FIGURE 6.3:
Keyboard Editor dialog box

2. Pull down the Item Types box and select Text.

3. Select Add to display the dialog box shown in Figure 6.4.

4. Type **Phonetic A** in the Name box, and then press Tab to reach the Text box.

5. Press Ctrl-W to display the WordPerfect Characters dialog box, and then type **11,12** to select the phonetic A character in the Japanese set.

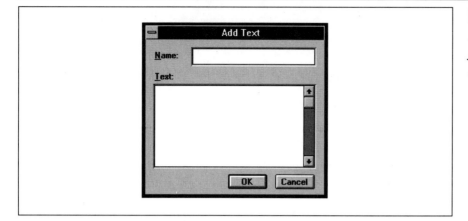

FIGURE 6.4:

*Add Text dialog box
for adding text to a
keyboard definition*

6. Select Insert and Close to return to the Add Text dialog box, then OK to return to the Keyboard Editor.

7. Select Phonetic A in the list box, press Ctrl-A, and choose the Assign button (at the bottom of the Change Assignment section).

8. To assign another character to the keyboard, select Add.

9. Type **Phonetic I** and press Tab.

10. press Ctrl-W, type **11,13**, select Insert and Close, and select OK.

11. Select Phonetic I in the list box and press Ctrl-I. In the Change Assignment section of the dialog box, WordPerfect will indicate that the Ctrl-I combination is currently assigned to the FontItalic command.

12. Select Assign to change the assignment.

13. Select Save As, type **Japan**, and select Save.

14. Select OK. In the Keyboard dialog box, your new keyboard is already selected.

15. Select OK to return to the document, and then press Ctrl-A and Ctrl-I to insert the two characters.

16. Select File ➤ Close, then No to close the document without saving it.

17. To reset the default keyboard, select File ➤ Preference ➤ Keyboard ➤ Default (CUA). Then select Close.

To use your custom keyboard, select File ➤ Preferences ➤ Keyboard ➤ Select. Double-click on the keyboard name in the list box, and then select Close in the Keyboard dialog box.

CREATING EQUATIONS

WordPerfect's Equation Editor provides tools for typing equations. It is used to format and print equations, not to perform the actual calculations. The Equation Editor translates the equation text into a graphic element that you can insert in a document.

To access the Equation Editor, select Graphics ➤ Equation ➤ Create. (You can also choose to create a table or user box with the Equation Editor.) As shown in Figure 6.5, the Equation Editor window has three panes:

◆ The Editing pane (top of the window) contains the characters, symbols, and equation commands used to create a equation.

◆ The Display pane (bottom of the window) shows a graphic representation of the equation.

◆ The Equation palette (along the left side of the window) shows available commands, functions, and symbols.

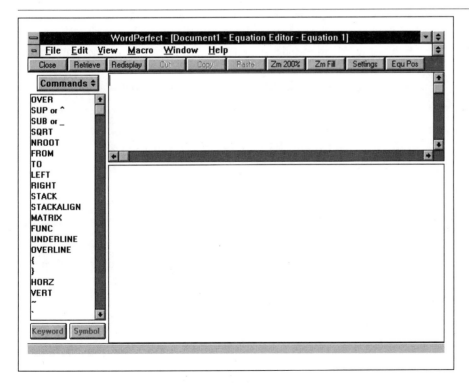

FIGURE 6.5:

Equation Editor window

CHANGING THE EQUATION PALETTE

WordPerfect has eight sets of Equation palette options:

♦ **Commands:** Common formats and symbols

♦ **Large:** Popular mathematical symbols from character set 7

♦ **Symbols:** Miscellaneous symbols from character sets 3, 4, 5, and 6

♦ **Greek:** Greek characters from set 10

♦ **Arrows:** Arrows, triangles, squares, and circles from set 6

♦ **Sets:** Set symbols and relational operators from set 6

♦ **Other:** Diacritical marks and ellipses from set 6

♦ **Functions:** Mathematical functions

Pull down the list box on top of the palette and select the set you want to use. Using the keyboard, press F6 to enter the palette area, press Shift-Tab to activate the list box, and then press ↑ or ↓ to cycle through the sets. Press Tab to enter the palette area to select a command.

Below the Equation palette are two buttons: Keyboard and Symbol. For some characters or commands, you can select to insert its word or the actual symbol that it represents. With either option, the symbol will appear in the Display pane.

USING THE EQUATION EDITOR BUTTON BAR

The Equation Editor Button Bar is along the top of the window, below the menu bar. It contains the following buttons:

♦ **Close:** Closes the Equation Editor window and inserts the equation (in an equation box) into the document.

♦ **Retrieve:** Recalls an equation from disk into the Equation Editor window.

♦ **Redisplay:** Updates the Display pane.

♦ **Cut:** Cuts the selected portion of the equation into the clipboard.

♦ **Copy:** Copies the selected portion of the equation into the clipboard.

♦ **Paste:** Inserts the contents of the clipboard at the position of the insertion point in the Editing pane.

◆ **Zoom 200%:** Displays the equation at 200% magnification (twice the actual size).

◆ **Zoom Fill:** Enlarges the equation to fill the Display pane.

◆ **Settings:** Displays the Equation Settings dialog box.

◆ **Equ Pos:** Displays the Box Position and Size dialog box.

You can also use the items on the File, Edit, and View menu to access these functions.

ENTERING EQUATION SYMBOLS AND COMMANDS

There are several ways to enter symbols and equation commands in the Editing pane. For example, you can enter the capital sigma (Σ) by typing the keywords SIGMA, SUM, or SMALLSUM, or by selecting the keyword or symbol in the Equation palette. With a mouse, you can quickly insert a character by double-clicking on it in the palette.

You can also enter the character by selecting it from the WordPerfect Characters dialog box (press Ctrl-W or select Edit ➤ WP Character). If you type or select the keyword, the word itself will be displayed in the Editing pane, but it will appear as the symbol in the Display pane when you select Redisplay.

If you would like to be able to type equation characters, you can switch to the Equation keyboard. With this keyboard, equation characters and commands are assigned to Ctrl-key combinations, as shown in Figure 6.6.

To change to the Equation keyboard, select File ➤ Preferences ➤ Keyboard ➤ Select and double-click on it in the list box. If you want the Equation keyboard to be active every time you use the Equation Editor, select File ➤ Preferences ➤ Equations ➤ Select to display the Keyboard dialog box, and then choose Equation in the list box. Selecting the keyboard in this way makes it available in the Equation Editor but not in the document window.

Figure 6.7 shows the sigma character entered several different ways. Left to right, they have been entered by using the WordPerfect Characters dialog box, by typing the three keywords, by selecting the symbols in the Large palette, and by selecting the keyword in the Greek palette. The Large palette contains two sizes of most characters in the set. No matter how it appears in the Editing pane, the symbol itself appears in the Display pane.

If you make a mistake in the Editing pane, delete characters by pressing the Del or Backspace key. You can use the arrow keys to move the insertion point in the pane and press Ins to turn on Typeover mode.

Keystroke	Inserts
Ctrl-A	α
Ctrl-Shift-A	SUP
Ctrl-B	β
Ctrl-Shift-B	BAR
Ctrl-C	CONG
Ctrl-Shift-D	Δ
Ctrl-D	δ
Ctrl-E	ε
Ctrl-Shift-E	IN
Ctrl-F	φ
Ctrl-Shift-F	From-To
Ctrl-G	γ
Ctrl-Shift-G	GRAD
Ctrl-I	INF
Ctrl-Shift-I	INT
Ctrl-L	λ
Ctrl-Shift-L	OVERLINE
Ctrl-M	μ
Ctrl-N	η
Ctrl-Shift-N	GRAD
Ctrl-O	ω
Ctrl-Shift-O	OVER
Ctrl-P	π
Ctrl-Shift-P	PARTIAL
Ctrl-Q	SIMEQ
Ctrl-Shift-Q	SQRT
Ctrl-R	ρ
Ctrl-S	σ
Ctrl-Shift-S	SUM
Ctrl-T	θ
Ctrl-Tab	→
Ctrl-Shift-Tab	←
Ctrl-U	<=
Ctrl-Shift-U	>=
Ctrl-X	!=
Ctrl-Z	LINE
Ctrl-Shift-Z	SUB

The Display pane is not updated automatically as you form the equation. To see how the equation looks at any time, select Redisplay or press Ctrl-F3. If the message

ERROR: Incorrect syntax

appears in the status bar when you try to update the Display pane, something is wrong with your equation. Correct the equation and try updating the Display pane again.

Commands such as SUB and OVER are not case sensitive. They can be entered in any combination of uppercase and lowercase. Variables will appear in the exact case in which you enter them.

We will now create a typical equation, with variables and subscripts.

1. Select Graphics ➤ Equation ➤ Create.

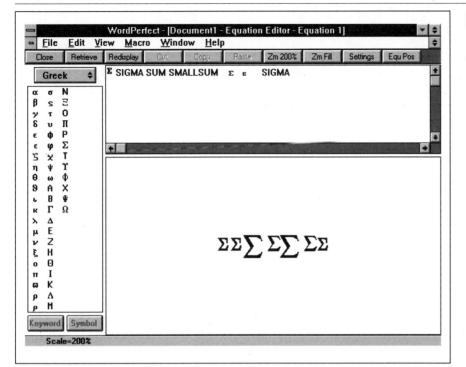

2. Type **db loss =**, and then select Redisplay (Ctrl-F3). The characters in the Editing pane now appear in the Display pane.

The 200% shown in the status bar means that the image shown in the Display pane is twice the actual size. Notice that the words *db loss* are in italics. When you enter words that are not equation commands, functions, or keywords, WordPerfect assumes they are variables of the equation and prints them in italic. Also notice that the spaces you entered in the Editing pane do not appear in the Display pane. Spaces are reserved for use as delimiters to identify equation commands. Any spaces that you type or see in the Editing pane are ignored when the display is updated.

3. Place the insertion point immediately after *db* and type ~, the tilde symbol. WordPerfect uses the tilde to indicate a full space. The backward accent (`) stands for a quarter space.

4. In the same way, enter the tilde after the word *loss*, and then place the insertion point at the end of the equation.

5. Select Redisplay to update the screen. Spaces now appear where you typed tildes in the Editing pane.

6. Type **~20~log**, and then select Redisplay (Ctrl-F3) to update the display.

7. If the Command palette is not shown, switch to that set. Then click on the word SUB in the Equation palette. If you are using the keyboard, press F6 to activate the palette, then press ↓ to highlight the word.

Notice that the status bar now includes the notation

Subscrpt: x Sub y or x_y

When you highlight an item in the palette, its full name and a sample or description of its use will appear in the status bar. In this case, it shows you can also subscript a character by using the underline symbol instead of the SUB keyword.

8. Press ↵. The word *SUB* appears in the Editing pane.

Notice that there is a space before and after the word *SUB* in the Editing pane. The Equation Editor automatically adds the spaces to differentiate commands from text. If you had typed SUB without any space before it, WordPerfect would interpret it as a variable, and the characters SUB would appear in the Display pane (and print): db loss = 20 logSUB10.

9. Type **10**, making sure there is at least one space after the word *SUB*, and then select Redisplay to update the Display pane. WordPerfect subscripted the number 10.

All numeric characters followed by a SUB command (or SUP for a superscript) will be formatted correctly. The subscript or superscript stops at the first non-numeric character. So, for example, the command log SUB 10X would result in $\log_{10}$x. If you want to subscript or superscript nonnumeric characters, they must be classified as a group and included in braces. Using groups, log SUB {10x} would result in $\log_{10x}$.

If you typed the (character into the equation now, it would appear in its normal size rather than enlarged to enclose the remainder of the equation. To format the equation properly, we will use the Left command, which tells WordPerfect to print the next enclosing character, such as a brace or parenthesis, large enough for the subgroup that follows.

10. Select the word LEFT in the Equation palette. (If you type the word yourself, remember to insert spaces.)

Note that if you tried to update the display at this point, you would see the Incorrect Syntax error message. Each Left command requires a corresponding Right command.

11. Type **(**, and then select SQRT, the square root command.

Now that the square root command is inserted, WordPerfect needs to know which of the next characters should go under the symbol. It also has to determine which characters are above the division line and which are under the line. The proper positioning is indicated by the group indicators { and }.

The equation commands to create the text inside the square root are Z SUB 1 OVER Z SUB 2. This means to place Z SUB 1 on a line over Z SUB 2. If you entered

SQRT Z SUB 1 OVER Z SUB 2

only Z_1 would appear under the square root sign in the Display pane. To correct this, you must surround the entire group with braces.

12. Type **{ Z SUB 1 OVER Z SUB 2 }**. Enter the braces by typing them or by selecting them from the palette. Make sure that at least one space surrounds each SUB and OVER.

13. Enter **+ SQRT { Z SUB 1 OVER Z SUB 2 -1 } RIGHT)**.

The −1 will not be subscripted because it starts with a nonnumeric character. However, it will appear under the second square root symbol because it is within its group (the opening and closing braces).

14. Select Redisplay (Ctrl-F3) to see the completed equation. It should look like the one shown in Figure 6.8.

Before leaving the Equation Editor, look carefully at the final form of the equation:

db~loss~=~20~log SUB 10 LEFT (SQRT { Z SUB 1 OVER Z SUB 2 } + SQRT { Z SUB 1 OVER Z SUB 2 −1 } RIGHT)

15. Select Close to accept the equation and return to the document. Within the document, you can adjust the position and size of the equation box, as explained in Chapter 4.

16. Select File ➤ Print (F5) ➤ Print to print the final equation.

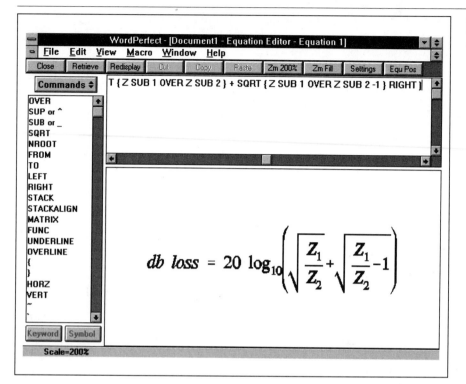

CHANGING EQUATION SETTINGS

By default, all the characters in an equation are in the same point size as the document's default font and centered in the equation box. To change the point size or position of the equation within the box, select Settings (from the Button Bar or File menu) in the Equation Editor.

The Equation Settings dialog box, shown in Figure 6.9, contains Graphic Font Size and Alignment options. You can select Point Size and enter a new type size for the equation or adjust its horizontal and vertical alignment. The Horizontal choices are Left, Center, and Right; the Vertical options are Top, Center, and Bottom.

The dialog box also includes the Print as Graphics option. When it is selected (the default), WordPerfect produces and prints each character and symbol graphically. If you turn off Print as Graphics, WordPerfect will print the equation using your printer's available fonts. If a character is not available, it will be generated graphically to complete the equation. Consider turning off Print as Graphics if you have high-resolution printer fonts that include all the symbols in the equation.

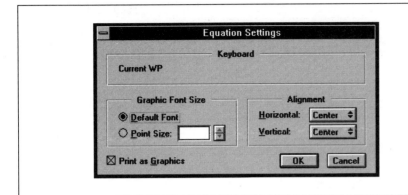

To change the default settings for equations, select File ➤ Preferences ➤ Equations. The options in the Equation dialog box are the same as those in the Equation Settings dialog box, but the type size and alignment you set here apply to all new equations.

To change the font for an equation, the font code must appear before the equation options code (which should precede the equation box code):

[Font][Equ Opt][Equ Box]

Insert the equation options code by selecting Graphics ➤ Equation ➤ Options ➤ OK. Reveal the codes (Alt-F3) to make sure the equation codes are in the proper order.

SAVING AND RETRIEVING EQUATIONS

You can save an equation in its own file, separate from the document. This is useful when you are constructing complex equations and you don't want to exit the equation function to save your work. In the Equation Editor window, select File ➤ Save As (F3), enter a file name with a .EQN extension, and select Save. This saves only the equation, not the document in the document window.

To recall the file into the Equation Editor, select the Retrieve button or File ➤ Retrieve. Then choose the name from the list box and select Retrieve.

USING THE INLINE EQUATION MACRO

WordPerfect provides the Inline macro for adding equations within a line of text, as shown in Figure 6.10. The macro creates a user box (without borders)

The $\sqrt{\pi}$ equals 1.77 and the $\sqrt{\frac{\pi}{2}}$ equals 1.25.

FIGURE 6.10:

Equation created with the Inline macro

and displays the Equation Editor window. The equation box is set with a character anchor, baseline vertical positioning, and auto both for the size. To run the macro, select Macro ➤ Play (Alt-F10), type **Inline**, and select Play. Enter your equation in the Equation Editor window, and then select Close.

As with other equations, you can adjust the size of the equation characters if the equation appears too small or large for the text. Redisplay the Equation Editor window and use the Equation Settings dialog box to change the point size.

CREATING HEADLINES WITH THE EQUATION EDITOR

If your printer does not have built-in headline fonts and you do not want to purchase a scalable font program, you can create headlines with the Equation Editor. Select to create an equation box (Graphics ➤ Equation ➤ Create), choose Settings, and set the Point Size for a larger size, such as 36. You can also change the alignment of the text by adjusting the settings in the Settings dialog box.

Enter the text in the Equation Editor window. If you want to insert special characters, use the WordPerfect Characters dialog box (Ctrl-W). When you print the document, the text will print as a graphic image, producing a headline even on printers without large fonts.

Because the Equation Editor considers regular text as variables, the headline is in italics. To print the text in normal type, precede the headline with the FUNC command, as in

FUNC {One~Day~Sale}

You can format text within the function using the BOLD and ITAL commands. For example, to produce the headline

This is the **last** day of the *sale*

enter

FUNC {This~is~the~BOLD last} FUNC {~day~of~the~} sale

To enter text on more than one line, use the # character, as in

For~Sale#
Today~Only

To change the size of individual characters within the equation, use the SCALESYM command. The syntax is

SCALESYM *Percentage Character*

For example, entering the command

SCALESYM 200 1~Day~Only

will print the number *1* twice as large as the other characters.

If the vertical or horizontal spacing of the enlarged character is incorrect, try using the HORZ or VERT commands to adjust the position. The syntax is

HORZ *x*
VERT *x*

where *x* is the percentage of the font size. For example, if you are using a 24-point font, the command

HORZ 50 A

shifts the character *A* up 12 points.

CREATING GRAPHICS WITH THE EQUATION EDITOR

You can also create graphic images with the Equation Editor. Figure 6.11 shows a picture of an old-fashioned camera created by using the SCALESYM, HORZ, and VERT commands. The body of the camera and the lens use the square symbol from the Arrows set. The diagonal lines are WordPerfect characters 6,6 and 6,7. The point size was set at 36 to enlarge the graphic.

Figure 6.12 shows another example of a graphic image designed with equation boxes. It consists of four triangles positioned to form the star. The Wrap Text Around Box feature was turned off for all the boxes so that they could be positioned.

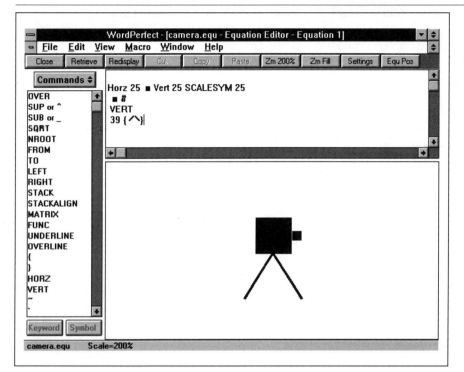

Drawing created with equation commands

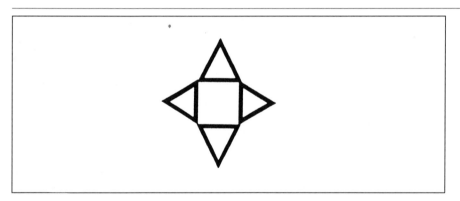

FIGURE 6.12:
Star created with four equation boxes

To combine text and symbols (or other special characters) in a design, type the text normally in the document window, and then add the symbol in an equation box. This technique is useful if you want to use your printer's high-quality fonts but the graphic symbol is not in your symbol set. For example, here are the steps for creating the logo shown in Figure 6.13:

1. In a new document, press ↵ eight times, and then press Shift-F7 to center the insertion point.

2. Select an 18-point font and type **Pyramid Sales Company**. Insert four spaces before and after the word *Sales.*

3. Select Graphics ➤ Equation ➤ Create ➤ Settings.

4. Select Point Size, enter **200** in the text box, and select OK.

5. In the Equation palette, select the Arrows set, then the triangle character.

6. Select the Equ Pos button (or File ➤ Box Position), set Anchor To to Page, turn off Wrap Text Around Box, select OK, and then choose Close.

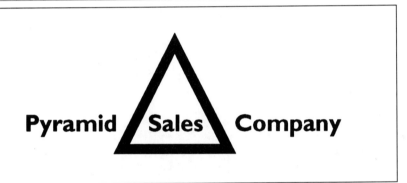

FIGURE 6.13:

Logo created with the Equation Editor

When Wrap Text Around Box is turned off, you can superimpose the text and graphics. You also must use the right mouse button to select a box.

7. Click on the graphic with the right mouse button and choose Select Box.

8. Drag the box so it is centered over the text and release the mouse button.

Experiment with the Equation Editor graphics capabilities. You can combine text and symbols for a variety of designs.

TYPESETTING TECHNIQUES AND OPTIONS

When your document requires precise spacing, adjust the settings in the Typesetting dialog box, shown in Figure 6.14. Select Layout ➤ Typesetting to display the dialog box.

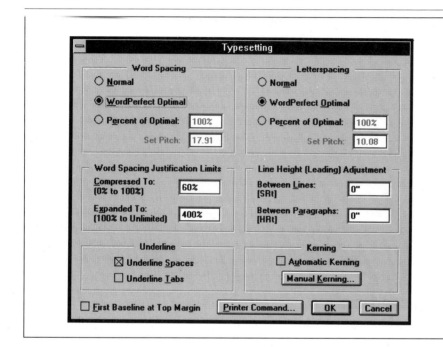

FIGURE 6.14:

Typesetting dialog box

SPACING WORDS AND CHARACTERS

The Word Spacing settings in the Typesetting dialog box control the spacing between words. Normal is the spacing set by the font manufacturer. Word-Perfect Optimal, the default, is spacing selected by WordPerfect. With fixed-width fonts, the Normal and WordPerfect Optimal spacing are the same.

To modify the default spacing, select Percent of Optimal and enter a percentage of the default spacing. Values less than 100 reduce the spacing between words; those higher than 100 increase the spacing. If you want to maximize the number of words on a page without changing the margins, try reducing the percentage slightly. When a typeface appears tightly spaced, with the words too close together, increase the word spacing. To print a specific number of characters per inch, enter the number in the Set Pitch text box.

Use the Word Spacing Justification options to control the spacing between words in fully justified text. In the Compressed To and Expanded To text boxes, enter the minimum and maximum amount that words can be spaced as a percentage. By default, WordPerfect will reduce the spacing between words to as little as 60 percent or increase spacing by as much as 400 percent. If the words in fully justified text appear too close together, increase the Compress To measurement. When the words are too far apart, reduce the Expanded To measurement.

The Letterspacing options control the spacing between letters. You may want to change the letter spacing of some proportionally spaced fonts if the characters appear too tightly or loosely spaced.

ADJUSTING THE LINE SPACING

The Line Height (Leading) Adjustment options in the Typesetting dialog box control the spacing between lines of text. Enter any *extra* space that you want between lines.

The Between Lines setting determines the spacing of lines within a paragraph. Use the Between Paragraphs setting to control the spacing inserted when you press ↵. For example, to automatically double-space between paragraphs, enter a measurement equal to the font size in the Between Paragraphs text box.

You cannot use the Typesetting dialog box to reduce the amount of spacing between lines. To *reduce* the default spacing between text lines, select Layout ➤ Line (Shift F-9)➤ Height ➤ Fixed, and then enter a line height in the text box. If you enter a size in points, follow the number by *p*, as in 14p.

With proportionally spaced fonts, WordPerfect adds 2 points to the font size to determine the default line height. For example, a 12-point font will appear with a line height of 14 points. If you want to decrease the leading, enter a line height of less than 14 points, such as 12p.

CONTROLLING UNDERLINING

By default, when you select to underline text, the line will appear under words and the spaces between words. If you prefer to underline text only, not spaces, turn off the Underline Spaces option in the Typesetting dialog box.

The Underline Tabs option underlines tab spaces (the blank area between the text), as in

President_____John Brown

Vice President_____Ann Johnson

Treasurer_____Mary Jones

If you do not want tab spaces underlined, turn this underlining option off.

ADJUSTING THE SPACING BETWEEN CHARACTERS

The Kerning options in the Typesetting dialog box allow you to adjust the spacing between two characters. Select Automatic Kerning to have Word-Perfect automatically reduce the spacing between certain letters. The [Kern; On] code is inserted in the document and affects text to the end of the document or until you turn off automatic kerning.

Select Manual Kerning to adjust the space between characters to the left and right of the insertion point. In the Manual Kerning dialog box, shown in Figure 6.15, click on the down arrow under Amount to reduce the space between characters; click on the up arrow to increase the space. You can reduce the space between characters so that they print on top of each other or even change position. When you are satisfied with the appearance of the characters shown in the Preview box, select OK to return to the Typesetting dialog box.

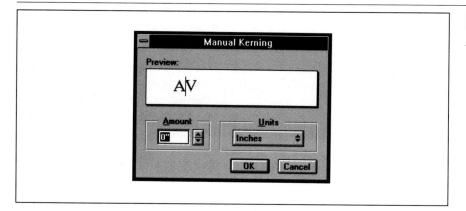

FIGURE 6.15:

Kerning dialog box

You can also use kerning to create interesting effects with standard characters. For example, by reducing the space between the characters *A* and *V,* you can make them appear to share a common stroke, as shown in Figure 6.16.

POSITIONING THE BASELINE

Select the First Baseline at Top Margin button at the bottom of the Typesetting dialog box if you want the first line of text to be referenced from the position of the top margin. The top margin setting determines where the top of the first line of text begins. The distance of the baseline below the top margin (the line on which text sits) is determined by the point size of the font. For example, for a 12-point font, the bottom of the first line of text will begin 84 points from the top of the page. With a 24-point font, the bottom of the first line is 96 points from the top of the page.

Use this option, combined with a fixed line height, to position text at exact locations for printing on preprinted forms. Selecting First Baseline at Top Margin will not cause the first line of text to print in the margin area.

ENTERING PRINTER COMMANDS

The Printer Command button at the bottom of the Typesetting dialog box allows you to control functions of your printer that are not recognized by the WordPerfect printer driver. You can also specify a file that you want downloaded to the printer. This option cannot be used with Windows printer drivers.

When you select Printer Command, you can enter any codes that you want transmitted to your printer at that location in the document. Your printer manual should include a complete list of commands. Enter commands in decimal format, between angle brackets, as in <18>. Enter the Escape character, which must precede commands for many printers, as <27>.

CREATING OVERSTRIKE CHARACTERS

Overstrike characters are two or more characters that print in the same position, so they appear superimposed. You can create this effect by manual kerning, but

WordPerfect also provides an overstrike function. Select Font ➤ Overstrike ➤ Create to display the Create/Edit Overstrike dialog box.

Type the overstrike characters in the text box. If you want to format or change the size of the characters, click on the left-pointing triangle at the end of the text box to select from the drop-down menu. The characters you entered will appear superimposed on the screen and on the printed page.

CHAPTER 7

Formatting newspaper and
parallel columns
Creating spreadsheets and invoices
Using tables for questionaires
and graphics

Formatting Text in Columns and Tables

f you produce newsletters or other multicolumn documents, you can take advantage of WordPerfect's column features. To format tables, use the table features. Tables are most often used to display statistical data, but they are also ideal for creating ruled forms of all types and a variety of special documents that would be difficult to create in any other way. In fact, the more you know about WordPerfect tables, the more uses you will find for them.

PRINTING TEXT IN COLUMNS

WordPerfect can automatically format text as either newspaper or parallel columns. *Newspaper columns* flow text from one column to the next one on the page, from left to right. When the far right column is filled, the text moves to the left column on the next page. If you delete or insert text, WordPerfect will move the text from column to column or page to page as necessary to accommodate your changes. *Parallel columns* remain next to each other, no matter how much text is added or deleted, instead of flowing from one column to the next.

CREATING COLUMNS WITH A MOUSE

With a mouse, you can quickly create up to five newspaper columns. Place the insertion point where you want the columns to begin, pull down the column icon in the ruler (the third icon from the right), and select the number of columns you want to use. Text following the insertion point will flow from column to column and from page to page. In the status bar, you will see the Col indicator followed by the number of the column that contains the insertion point.

The ruler shows the width of each column; the gray area indicates the gutters (the space between columns). You can change the width of a column by dragging its left or right margin indicator in the ruler.

To manually end a column, press Ctrl-↵. If you press Ctrl-↵ at the rightmost column, WordPerfect will insert a page break and begin the left column on the next page. To type single-column text again, press Ctrl-↵ to end the last column, pull down the column icon in the ruler, and select Columns Off. Unlike the columns in which WordPerfect entered a soft column/page end code to end the page or column, the hard column/page end code that you insert with Ctrl-↵ isolates that column from the others. Adding or deleting text in that column will not affect the other columns.

USING THE DIALOG BOX TO FORMAT COLUMNS

You can use the Define Columns dialog box, shown in Figure 7.1, to set up any number of columns. Select Layout ➤ Columns (Alt-Shift-F9) ➤ Define to see the dialog box.

By default, WordPerfect evenly spaces the columns across the page. When you type the number of columns in the Number of Columns text box, WordPerfect calculates the left and right margins of each column and enters the measurements for evenly spaced columns in the Margins text boxes. You can replace these entries with your own left and right margin settings for each column.

The Options section of the dialog box contains two items. If you enter new margins, WordPerfect will automatically turn off the Evenly Spaced option. The Columns On option puts the column format into effect as soon as you close the dialog box. Turn if off to type single-column text.

To change column widths with the keyboard, delete the [Col Def] code and then redefine the column format through the Define Columns dialog box.

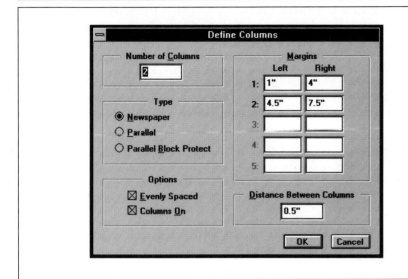

FIGURE 7.1:

*Define Columns
dialog box*

When you define a new format, the text will automatically adjust because the [Col On] code is still in the text.

CREATING PARALLEL COLUMNS

The default format, Newspaper, is selected in the Type section of the Define Columns dialog box. The other two types create parallel columns. Use parallel columns when you do not want the text to flow freely from column to column, page to page. For example, in some documents, material in a paragraph on the right relates directly to text on the left, and they should always be side by side.

Select Parallel to create regular parallel columns, in which longer columns will span a page break if necessary. Choose Parallel Block Protect to keep the columns next to each other even if it means moving all the text in each column to a new page.

When you are entering text in parallel columns, you press Ctrl-↵ to move the insertion point from one column to another. Unlike in newspaper columns, this key combination does not insert a page break when you press it from the rightmost parallel column.

You can use parallel columns to format brochures. For example, if you are creating a four-page folder—one sheet of paper folded in half—select a landscape form, and then define two evenly spaced parallel columns. Type the text for one page, press Ctrl-↵, and enter the text for the page to be printed next to it. Type the text for the pages in this order: 4, 1, 2, 3.

Note that in many cases it is more efficient to create documents that require parallel columns as labels or as tables. For example, columnar mailing lists are easier to create and manipulate by using a label form. A label format ensures that addresses do not break across columns (with the start of an address at the bottom of one column and the remainder at the top of the next). You can also print specific addresses by entering their page numbers in the Multiple Pages dialog box. (Label forms are described in Chapter 3.)

CONVERTING COLUMNS TO SINGLE-COLUMN FORMAT

Two codes are required to enter columns: the column definition code, [Col Def], and the column on code, [Col On]. Both codes precede the column text.

To convert multicolumns to a single column, delete the [Col On] code. The [Col Def] code will remain in the text, but it will have no effect until you turn on the column feature again and insert another [Col On] code. You can also delete the [Col Def] code, but then you must create or define the columns again when you want to format the text in columns.

Another way to convert multicolumn text to a single column is to place the insertion point at the start of the columns and select Layout ➤ Columns (Alt-Shift-F9) ➤ Columns Off. This inserts the [Col Off] code. To return the text to multiple columns, delete the [Col Off] code.

TURNING OFF THE SIDE-BY-SIDE DISPLAY

If you find the side-by-side display of columns distracting, you can view the columns separately. Select File ➤ Preferences ➤ Display and turn off the Columns Side-by-Side option.

Each column will appear on a separate page but in its proper position. For example, in a two-column format, columns will appear on the left or right side of the window. The columns will still print side by side, no matter how they appear on the screen. Turn the Columns Side-by-Side option back on to display the columns together.

DEFINING COLUMN STYLES

If you use columns often, consider creating styles for their formats. For example, you could create a stylesheet with all the formats needed for a standard monthly newsletter:

◆   A style that contains all the text and formatting codes for the masthead.

◆ A style for large column headings; for example, a paired style that turns on extra-large printing and centers the insertion point.

◆ A third style that defines and turns on the number of columns that you use.

Creating and retrieving stylesheets are covered in Chapter 2.

PLACING GRAPHICS IN COLUMNS

With a mouse, you can easily move and scale a graphic image to place it within a column or across several columns. You can also use the Box Position and Size dialog box to position the image. Set the Anchor To option to Page, and then select the appropriate Horizontal Position:

◆ **Column, Left:** Aligns the graphic image with the column's left margin.

◆ **Column, Right:** Aligns the image with the column's right margin.

◆ **Columns Full:** Aligns the image with both of the column's margins.

◆ **Columns Center:** Centers the image in the column.

When you select one of these options, the Horizontal Position text box changes to Columns. Enter the number of the column or columns with which you want the graphic image to align.

CREATING TABLES

You access WordPerfect's table features by selecting Tables from the Layout menu or by clicking on the table icon on the ruler. Before you begin to set up a table, decide how many rows and columns you will need. Although you can add or delete rows and columns, your table will be easier to work with when its structure is appropriate for your purposes. With the default row height and 1-inch top and bottom margins, 31 rows will fit on an $8\frac{1}{2}$-inch-by-11-inch page.

With a mouse, you can use the table icon on the ruler to create a table of up to 32 columns (the maximum that WordPerfect allows) and 45 rows. To create a table with more rows, or if you do not have a mouse, select Layout ➤ Tables (Ctrl-F9) ➤ Create.

USING THE TABLE BUTTON BAR OR SUBMENU

If you have a mouse, you can use WordPerfect's Table Button Bar. Select View ➤ Button Bar Setup ➤ Select. In the dialog box, which lists the Button Bar files in the WPWIN/MACROS subdirectory, double-click on TABLES.WWB.

The Button Bar contains buttons for the Layout ➤ Tables submenu options, from left to right as follows:

BUTTON BAR	LAYOUT ➤ TABLES MENU
Table	Create
Tbl Opts	Options
Tbl Join	Join
Tbl Split	Split
Tbl Insert	Insert
Tbl Del	Delete
Tbl Cell	Cell
Tbl Col	Column
Tbl Row	Row
Tbl Lines	Lines
Tbl Form	Formula
Tbl Calc	Calculate

To scroll the Button Bar, click on the left and right arrows on the left side of the bar.

To display the default Button Bar again, select WP{WP}.WWB from the Select Button Bar dialog box. You can turn the currently selected Button Bar off and on by selecting View ➤ Button Bar.

Note that when you select to delete a table, you will be presented with three choices:

◆ **Entire Table:** Deletes the table from the document

◆ **Contents (Text Only):** Deletes the text in the cells but not the table. The blank table remains in the document.

◆ **Table Structure (Leave Text):** Deletes the table but not the text. The text will be converted to tabular columns (defined by tab stops).

CREATING A SPREADSHEET

WordPerfect's table features are especially useful for designing and working with spreadsheets. We will create the sample spreadsheet shown in Figure 7.2, which uses formulas and contains special formatting.

FIGURE 7.2:

Sample table

	Sun Manufacturing Company Comparative Analysis					
	All figures in thousands of dollars					
Sales		1246		1321		1282
Rentals		89		91		92
Total Income	1 9 9 3	1,335	1 9 9 4	1,412	1 9 9 5	1,374
Salaries		543		552		522
Office		99		102		98
Total Expenses		642		654		620
Net		693		758		754
Net % of Sales		51.52		49.51		48.36
All figures are subject to audit						

Defining the Table Size

If you do not have a mouse, select Layout ➤ Tables (Ctrl-F9) ➤ Create. In the Create Table dialog box, type **7** for Columns and **12** for Rows. Select OK, and the blank table will appear on the screen.

To create the blank table with a mouse, follow these steps:

1. Select a 12-point font. The size of the font determines the size of the table cells. Choosing a 12-point font ensures that you will see the entire table on the screen without having to scroll horizontally or vertically.

2. Display the ruler (Alt-Shift-F3), point to the ruler's table icon, and hold down the left mouse button. A miniature grid appears, representing the rows and columns of a table, as shown in Figure 7.3.

3. Drag the mouse slightly down and to the right. As you drag the mouse, squares in the grid will become selected. The notation No Table on top of the grid will change to reflect the number of rows and columns indicated by the selected squares.

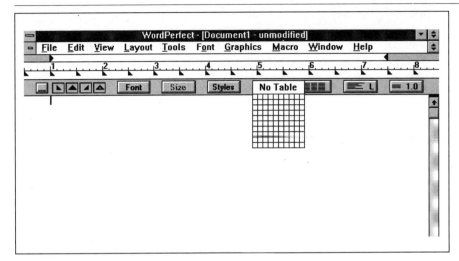

FIGURE 7.3:
Miniature grid representing table

4. Move the mouse until the table says 7,12 (for 7 columns and 12 rows), and then release the mouse button. A blank table will appear at the top of the screen, as shown in Figure 7.4.

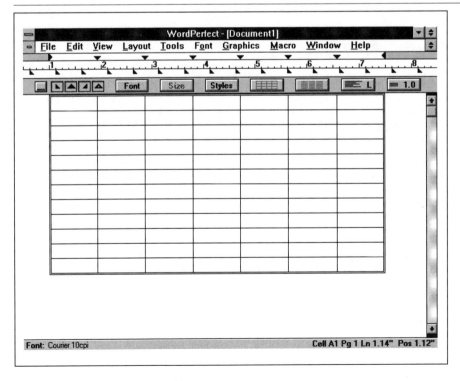

FIGURE 7.4:
Blank table on the screen

The down-pointing triangles in the ruler, between the left and right margin indicators, show the width of the columns. You can quickly change a column width by dragging the marker to the left or right.

As in a spreadsheet, each cell in the table is referenced by its column letter (A through G in the seven-column table) and row number (1 through 12). The top-left cell is A1.

Entering Text in Cells

To enter text in a cell, place the insertion point in the cell and type. To place the insertion point in a cell, click on the cell with the mouse. The row and column of the cell will be shown in the status bar next to the Pg indicator. To position the insertion point using the keyboard, use the keystrokes listed in Table 7.1. If the insertion point is in a blank cell, you can use the arrow keys to move to cells in any direction.

KEYSTROKE	INSERTION-POINT MOVEMENT
Tab	One cell to the right
Shift-Tab	One cell to the left
Home Home	To the first cell in the row
End End	To the last cell in the row
Alt-←	One cell to the left
Alt-→	One cell to the right
Alt-↑	One cell up
Alt-↓	One cell down
Alt-Home	The top line of a multiline cell
Alt-End	The bottom line of a multiline cell

TABLE 7.1:

Keystrokes for Moving to Table Cells

When you press ↵ within a cell or word wrap takes effect in a long entry, the cell's height will increase by one line. If you press ↵ by mistake, press Backspace to return the row to its original height.

Now we will enter some text and numbers in the blank table. Do not be concerned with alignment or cell size. We will format the table after it contains the data.

Enter the following text in the cells in the first column. Remember, do not press ↵ to move down to the next cell; use the mouse or keystrokes listed in Table 7.1.

Cell A3: **Sales**

Cell A4: **Rentals**

Cell A5: **Total Income**

Cell A6: **Salaries**

Cell A7: **Office**

Cell A8: **Total Expenses**

Cell A9: **Net**

Cell A10: **Net % of Sales**

Enter the text for the dates:

Cell B4: **1**	Cell D4: **1**	Cell F4: **1**
Cell B5: **9**	Cell D5: **9**	Cell F5: **9**
Cell B6: **9**	Cell D6: **9**	Cell F6: **9**
Cell B7: **3**	Cell D7: **4**	Cell F7: **5**

Enter the figures in the columns. We are not entering amounts in rows 5, 8, 9, and 10. These entries will later be calculated and inserted by WordPerfect.

Cell C3: **1246**	Cell E3: **1321**	Cell G3: **1282**
Cell C4: **89**	Cell E4: **91**	Cell G4: **92**
Cell C6: **543**	Cell E6: **552**	Cell G6: **522**
Cell C7: **99**	Cell E7: **102**	Cell G7: **98**

After you finish making these entries, your table should look like the one shown in Figure 7.5.

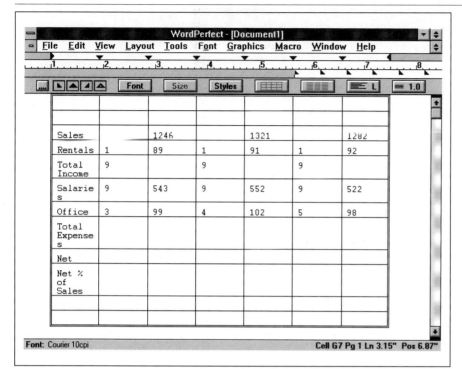

Selecting and Moving Cells

You must select cells in order to perform some table operations. With a mouse, place the pointer on the vertical line on the left side of the first cell you want to select, and then move the pointer until it changes into a left-pointing arrow. Then click the mouse button the number of times that corresponds to the cells you want to select: once to select the cell, twice to select the row, or three times to select the entire table.

To select a column, point to a horizontal line to change the pointer to an up-pointing arrow and click the mouse twice. You can also point to a cell and drag to select a group of cells. Click the mouse again to deselect the cells.

To select a cell with the keyboard, place the insertion point in the cell and press Shift-F8. To extend the selection, hold down the Shift key and press the arrow keys. The other keystrokes you can use while in Extend mode are listed in Table 7.2.

To move the contents of a cell, row, or column, select it then select Edit ➤ Cut (Shift-Del) or Edit ➤ Copy (Ctrl-Ins). In the dialog box that appears,

KEYSTROKE	SELECTION
Shift-Alt-Arrow	Extends the selection (but not outside the table)
Shift-Home	Selects to the start of the row
Shift-End	Selects to the end of the row
Ctrl-← or →	Selects the row
Ctrl-↑ or ↓	Selects the column
Shift-Ctrl-Home	Selects the text from the insertion point to the beginning of the document, without selecting the cells themselves. Use this to delete cell contents without deleting the cells.
Shift-Ctrl-End	Selects the text from the insertion point to the end of the document, without selecting the cells themselves.

TABLE 7.2:

Keystrokes for Selecting Cells in a Table

select to cut or copy the selected cells (Selection), rows, or columns. Then move the insertion point to where you want to insert the text and select Edit ➤ Paste (Shift-Ins).

Joining Cells

When you join cells, the lines separating the cells will disappear, and the area appears as one large cell. We will join several sets of cells in the table and then enter some text.

1. Select cells A1 and B1, the first two cells in the first row.

2. Select Layout ➤ Tables (Ctrl-F9) ➤ Join, or click on the Tbl Join button in the Button Bar. Cell B1 no longer exists.

3. Use the same procedure to join the following cells:

Cells C1 through G1
Cells A2 and B2
Cells C2 through G2
Cells A11 through G11
Cells A12 through G12
Cells B3 through B10
Cells D3 through D10
Cells F3 through F10

4. In cell C1, type **Sun Manufacturing Company**, press ↵, and type **Comparative Analysis**. Figure 7.6 shows how the table appears at this point.

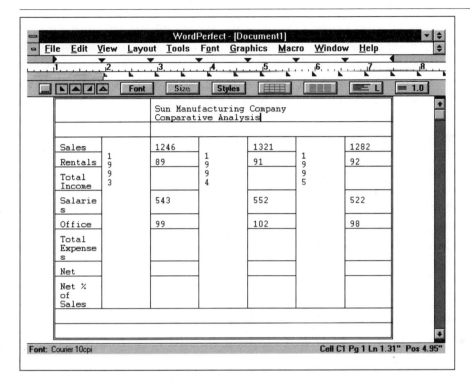

5. In cell C2, type **All figures in thousands of dollars**.

6. In cell A12, type **All figures are subject to audit**.

You may have a problem joining cells in more than one row, especially if you join other groups of cells in those rows in another column. For example, suppose that you joined cells C1 through G2, then cells A1 through B2. Cells C1 through G2 will appear to be one large cell (without any separating lines), but cells C2 through G2 will still be there. You will be able to move the insertion point to these cells and see them indicated in the status bar. If you reveal codes, you will see a [Cell] code for each of them. In fact, if you type text in cell C2 and press ↵, the row height will increase even though there appears to be a second empty line in the cell. To join those cells, reselect the block of cells and select to join them again.

Changing Column Widths

If you do not have a mouse, you must use the Format Column dialog box, shown in Figure 7.7, to change the widths of the table columns. The insertion point can be anywhere within the column you want to adjust. Place the insertion point in cell A3 of our sample table, and select Layout ➤ Tables (Ctrl-F9) ➤ Column to display this dialog box. In the Column Width text box, type **1.75**, and then select OK. Use this same procedure to change the widths of columns B, D, and F to **.375**. Change the width of columns C, E, and G to **1.15**.

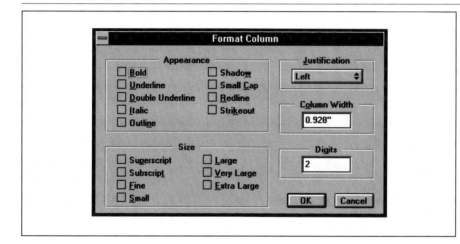

FIGURE 7.7:

Format Column dialog box

With a mouse, you can adjust column widths by dragging one of the down-pointing triangles on the ruler, which represent the column margins. Follow these steps to change the widths of the columns in our table:

1. Point to the triangle to the left of the 2-inch position on the ruler and drag it to the right. The status bar will show the notation Tables Split followed by the location of the pointer on the ruler.

2. Drag the mouse to the 2.75-inch position, then release the mouse button.

3. To reduce the width of the column that contains the year 1993, drag the triangle representing the column's right margin to the left to the 3.13-inch position. This is as far as WordPerfect will allow you to go using the mouse.

4. In the same way, drag the right margin of the 1994 column to the 4.31-inch position, and the right margin of the 1995 column to the 5.75-position.

If you have difficulty setting a column width to an exact size with the mouse, use the Format Column dialog box. We will do this now to make columns C, E, and G the same size.

5. Place the insertion point in cell G3 and select Layout ➤ Tables (Ctrl-F9) ➤ Column, or click on the Tbl Col button in the Button Bar, to display the Format Column dialog box.

6. In the Column Width box, enter **1.15**, and then select OK.

7. In the same way, set the width of columns C and E to **1.15**.

FORMATTING TABLES

Through the Table dialog boxes, you can set the formats for individual or selected cells, columns, rows, or the entire table. You can also change the format of text in cells in the same way that you format other text in a document. For example, use any of the Font or Layout menu items, such as Layout ➤ Justification ➤ Left (Ctrl-L). These settings override those in the Table dialog boxes.

FORMATTING COLUMNS AND ROWS

The settings in the Format Column dialog box affect the column in which the insertion point is located. As explained earlier in the chapter, you can use this dialog box to change column widths. You can also adjust the settings to change the appearance and size of characters. Use the Justification option to set the alignment of the text in the column to Left, Center, Right, or Decimal Align. In the Digits box, enter the number of digits you want to appear in decimal numbers.

To display the dialog box for formatting rows, select Layout ➤ Table (Ctrl-F9) ➤ Row, or click on the Tbl Row button in the Button Bar. The dialog box contains two settings:

◆ **Lines Per Row:** Sets the cells in the row as single line or multiline. With the Single Line setting, only one line of text can be entered in the cell, and pressing ↵ will move the insertion point to the next cell.

◆ **Row Height:** Sets the height to Auto or Fixed. With the default Auto setting, the row height will expand to accommodate the size of the font. Select Fixed to enter a specific height for the row. The row will remain that size no matter which font you use. If the font is too large to fit in the row, the characters will not print.

CONTROLLING THE FORMAT OF CELLS

You set the format of individual or selected cells through the Format Cell dialog box, shown in Figure 7.8. Select Layout ➤ Tables (Ctrl-F9) ➤ Cell, or click on the Tbl Cell button in the Button Bar, to display this dialog box.

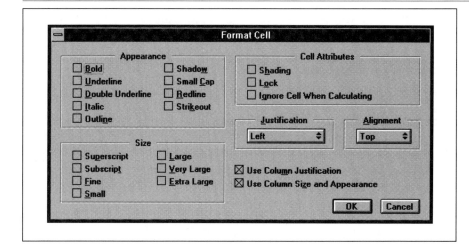

FIGURE 7.8:

Format Cell dialog box

You can choose Appearance and Size options for the selected cells, and those settings will override those set for the column in the Format Column dialog box. Additionally, you can select cell attributes and other options to format cells:

◆ **Shading:** Shades the selected cell. The degree of shading is set in the Table Options dialog box.

◆ **Lock:** Locks the cell so you cannot place the insertion point in it to change its contents. In the status bar, a locked cell is indicated by square brackets, as in [B4]. Turn off this attribute to unlock the cell, or use the Table Options dialog box to turn off all cell locks.

◆ **Ignore Cell When Calculating:** Has WordPerfect ignore a formula in the selected cell when performing calculations. In the status bar, an ignored cell is indicated by quotation marks, as in "B4.

◆ **Justification:** Aligns characters between the left and right borders of the cell. The choices are Left, Right, Center, and Decimal.

◆ **Alignment:** Aligns characters between the top and bottom borders of the cell. The choices are Top, Center, and Bottom.

◆ **Use Column Justification:** Returns the alignment of the selected cell to the column format.

◆ **Use Column Size and Appearance:** Returns the size and appearance of the selected cell to the column format.

We will format some cells in the table to center the notations, format the digits for the years, and align amounts.

1. Place the insertion point in cell A12 (*All figures are subject to audit*) and select Layout ➤ Tables (Ctrl-F9) ➤ Cell or click on the Tbl Cell button in the Button Bar.

2. For Justification, select Center, and then select OK.

3. Place the insertion point in cell C2 (*All figures in thousands of dollars*) and press Ctrl-J.

4. Place the insertion point in the top line of cell C1 (*Sun Manufacturing Company*) and press Ctrl-J.

5. Place the insertion point in cell B3 above the number *1* and press ↵ three times to move the year down.

6. Display the Format Cell dialog box and select Center for Justification.

7. In the same manner, center the digits for 1994 and 1995 in cells D3 and F3.

8. Place the insertion point in cell C3 (the first amount) and select Layout ➤ Tables (Ctrl-F9) ➤ Column, or click on the Tbl Col button.

9. For Justification, select Right, and then select OK.

10. In the same way, right align the amounts in columns E and G.

CHANGING THE FORMAT OF THE WHOLE TABLE

Formats that affect the entire table include its size, position, and cell margins. Another feature of a table that you can adjust is the appearance of the lines that divide the cells.

Setting Table Options

To display the Table Options dialog box, shown in Figure 7.9, select Layout
➤ Tables (Ctrl-F9) ➤ Options, or click on the Tbl Opts button in the Button
Bar. This dialog box contains the following settings:

◆ **Table Size:** Changes the size of the table. Enter the number of columns
and rows for the new size.

◆ **Position:** Sets the position of the table between the left and right margins of the page. You can also specify the distance from the left edge
by selecting that button and entering a measurement in the text box.

◆ **Cell Margins:** Sets the amount of space between text in cells and cell
borders.

◆ **Shading:** Specifies the degree of shading in cells with shading. With
some printers, setting the shading at 100 will print characters in
reverse. Otherwise, 100% shading will print a solid black cell,
covering the cell's contents.

◆ **Negative Result Display:** Determines the display of negative numbers resulting from calculations. Choose between a minus sign and
parentheses.

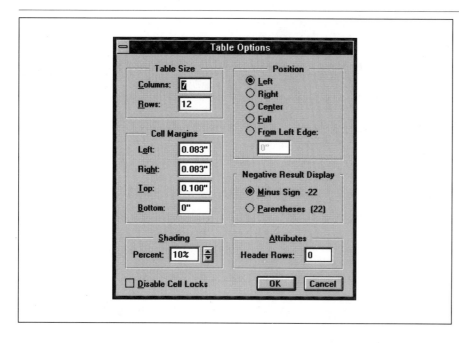

FIGURE 7.9:
*Table Options
dialog box*

◆ **Attributes:** Sets the number of header rows for tables that are longer than a page. Header rows automatically appear at the start of the table on each page. In the status bar, header cells are indicated by an asterisk, as in B4*.

◆ **Disable Cell Locks:** Unlocks all locked cells in the table.

You can also change the size of a table by inserting or deleting rows and columns. Use the Insert and Delete items in the Layout Table submenu, or use the key combinations: Alt-Ins to insert a row above the insertion point, Alt-Shift-Ins to insert a row below insertion point, or Alt-Del to delete the row containing the insertion point.

Adjusting Table Lines

WordPerfect places lines along the top and left sides of each cell. The lines along a cell's bottom and right are formed by the top line on the cell underneath it and the left line of the cell to the right. All cells but the ones in the rightmost column and bottom row are outlined in this manner. However, even though the cell borders are formed this way, you can control the appearance of each line individually.

Select different lines or remove lines completely by using the Table Lines dialog box, shown in Figure 7.10. Select Layout ➤ Tables (Ctrl-F9) ➤ Lines, or click on the Tbl Lines button in the Button Bar, to display this dialog box.

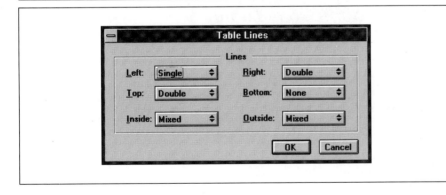

FIGURE 7.10:

Table Lines dialog box

The choices for each line are Single, Double, None, or Thick. Selecting None to remove lines deletes them from the display without joining the cells; the cell is still considered separate from its adjoining cells. Selecting another choice will change the existing line or add a line. For example, if you choose a single line for the bottom of a cell, that line will print in addition to the top line of the adjacent cell, with no spaces in between, creating a thicker line.

By combining adjacent lines, you can create line thicknesses and appearances that are not available elsewhere. Figure 7.11 shows how table line settings can be used to create special formats. Although the row numbers and column letters appear to be outside the table, they are centered in cells that have had their lines removed. If you actually typed the letters outside the table, they would be difficult to center over the columns. And if you changed the columns widths, you would have to recenter the letters.

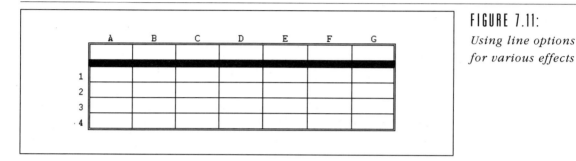

FIGURE 7.11:

Using line options for various effects

The outside lines in the second row were changed to double to match the other outside lines. The thick line under the second row (which appears to be the first line in the table) separates the labels from the table.

Adding a Graphic to a Table

You add a graphic image to a table in the same way that you insert one in a document: create a box and retrieve the graphic file into the Figure Editor (see Chapter 5). If you create a box that include borders, they will print in addition to the cell lines.

Our sample table has a picture in its top-left corner. We will format the table using the Table dialog boxes and then add the image.

1. In the Table Options dialog box, select Center for Position and increase Shading to 20%.

2. Place the insertion point in cell A2, display the Format Cell dialog box and select Shading.

3. Place the insertion point in cell C1, display the Table Lines dialog box, and select None from the Left list box.

4. Place the insertion point in cell A1, select to create a user box with the Figure Editor, and retrieve the Manufact.wpg graphic file.

5. In the Box Position and Size dialog box, set Anchor To to Page and Horizontal Position to Margin Left. Turn off Wrap Text Around Box. Select OK, then Close to insert the image in the table.

6. Point to the graphic image, click the right mouse button, choose Select Box, and drag the box to the center of the cell. Then click the right mouse button and choose Unselect Box. With the keyboard, use the Box Position and Size dialog box to set the vertical position to **.846** and the horizontal position to **1.38** (you may have to adjust this position slightly).

PERFORMING MATH IN TABLES

If you are using a version of Word-Perfect 5.1 for Windows dated after April 1992, refer to Appendix C for more information on this feature.

You could use a calculator to compute the results of formulas and type them in yourself, but inserting table formulas is much more efficient. By using formulas, you can change any of the numbers and have WordPerfect recalculate the formula for you. Locked cells will be calculated if they contain formulas.

You enter formulas in the Tables Formula dialog box, shown in Figure 7.12. Select Layout ➤ Tables (Ctrl-F9) ➤ Formula, or click on the Tbl Form button in the Button Bar to display the dialog box.

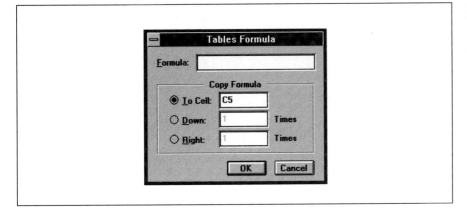

FIGURE 7.12:

Tables Formula dialog box

In the Formula text box, type the symbol for a function or an entire equation. Use the following function symbols:

SYMBOL (KEYPRESS)	FUNCTION	PURPOSE
+ (plus sign)	Subtotal	Adds the numbers in the cells above, up to another function.
= (equal sign)	Total	Computes the sum of all subtotals in the cells above.
* (asterisk)	Grand total	Computes the sum of all totals in the cells above.

The Tables Formula dialog box also contains options for copying formulas. Like a spreadsheet program, WordPerfect copies formulas in a relative way. A copied formula will adjust for the new row and column. The Down and Right options let you copy a value or formula to cells that are either below or to the right of the selected cell.

The final step in creating the sample table is to add formulas. We will have WordPerfect calculate the total, net, and percentage figures.

1. Place the insertion point in cell C5 and select Layout ➤ Tables (Ctrl-F9) ➤ Formula, or click on the Tbl Form button.

2. In the Tables Formula dialog box, type **+**, and then select OK. WordPerfect will calculate the total of the numbers in the cells above and display it in the cell with two decimal places.

3. Place the insertion point in cell C8, display the Tables Formula dialog box, type **+**, and select OK.

4. In the same way, enter the + function in cells E5, E8, G5, and G8.

5. Place the insertion point in cell C9, display the Tables Formula dialog box, type **C5-C8**, and select OK. This tells WordPerfect to calculate and insert the difference between cells C5 and C8, or subtract the expenses from the income.

6. With the insertion point in cell C9, display the Tables Formula dialog box. In the To Cell text box, type **E9**, and then select OK. Instead of repeating the formula C5-C8 in cell E9, WordPerfect will change it to E6-E9.

7. Display the Tables Formula dialog box, type **G9** in the To Cell text box, and select OK.

8. Place the insertion point in cell C10, display the Tables Formula dialog box, type **(C8/C3)*100**, and select OK. This formula is for calculating the percentage.

9. Display the Tables Formula dialog box, type **E10** in the To Cell text box, and select OK.

10. Display the Tables Formula dialog box, type **G10** in the To Cell text box, and select OK.

11. To delete the decimal places in the dollar figures, place the insertion point in cell A1, select Edit ➤ Replace (Ctrl-F2), type **.00** in the Search For text box, and then select Replace All. Select Close to remove the Replace dialog box.

We could have entered 0 in the digits text box when formatting the columns to prevent the decimal places from being inserted. However, the percentage would also be displayed without decimal places.

12. Select File ➤ Print (F5), then Print to print a copy of the completed table.

13. Select File ➤ Exit (Alt-F4), then No to exit WordPerfect without saving the document.

When you create your own spreadsheets, you may later change values in referenced cells. To update the calculations, select Layout ➤ Tables (Ctrl-F9) ➤ Calculate. If you edited the calculated figures, such as deleting decimal places as we did in our example, make the same changes before printing the updated table.

If there is more than one line of numbers in a cell, WordPerfect uses the bottom number in calculations. This may cause a problem if an operation creates a long number that wraps and causes the cell to expand. Make sure your cells are wide enough to display the number on one line before calculating formulas.

WordPerfect ignores spaces and nonnumeric characters when calculating. A cell that contains 23A 65, for example, will be treated as the value 2365 in a calculation.

CONVERTING COLUMNAR FORMATS

You can quickly convert tabular (created with tab stops) and parallel columns into a table. Select the columns, select Layout ➤ Tables (Ctrl-F9) ➤ Create, and choose which type of column you are converting.

For tabular columns, WordPerfect converts each [Tab] code to a cell boundary, and each hard carriage return to the end of a row. Each parallel column is converted to a table column.

To convert a table to text, delete the table definition code, [Tab Def]. WordPerfect will create tabular columns, each column separated by a tab stop.

WordPerfect will not let you directly insert a table in a newspaper column so that text in the other columns wraps around it. The solution is to insert the table in a text, table, or user box. If you create a table or user box, choose the Text Box Editor. If you want to add table captions, create a table box.

IMPORTING SPREADSHEETS

You can import or link Excel or Lotus 1-2-3 spreadsheets into WordPerfect and use its table features to edit and format the data. (However, if the spreadsheet is from software released after your version of WordPerfect for Windows, it may not be compatible.) You can even import a three-dimensional spreadsheet. Each dimension will be inserted as a separate table.

To import a spreadsheet, so that changes in the original spreadsheet do not affect the WordPerfect table, select Tools ➤ Spreadsheet ➤ Import. To insert the spreadsheet as well as a link to the original file, select Tools ➤ Spreadsheet ➤ Create Link. When you create a link, the most recent version will be displayed and printed with the WordPerfect document.

The Import Spreadsheet dialog box, shown in Figure 7.13, and the Create Spreadsheet Link dialog box contain the following specifications:

◆ **Filename:** The path and name of the spreadsheet file.

◆ **Range:** The portion of the spreadsheet to be imported (if you do not want the entire spreadsheet). Enter the range as the upper-left and lower-right corners of the group of cells, separated by a colon, period, or two periods, as in A1:C4, A1.C4, or A1..C4.

◆ **Range Name:** The names of ranges in the spreadsheet (if it contains any named ranges). Select the range you want to import or link.

◆ **Type:** Inserts the spreadsheet as a table or as text (tabular columns).

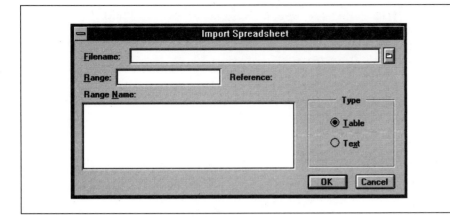

The other items on the Tools ➤ Spreadsheet submenu pertain to linked spreadsheets. Edit Link allows you to change the spreadsheet or range linked to the document. Update All Links retrieves the latest versions of all spreadsheets. Link Options offers two choices: Update on Retrieve, which automatically updates the link when you retrieve the document, and Show Link Codes, which displays a code showing that the spreadsheet is linked.

SPECIAL TABLE APPLICATIONS

WordPerfect's table features can be used to create a wide variety of useful forms, such as invoices, attendance sheets, and questionnaires. You can also design graphics as tables.

Designing a Calculating Invoice

With WordPerfect's table features, you can create an invoice form that automatically adds the sales tax and calculates the total amount due. Using the invoice form shown in Figure 7.14, you enter only the item number, description, and quantity for each item. Then select Layout ➤ Tables ➤ Calculate to compute the item totals, tax, and grand total. (The camera graphic on the form was added in a user box created with the Equation Editor, as described in Chapter 6.)

We will use this invoice form in later chapters to illustrate how to automate operations using macros and merge commands. Even if you do not produce invoices, create this table so that you can see how the other techniques work.

Aardvark Photography

354 West 88th Avenue
Weston, NJ 08761
609-555-1212

The one stop store for all of your photographic needs

Sold To:

Date:

Item #	Description	Quantity	Cost	Total
				0.00
				0.00
				0.00
				0.00
				0.00
				0.00
				0.00
				0.00
				0.00
				0.00
				0.00
				0.00
				0.00
				0.00
				0.00
				0.00
			Item Total	0.00
Thanks for the order!			Sales Tax	0.00
			Total	0.00

FIGURE 7.14:
Invoice form created using a table

The Total column in the table contains the formulas shown in Figure 7.15. In addition, use the following formats:

◆ Create a table with 5 columns and 20 rows.

◆ Delete the lines separating the cells in the first row, without joining the cells (in the Table Lines dialog box, select None for Inside and Bottom, Single for Outside).

◆ Join cells A18 through B20.

Total
C2*D2
C3*D3
C4*D4
C5*D5
C6*D6
C7*D7
C8*D8
C9*D9
C10*D10
C11*D11
C12*D12
C13*D13
C14*D14
C15*D14
C16*D16
C17*D17
+
E18*0.06
E18+E19

FIGURE 7.15:

Formulas used in the invoice

◆ Join cells C18 and D18, C19 and D19, C20 and D20.

◆ Set the Quantity column to right justification; the Cost and Total columns to decimal justification.

◆ For all of the rows, set Lines Per Row (in the Table Row dialog box) to Single Line and Line Height to Fixed. This prevent cells from being expanded and pushing rows onto the next page.

◆ Lock the cells containing formulas to ensure that these figures cannot be altered.

CREATING WIDE AND IRREGULAR-SHAPED TABLES

WordPerfect create tables up to 32 columns wide. However, if your printer can print in landscape orientation, you can set up wider tables. The trick is to create two tables and use the Layout ➤ Advance command to position them side by side.

For example, you could use this technique to create student attendance forms for 10-week classes. The table needs 51 columns: one to hold the student's name and 50 for the daily attendance record. If you have 20 students in each class, you need 20 rows in the table.

We will create a 51-by-20 table, using legal-size paper in landscape orientation, with ½-inch right and left margins. The first column will be 1-inch wide, and the remaining columns will be 0.24-inch wide. The column width is determined by subtracting the margins (1 inch total) and the first column width from the overall 14-inch width of the paper in landscape orientation. Dividing the remaining 12 inches by 50 columns results in 0.24 inch per column.

Depending on your computer system, it may take WordPerfect quite some time to change the display when you are working with large tables. For example, when you click three times to select the table, you may wait several seconds or longer for the table to be highlighted. To speed the process, create a table using just one or two rows. After making the necessary adjustments, use the Table Options dialog box to increase the table to the proper size. We will use this technique here.

1. Select the legal landscape page size and set the left and right margins to **.5"**.

2. Select a 12-point font, and then use either the ruler or the Create Table dialog box to create a table with 30 columns and 2 rows.

3. Display the Table Options dialog box and set the left and right cell margins to **0**. This will allow you to create the narrow columns.

4. To select the entire table, position the insertion point on one of the table lines until it becomes an arrow, and then click the mouse button three times.

5. Display the Format Column dialog box and set the column width to **.24"**.

6. Use the ruler or the Format column dialog box to change the first column to 1-inch wide.

7. Select the last column in the table and display the Table Lines dialog box. Change the right option to None. The right end of that column will be drawn by the left border of the second table.

8. Place the insertion point at the start of the line immediately after the table and set the left margin of the document to **8.46"**. This is calculated by adding the left margin and first 1-inch column to the space required by 29 cells that are 0.24 inch: 0.5 inch + 1 inch + (29 * 0.24 inch). You may have to adjust the left margin for your printer.

9. Select Layout ➤ Advance to display the Advance dialog box. Select To Line, enter **1"** in the Advance text box, and select OK. This code will move the second table to the 1-inch position. The left and right margin settings will place the two tables side by side.

10. Create a new table with 21 columns and 2 rows. Because of the margin settings, the cells will automatically be 0.24-inch wide.

11. Select the first column in the table, display the Table Lines dialog box, and change Left to Single.

12. Deselect the column. With the insertion point still in the second table, use the Table Options dialog box to set the number of rows to **20**. Be patient while WordPerfect expands the table.

13. Use the same method to set the number of rows for the first table to **20**.

14. Select File ➤ Print Preview (Shift-F5) ➤ Full Page. The second table will appear next to the first in Print Preview mode, as shown in Figure 7.16, as well as when printed.

15. Close the Print Preview window, then close or print the document.

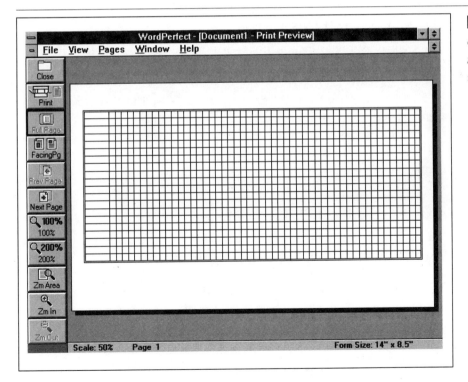

FIGURE 7.16:

Completed 51-column table in Print Preview mode

You can also combine tables to create ones that are not rectangular, such as the one shown in Figure 7.17. The table is actually two tables that share a common line. It was formed by creating a 6-by-8 table, followed by a 3-by-3 table. The column widths in the second table were set to match those in the first, and then the lines were adjusted to place single lines between each of the adjoining cells.

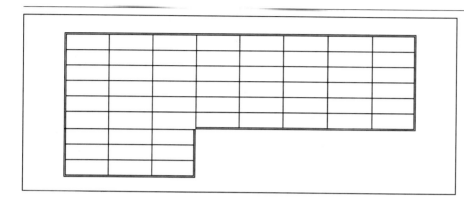

FIGURE 7.17:

Irregular-shaped table

CREATING QUESTIONNAIRES

Questionnaires usually include boxes that can be checked and lines in which to write responses. You can create this type of format as a table, as shown in Figure 7.18.

The large boxes in the sample form are cells. The small check boxes were created with a WordPerfect special character: 5,24 in 18-point type. The check mark is special character 5.23, manually kerned to print in the same position as the check box. WordPerfect special characters are discussed in Chapter 6.

ENHANCING PARALLEL COLUMNS

You can increase the visual impact of parallel columns by using the shading and line options for tables. Figure 7.19 shows an example of two columns created with this technique.

The entire document shown in the figure is one table, with the lines removed or modified. Although you could create this format with graphic text boxes, they would be very difficult to align properly.

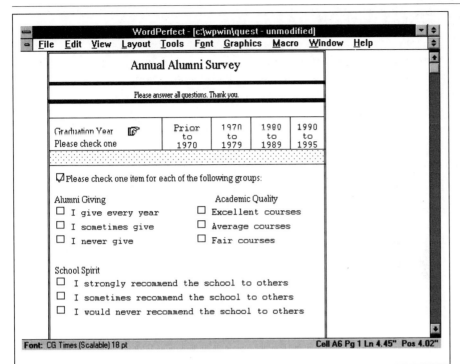

FIGURE 7.18:

Questionnaire created as a table

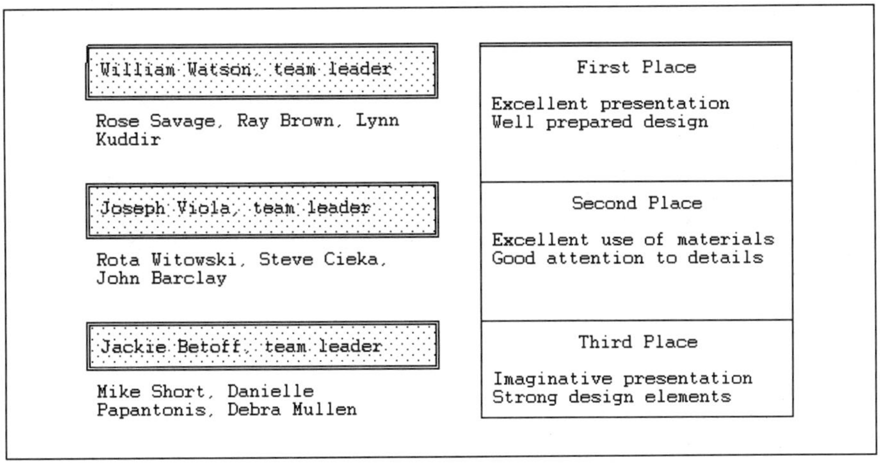

FIGURE 7.19:

Parallel columns with table formatting

CREATING GRAPHICS AS TABLES

With a little imagination, you can use tables to create some interesting graphic images. For example, the piano keyboard shown in Figure 7.20 is a Word-Perfect table with the shading set at 100%. It was created from a table of 13 columns and 6 rows. Cells were joined then shaded to form the black keys. The white keys were formed by joining cells and changing lines.

The figure also shows a chart structure formed from a table. You can create organization charts, family trees, and other documents that require lines, boxes, rows, or columns. For a complex drawing, plan the design ahead of time using graph paper.

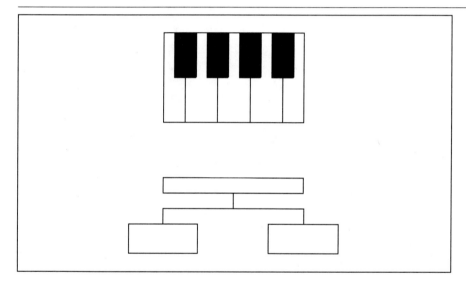

FIGURE 7.20:

Graphics created as tables

CHAPTER 8

Recording and playing macros
Editing and writing macros
Creating your own Button Bars

Streamlining Your Work with Macros and Button Bars

 *macro* is a series of keystrokes stored on disk. You can repeat the keystrokes automatically by playing the macro. Macros can be used to repeat text, such as your company's name, or complex formatting commands, such as changing the paper size and inserting a header or footer.

This chapter describes how to record, edit, and write macros. It also explains how to create custom Button Bars that include your macros. More advanced macro functions are discussed in Chapter 9.

RECORDING MACROS

The simplest way to create a macro is to record the keystrokes to complete the task you want the macro to perform. After you have recorded and saved a macro, you can run it to perform the task.

Select Macro ➤ Record (Ctrl-F10) to display the Record Macro dialog box, shown in Figure 8.1. In this dialog box, you can assign a file name to your macro. WordPerfect will add the .WCM extension when it saves the macro. If the macro name is more than eight characters, the macro will be saved under the first eight, and you must add the file name extension yourself. If you give the macro the same name as an existing one, WordPerfect will ask if you want to replace that macro with the new one.

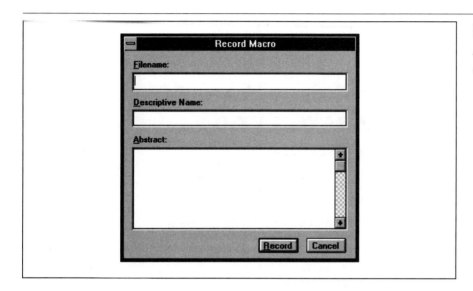

ΓIGURE 8.1:

Record Macro dialog box

Instead of a file name, you can enter a key combination that you want to use to execute the macro. The following combinations are accepted:

◆ Ctrl-A through Ctrl-Z

◆ Ctrl-0 through Ctrl-9

◆ Ctrl-Shift-A through Ctrl-Shift-Z

◆ Ctrl-Shift-0 through Ctrl-Shift-9

Note that if you use a combination already assigned to the keyboard, the keyboard function will be performed when you press the keys, not your macro. To use the combination for the macro, you must remove the keyboard assignment or change to a keyboard that does not define those keystrokes. However, you can always run the macro through the Play Macro dialog box.

In the Descriptive Name text box, you can enter the purpose of the macro, using up to 68 characters. Add a more thorough explanation of up to 762 characters under Abstract. Text in the Abstract box will word wrap as you type. To manually start a new line, press Ctrl-↵; pressing ↵ by itself will close the dialog box.

When you are recording a macro, the mouse can be used only to select menu and dialog box options. You must select text and move the insertion point with the keyboard. To ensure that your macros run correctly, it's a good idea to avoid using the mouse.

CREATING A LETTERHEAD MACRO

The first macro we will record will insert text and formatting commands to produce a letterhead. Start WordPerfect (or open a new document) and follow these steps:

1. Select Macro ➤ Record (Ctrl-F10), type **Lethead** as the macro name, and select Record. The mouse pointer will change to the international "don't" sign when it is in the text area of the screen, indicating that the mouse cannot be used to select text.

2. Press Ctrl-J to center the insertion point, type your name, and press ↵. If you make a typing error, just correct it as usual.

3. Type your street address and press ↵.

4. Type your city, state, and zip code, and then press ↵ twice.

5. Select Tools ➤ Date Code (Ctrl-Shift-F5) to insert the date function and press ↵.

6. Press Ctrl-L, and then press ↵.

7. Select Macro ➤ Stop (Ctrl-Shift-F10) to end keystroke recording.

WordPerfect automatically saves the macro on your disk in a file called Lethead.wcm.

RECORDING FORMATTING MACROS

Now record two macros to format text:

◆ To record a triple-spacing macro, press Ctrl-3 in the Filename text box in the Record Macro dialog box (Ctrl3.wcm appears as the name) and choose Record. Select Layout ➤ Line (Shift-F9) ➤ Spacing, type **3**, and select OK. Then select Macro ➤ Stop to end the macro definition.

◆ To record a macro to switch the position of two paragraphs, type **Paragraph one**, press ↵, type **Paragraph two**, and press ↵. Place the insertion point anywhere in the second sentence, and choose to record the macro under the name **Swap**. Select and cut the paragraph, press Ctrl-↑ then Home, and paste the paragraph. (Pressing Home ensures that this macro will work with an indented paragraph by placing the insertion point before any formatting codes.) Then end the macro recording.

When you are finished recording the two macros, close the document without saving it.

ASSIGNING MACROS TO THE MACRO MENU

In addition to assigning macros to keystrokes, you can add them to the Macro menu. This makes macros that you use frequently easily accessible. Select Macro ➤ Assign to Menu ➤ Insert to display the dialog box shown in Figure 8.2.

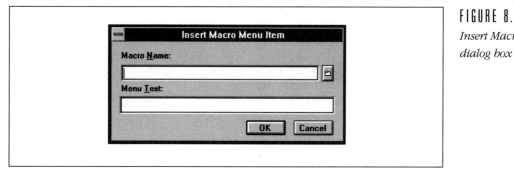

Insert Macro Menu Item dialog box

In the Macro Name box, type the name of the macro you want to add to the menu. In the Menu Text box, enter how you want this macro to be listed on the menu. For example, if you decided to add the Swap macro (for switching paragraphs) to the Macro menu, you might want to list it as Transpose. If you leave the Menu Text box blank, the macro name will appear.

If you later want to delete the macro from the menu, highlight its name in this dialog box, then select Remove. To change the menu text, select Edit.

ASSIGNING MACROS TO THE KEYBOARD

You assign a macro to the keyboard in much the same way that you assign a special character (see Chapter 6). However, you cannot add a macro to the keyboard until it has been compiled. To compile the macro, run it once.

After running the macro, select File ➤ Preferences ➤ Keyboard ➤ Create or Edit. In the Keyboard Editor dialog box, select Macros from the Item Types drop-down list. Then select Add to display a list of macros in the MACROS subdirectory. If your macro is in another directory, select the path in the Directories list box, then the macro, then Import. Highlight the macro in the list box, press the key combination you want to assign to it, and select Assign. After you choose OK, select Yes to save the keyboard.

RUNNING MACROS

You can run any macro from the Play Macro dialog box, shown in Figure 8.3. Other macros can be run from the Macro menu or keyboard, depending on how you defined them.

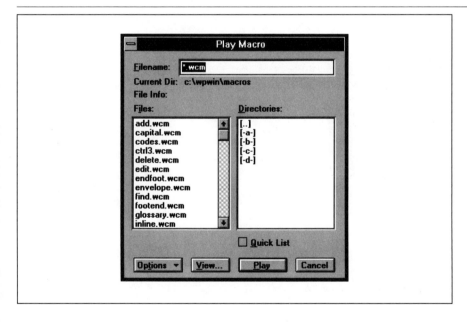

FIGURE 8.3:

Play Macro dialog box

USING MACROS IN A DOCUMENT

We will use two of our recorded macros to create a new document:

◆ Select Macro ➤ Play (Alt-F10), scroll through the list of macro files to select Lethead.wcm, and then choose Play. The macro is compiled, and then your address appears on the screen just as you typed it.

◆ Place the insertion point at the start of the document and press Ctrl-3 to run the triple-spacing macro.

After running the two macros, close the document without saving it.

If you press a key combination that has not been assigned to a macro, or the macro is not in the MACROS directory, WordPerfect will display the message

File XXXX.WCM not found -- Search for file?

Select Yes to display the Play Macro dialog box.

If you press a key combination to play a macro and WordPerfect performs some other function, that key combination has been assigned to the active keyboard. However, you can still run the macro from the Play Macro dialog box.

RUNNING A MACRO ON STARTUP

You can start WordPerfect and run one of your macros automatically. In Program Manager, select File ➤ Run. Type **WPWIN /M-** followed by the macro name, as in WPWIN /M-LETHEAD. The macro will be executed as soon as the program is loaded.

To run a macro every time you start WordPerfect, change the command that executes when you select the WordPerfect icon in Program Manager. In Program Manager, highlight the WPWIN icon, and then select File ➤ Properties. The Properties dialog box contains a Command Line item containing an entry like this:

C:\WPWIN\WPWIN.EXE

Edit the entry to include the /M- switch and the name of the macro:

C:\WPWIN\WPWIN.EXE /M-LETHEAD

Be sure to leave a space after the .EXE extension. The macro will be played whenever you click on the icon to start WordPerfect. When you no longer want the macro to run, delete the switch and macro name from the command line.

EDITING MACROS

Editing a macro allows you to correct any mistakes you made when recording the macro. It is easy to correct typographical errors or add text to a macro, but making more complex changes requires knowledge of WordPerfect's macro language.

OPENING A MACRO FILE

To edit a macro, open it as a document and change its text. Open the Lethead.wcm macro now to see its text in a document window: select File ➤ Open (F4), select the MACROS subdirectory in the directories list box, choose Lethead.wcm in the File list box, and then select Open. The text of the macro will appear in the editing window, as shown in Figure 8.4.

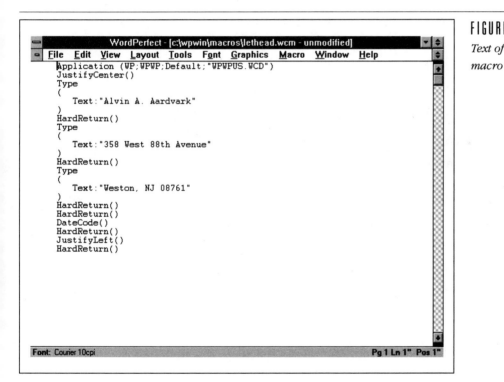

FIGURE 8.4:

Text of the Lethead macro

Each of the functions and commands in the displayed macro are listed in WordPerfect's macro language:

Application(WP;WPWP;Default;"WPWPUS.WCD")

	Designates the start of the macro and the application in which the commands will be run. It indicates that the syntax for the commands can be found in the WPWPUS.WCD file.
JustifyCenter( )	Centers the insertion point, performing the Layout ➤ Justification ➤ Center (Ctrl-J) command.
Type	Inserts the text enclosed in quotation marks into the document.
HardReturn( )	Inserts a carriage return (like pressing ↵).
DateCode( )	Inserts the date code.
JustifyLeft( )	Left aligns the text, performing the Layout ➤ Justification ➤ Left (Ctrl-L) command.

CHANGING MACRO TEXT

If you want to change the text that a macro generates, edit any of the text within the quotation marks. To insert new text, add a Type command. We will use this method to change the Lethead macro to include your telephone number.

1. With the text of the Lethead.wcm file on the screen, move the insertion point to the end of the line containing the closing parenthesis for the city, state, and zip code Type command, and press ↵. This performs a carriage return, inserting a blank line, but it will not insert a carriage return in the document when the macro is run.

2. Type **HardReturn( )** and press ↵.

3. Type **Type("**, then your telephone number, then a quotation mark and closing parenthesis. It should appear something like this:

   Type("555-1212")

Notice that we entered this Type instruction all on one line, rather than on separate lines as in the macro, and without the notation *Text:*. Spacing the command over several lines makes it easier to read but is not required.

4. Select File ➤ Save (Shift-F3) to save the edited macro.

If you made any syntax errors while editing a macro, when you try to play that macro, WordPerfect will detect them and display a dialog box. For example, the dialog box shown in Figure 8.5 appeared because of a missing parenthesis in a Type command. The dialog box contains a general description of the problem and the location of the problem within the macro. In this case, the error is reported in the line following the one with the missing parenthesis.

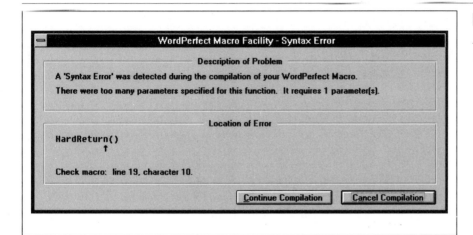

FIGURE 8.5:

Dialog box reporting a macro error

If this dialog box appears when you play a macro, select either Continue Compilation to look for additional errors, or Cancel Compilation to stop the process at this point. Correct the errors, then try playing the macro again.

WRITING MACROS

Macros created by recording keystrokes are useful, but they only touch upon the power of WordPerfect's macro language. By writing a macro, you can create entire applications.

You type the programming instructions for a macro, starting with the Application command, in a new document, and then save the macro with a file name using the .WCM extension. Save your macros in the MACROS subdirectory so that they will be easy to access. WordPerfect will ignore most formatting codes, so you can type macros with any line spacing and in any font.

Many macro programming instructions use *Product commands*, which execute a WordPerfect function that you could perform by using the mouse or keyboard. For example, you can include Product commands to select from dialog boxes or menus, move the insertion point, and insert text.

Pausing at Dialog Boxes

When you select options from a dialog box while recording a macro, the codes for the options are inserted; the dialog box will not appear when you run that macro. However, you can write a macro that includes Product commands to display a dialog box and then pause for you to make selections. The syntax of the command is

*Dialog-Box-Name*Dlg()

This means that you replace the text *Dialog-Box-Name* with the name of the dialog box you want to display, then follow the name with the characters Dlg( ). In some cases, the dialog box name is an abbreviation. For example, the command LineSpacingDlg( ) displays the Line Spacing dialog box. PreDateFormatDlg( ) displays the Preferences Date Format dialog box.

When the command is executed in a macro, the dialog box appears and the macro pauses until you select OK or Cancel. If you select OK, the codes for your dialog box selections will be inserted as codes into the document.

Inserting Dialog Box Actions

Some Product commands insert dialog box settings into the document without displaying the box on the screen. The syntax for these commands is

Dialog-Box-Name (Parameters)

The *Parameters* specify which dialog box settings should be inserted. For example, the command LineSpacing(Spacing:2) sets double line spacing. It will insert the code [LnSpacing:2] into the document, just as if it were entered from the keyboard.

These commands are useful when you will always want the same settings selected when you play the macro, or when you want to use a variable to specify the parameter value. You will learn how to input values into variables in Chapter 9. When you want to select the settings from the dialog box each time the macro is played, use the command to display the dialog box.

Including parameter names, such as Spacing, in commands is optional. You could type the double line spacing command as LineSpacing(2). However, since some commands have several parameters, entering parameter names makes your macros easier to read and interpret.

PERFORMING OTHER ACTIONS

Other Product commands duplicate keystroke entries. They include commands for moving the insertion point. For example, the command PosChar-Next( ) moves the insertion point one character to the right; HardReturn( ) inserts a carriage return.

There are also Product commands that select menu options. They are usually followed by the parameter On! or Off!. For example, change to Draft mode with the command DraftMode(On!). Use the InsertTypeover(Off!) command to ensure that Typeover mode is turned off.

The number 1 can be used in place of On!, and 0 can replace Off!, as in DraftMode(1), which turns on Draft mode. In many cases, a macro parameter can be a name, such as On!, or the number that represents it.

INSERTING TEXT

As explained earlier in the chapter, you use the Type command to have a macro insert text in a document. This command can include either text or a string variable as a parameter. A *string variable* is a variable that contains text, not a numeric value.

The parameter, or any text within quotation marks, can include up to 512 characters *without* hard carriage returns (let word wrap divide lines), tabs, or other layout codes. If you include any of these codes, WordPerfect will display an error message when you compile the macro. Font changes and character format codes in the parameter will be ignored; they will not cause an error.

To format text, you must include the appropriate Product commands. For example, to insert this text in a document

This is in **bold** and this is *italic*

you would use the commands

```
Application(WP;WPWP;Default;"WPWPUS.WCD") Type( "This is in ")
FontBold(On!)
Type("bold")
FontBold(Off!)
Type( " and this is " )
FontItalic(On!)
Type("italic")
FontItalic(Off!)
```

To center text and then return to left alignment, use the LineCenter( ) and Line-CenterEnd( ) commands:

```
LineCenter( )
Type("This is centered")
LineCenterEnd( )
HardReturn( )
Type("This is not centered")
```

DISPLAYING MACRO COMMAND RESULTS

The Display command controls whether changes made by the macro are displayed as the macro is running. By default, macros run with the display turned off. This means that all you see is the final result of the macro, not the result of each individual command.

Turning on the display is useful for checking how it works and locating errors. To see the changes as they are being made, insert the command

```
Display(On!)
```

If you later want to turn the display off, change the parameter to Off!. You can also turn it off by making the command a *comment*, which is represented by the characters //. WordPerfect ignores any text on a line preceded by these characters. Therefore, if you insert // at the start of the Display command line, the command will be treated as a comment and ignored. You can quickly turn the display back on by removing the slashes.

STRUCTURING PRODUCT COMMANDS

NOTE
NOTE
If you are using a version of Word-Perfect 5.1 for Windows dated after April 1992, refer to Appendix C for more information on this feature.

While you are writing macros, pay particular attention to differentiating the parentheses characters (and) from the brace characters { and }. They serve different purposes, and your macro will not compile correctly if you use one for the other.

The *Macros Manual*, available from WordPerfect Corporation, includes a complete description of the macro language as well as a program to help you insert macro commands and their parameters in your programs. You can learn command parameters by recording a macro that inserts the commands, such as displaying a dialog box and selecting the options desired, and then opening the macro as a document.

For example, if you record a macro that changes the margins to $1/2$ inch, it will appear with this command:

```
PageMargins
(
    Left:0.5”;
    Right:0.5”;
    Top:0.5”;
    Bottom:0.5”
)
```

You can then customize the macro by changing the measurements or replacing them with variables.

Commands are not case sensitive and can written in a neatly indented format (as above) or all on one line, as in

```
pagemargins(Left:0.5”;Right:0.5”;Top:0.5”;Bottom:0.5”)
```

or without any parameter names, as in

```
PageMargins(0.5”;0.5”;0.5”;0.5”)
```

You can include spaces and even carriage returns between a command and its list of parameters, as in

```
PageMargins ( 0.5” ; 0.5” ; 0.5” ; 0.5” )
```

Notice that spacing, indentation, and capitalization make the macro easier to read.

If you do not want to enter every option in the command, use parameter names or placeholders, unless the entries you do want to insert are in the correct order. For example, these two commands both set the left and bottom margins:

```
PageMargins(Left:0.05”;Bottom:0.05”)
PageMargins(0.05”;;;0.05”)
```

The first form uses parameter names. The second form sets the first parameter (Left), skips the next two, and sets the fourth one (Bottom). When you use parameter names, you do not have to include a placeholder (;) for a missing parameter, and the parameters can be in any order.

Entering the command

PageMargins(0.05";0.05")

would set just the left and right margins because it indicates the first two parameters.

You can also see a list of Product commands by opening the WPWPUS.WCD file in the WPC directory of your hard disk. However, be sure not to edit any text in WPWPUS.WCD or change the file in any way. If you do, WordPerfect may not be able to compile and run your macros.

The WPWPUS.WCD file shows all possible parameters for each command. For example, the Advance function appears like this:

```
function( 597 )
  Advance
    Where:{
      Up!=0;
      Down!=1;
      ToLine!=2;
      Left!=3;
      Right!=4;
      ToPosition!=5
    };
    Amount:wpunits
  )


function( 23 )
  AdvanceDlg()
```

The lines with the word *function* are for WordPerfect's internal use. Ignore them when writing your own macros. Groups of options in brackets indicate the possible values for the parameter. You can include only one in a group. With the Advance command, you can include one of the six parameters or its numeric equivalent: Up! or 0, Down! or 1, ToLine! or 2, Left! or 3, Right! or 4, or ToPosition! or 5.

For example, a macro that advances the position up $1/2$ inch would read

```
Application(WP;WPWP;Default;"WPWPUS.WCD")
Advance (
  Where:Up!;
  Amount:0.05"
)
```

You could also enter this command without the parameter names, as in

Advance(0;0.05")

CUSTOMIZING BUILT-IN MACROS

WordPerfect supplies a number of macros in the WPWIN\MACROS subdirectory. Table 8.1 lists the macros and their functions. You can use the macros as they are or modify them to suit your own tasks.

MACRO NAME	FUNCTION
Add	When a font attribute code is selected, displays the Font dialog box for adding attributes.
Capital	Capitalizes the first letter of a word.
Codes	Creates and prints a duplicate of the current document but with all codes displayed as text (like creating a document with codes revealed).
Delete	Deletes a line of text.
Edit	When a code is selected, displays the appropriate dialog box for changing the code.
Endfoot	Converts endnotes to footnotes.
Envelope	Formats and prints an envelope using address information in the active document window.
Find	Searches for and deletes <<<MARK>>> bookmarks.
Footend	Converts footnotes to endnotes.
Glossary	Expands common abbreviations.
Inline	Formats an equation to fit within the line of text at the location of the insertion point and displays the Equation Editor.
Insert	Inserts a blank line.
Justify	Displays a menu for setting justification.
Labels	Lets you select a label form to be inserted into the document and the current printer driver.

TABLE 8.1:

WordPerfect Built-In Macros

MACRO NAME	FUNCTION
Mark	Inserts the <<<MARK>>> bookmark.
Memo	Creates a memo, letter, or itinerary format.
Paper	Selects and inserts a paper size form.
Recalc	Locates a table in the document and recalculates formulas.
Replace	Searches for and replaces size and appearance attributes.

TABLE 8.1:

WordPerfect Built-In Macros (continued)

EDITING THE LABELS MACRO FOR WINDOWS PRINTER DRIVERS

As written, WordPerfect's Labels macro only works with WordPerfect printer drivers. However, you can easily edit the macro for use with Windows printer drivers and 8½-inch-by-11-inch label stock. The edited macro will not insert the form into the document, but it will add the label definition to the printer driver so that you can select it.

To edit the Labels macro to work with a Windows printer driver, follow these steps without making any other changes to the macro:

1. Select File ➤ Open (F4) and select the MACROS directory. Select Labels.wcm, then Open.

2. Select Edit ➤ Replace (Ctrl-F2). In the Search For text box, type **Other!**. In the Replace With text box, type **Labels!**. Then select Replace All.

3. When the replacements are made, select Close.

4. Select File ➤ Save As (F3), type **Wlabels.wcm**, and then select Save. Saving the edited macro under a new name ensures that the original macro is left unchanged (in case you make a mistake).

5. Select File ➤ Close (Ctrl-F4).

The replacement changed the Product command that started

```
PaperSizeAdd(
        Type:Other!;
```

to

```
PaperSizeAdd(
        Type:Labels!;
```

The edited command will add a label to a Windows printer driver.

When you run this macro (by selecting Wlabels.wcm in the Play Macro dialog box), make your selections from the lists and dialog boxes that appear, as explained in Chapter 3. If you are not sure you are using a Windows printer driver, select Yes when asked if you want to check whether you are using a WordPerfect printer driver, but select a Windows printer driver from the Select Printer dialog box. However, select No when the dialog box appears, asking if you want to insert a label form into the current document. If you select Yes, you will get an error message, but the label form would still be added to the driver. To use the label form, select it from the Paper Size dialog box (Layout ➤ Page ➤ Paper Size).

EDITING THE ENVELOPE MACRO

It is not practical to modify WordPerfect's envelope macro to work with Windows printer drivers. However, you can edit it to change the position of the address or to print on different size envelopes.

Open the Envelop.wcm file (in the MACROS directory). The instructions that format envelopes appear in the macro like this:

NOTE NOTE *If you are using a version of Word-Perfect 5.1 for Windows dated after April 1992, refer to Appendix C for more information on this feature.*

```
LABEL(PlaceIt@)
    PosDocTop()
    PageMargins
    (
    Left:4.5";
    Right:0.5";
    Top:2.0";
    Bottom:0.5"
    )
    EditPaste()
RETURN
```

If WordPerfect's Envelope macro prints the address in the wrong position on the envelope, change the margin measurements to correct the placement.

You can also adjust the margins to print addresses on other size envelopes. For example, if you use Monarch-size (7.5-by-3.88 inch) envelopes, use the Replace command to make these changes:

REPLACE	WITH
9.5	7.5
4.0	3.88
MacroEnv	MonEnv
Left:4.5	Left:2.5
Top:2.0	Top:1.25

This changes the length, width, and margins of the form, as well as the name of the form that will be used for selection.

Save the macro under the name **Monarch.wcm**, and then run it when you want to print on a Monarch-size envelope. The form will now be called MonEnv, not MacroEnv.

CREATING CUSTOM BUTTON BARS

 If you are using a version of Word-Perfect 5.1 for Windows dated after April 1992, refer to Appendix C for more information on this feature.

WordPerfect allows you to create your own Button Bars to contain the commands and macros you use frequently. This way, you can activate a function with a single click of the mouse. You can create and save on disk any number of different Button Bars. For example, you can create one Button Bar for use with academic papers, another for legal documents.

Button Bars are a powerful feature for automating your work. If you find yourself using the same dialog box or menu options, add the command to the Button Bar. If you repeat the same series of keystrokes often, create a macro and add the macro to the Button Bar. By combining macros and Button Bars, you can build your own interface for working with WordPerfect.

ADDING BUTTONS

You create a Button Bar by adding buttons to a blank bar. To add a command to the Button Bar, you select it from the menu. You add a macro by choosing from a list of files that appears when you select to assign a macro to a button. Even if you added the macro to the Macro menu, you cannot add it to the Button Bar by selecting it from the pull-down menu; you must choose the macro file.

We will now create a Button Bar and add two commands and two macros.

1. Select View ➤ Button Bar. The default Button Bar WP{WP}.WWB will appear.

2. Select View ➤ Button Bar Setup ➤ New. WordPerfect displays a blank Button Bar and the dialog box shown in Figure 8.6.

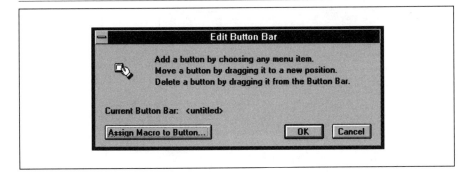

FIGURE 8.6:

Edit Button Bar dialog box

3. Select Font ➤ Bold. A boldfacing button will appear in the Button Bar.

4. Select Font ➤ Italic to add an italics button to the Button Bar.

5. Select Layout ➤ Margins to add a margins button.

6. In the Edit Button Bar dialog box, select Assign Macro to Button. You will see a dialog box with a list of the macros in the WPWIN\MACROS subdirectory.

In this dialog box, the Macro on Disk option is selected. With this setting, WordPerfect runs the macro from the disk file when the button is selected, so the most recent version of the macro will be used. If you do not want editing of the macro file to affect the function of the button, turn off the Macro on Disk option. Then the code of the macro will be added to the Button Bar file.

7. Select Swap.wcm, then Assign.

8. Select Assign Macro to Button, then Lethead.wcm, then Assign.

9. Select OK to close the Edit Button Bar dialog box. WordPerfect will display a dialog box for saving the Button Bar. Type **Myown** and select OK. The Button Bar will be saved on disk under the name Myown.wwm.

The completed Button Bar is shown in Figure 8.7. You can use the same procedure to add any commands you wish. You are not limited to the number of buttons displayed on the screen. If you add more buttons than will fit across the screen, you will be able to scroll them into view.

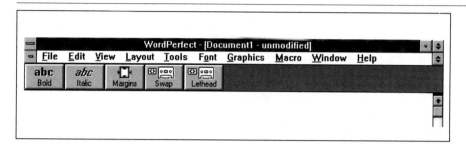

FIGURE 8.7:

Completed Button Bar

10. Click on the Margins button in the Button Bar. The button will appear pressed down and the dialog box will be displayed.

11. Type **1.5**, press Tab, type **1.5**, and select OK.

12. Click on the Lethead button to run the macro and insert your letterhead.

13. Click on the Bold button, type **This text is boldfaced**, and click on the Bold button again.

14. Select View ➤ Button Bar to turn off the Button Bar display.

15. Close the window without saving the document. Your custom bar will remain on the screen.

REFINING YOUR BUTTON BARS

Your Button Bars are very flexible. You can remove and rearrange the buttons, change the position of the entire bar, and select bar styles.

To delete or move buttons, drag them with the mouse. Reposition the bar or change the style used for the buttons through the Button Bar Options dialog box, shown in Figure 8.8. The Position options place the Button Bar across the top or bottom of the screen or down the left or right side. The Style options let you select what appears on the Button Bar: the name of the command (Text Only), a graphic icon representing the command (Picture Only), or both (Picture and Text).

Now we will edit our Button Bar to change the buttons and place the bar along the right side of the screen.

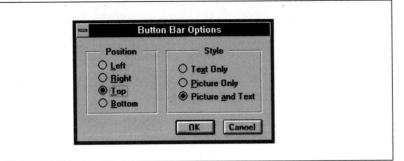

1. Select View ➤ Button Bar Setup ➤ Edit.

2. Drag the Italic button down off of the Button Bar. When you release the mouse button, the Font ➤ Italic command is deleted from the Button Bar.

3. Drag the Margins button across the Button Bar to the left of the Bold button, without dragging it down. When you release the mouse button, the positions of the buttons are reversed.

4. Select OK to close the dialog box.

5. Select View ➤ Button Bar Setup ➤ Options, and then choose Right in the Button Bar Options dialog box.

6. Select OK. The Button Bar will now appear down the right side of the document window.

7. Select View ➤ Button Bar Setup ➤ Options ➤ Top to return the Button Bar to its original position.

RESETTING THE DEFAULT BUTTON BAR

The most recently used Button Bar becomes the default—it will be displayed the next time you select to display the Button Bar. Follow these steps to reinstate the WordPerfect default Button Bar:

1. Select View ➤ Button Bar Setup ➤ Select.

2. Select WP{WP}.WWB, then choose the Select button.

3. Select View ➤ Button Bar to turn it off.

4. Select File ➤ Exit (Alt-F4), then No to exit WordPerfect without saving the document.

CREATING A BUTTON BAR FOR TEMPLATES

Chapter 2 explains how to set up templates to standardize documents. You can simplify the use of your templates by creating a button bar for selecting them.

Create a macro to open each template. Save the macros under the template names. Create another macro that displays the Save As dialog box. Then set up a new Button Bar and add buttons for the template and save as macros, as shown in Figure 8.9. Make this the default Button Bar.

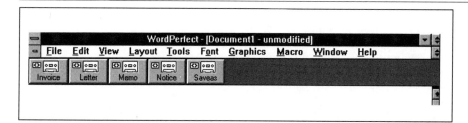

FIGURE 8.9:

Button Bar for selecting templates

Whenever you start WordPerfect, this Button Bar will automatically appear. Anyone who produces standard documents can easily see which templates are available, select the proper one, and use the Save As button to save the new document. You can use similar techniques to create other Button Bars that make complex formats, graphics, or other features easily accessible to every user.

CHAPTER 9

Getting user input
Creating decision-making macros
Using subroutines
Automating data entry

Advanced Programming with Macros

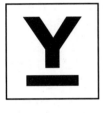

You can write sophisticated macro programs to automate a variety of tasks. For more advanced macros, use WordPerfect's Programming commands. These commands control the flow of a macro, make decisions, and perform complex operations.

This chapter introduces Programming commands and the purposes they can serve in your macros. Later chapters describe how the techniques presented here can be expanded to create fully automated applications.

PROGRAMMING COMMAND CONVENTIONS

WordPerfect's Programming commands are similar to commands found in most other computer languages. In fact, if you already know how to program in BASIC, Pascal, or a similar language, you will be able to program easily in WordPerfect. However, if you are not familiar with the logic and structure of some computer language, you should gain more programming experience before using WordPerfect's more advanced macro commands.

This chapter presents examples of macro code to illustrate the commands discussed. Although the examples perform a complete function, many of them are not complete macros because they do not include the Application command. To see how the sections work, write a macro beginning with the Application command, then add the series of instructions shown in the example.

In the macro code examples, the term *Var* represents a user-defined variable, and *Value* represents whatever value you have assigned to the variable. In WordPerfect macros, variables must be one word and start with a letter. Variables can contain either numeric values or text.

Remember that you cannot press ↵ within *any text surrounded by quotation marks*. In this book, some long command lines in the examples are divided into two lines. When typing the programs, let word wrap divide the text for you; do not press ↵. Also be sure to enter the punctuation marks correctly, differentiating between the colon and semicolon, parentheses and braces.

The macro programs in this and the remaining chapters follow these formatting conventions:

◆ Words or commands that you must replace with your own selections are shown in italics with hyphens between words, as in *Dialog-Box-Name*Dlg( ). Note that the characters Dlg( ) are not in italics, indicating that they are required in the command.

◆ Variable names and commands are shown in mixed uppercase and lowercase letters, as in NetIncomeTax. However, variable names are not case sensitive; the variables *NetIcomeTax*, *NETINCOMETAX* and *netincometax* are considered the same. The contents of string variables are case sensitive. For example, two string variables are not equal unless their values match letter by letter in the same case.

◆ Quotation marks indicate that the parameter must be surrounded by quotation marks. For example, the syntax

GetNumber(Count;"*Prompt* ";"*Title*")

indicates you must insert your own text for the prompt and title in quotation marks, as in

GetNumber(Count;"Please enter a number";"Sample dialog box")

◆ Programming commands are shown without spaces between the command and its parameters, although you can insert spaces in your own programs.

Spacing within commands is optional. For example, both of these formats are acceptable:

GetNumber(Count; "*Prompt*"; "*Title*")
GetNumber(Count ; "*Prompt*" ; "*Title*")

However, spaces within quotation marks will appear along with the text.

For more information about WordPerfect macro commands, print the file MACRO.DOC in the WPWIN directory or buy the book *WordPerfect 5.1 for Windows Macro Handbook* by Alan Simpson (SYBEX).

PROGRAMMING FOR USER INPUT

Using WordPerfect's Programming commands, you can write macros that allow the user to make entries or selections while the macro is running. You can also write macros with variables and use Programming commands to assign values to those variables.

ASSIGNING VALUES TO VARIABLES

One way to input information into a macro is by assigning values to variables. You can use the Assign command or the assign operator :=. A common mistake is to leave out the colon when using the assign operator.

The syntax of the Assign command is

Assign(*Var*;*Value*)

For example, the command to assign the value 35 to the variable Years is

Assign(Years;35)

The command

Assign(Int;1245*.05)

assigns the result of the calculation to the variable Int.

Using the operator, the form is

Years:=35

The command

Name:="Ted"

means that the variable Name will be the string Ted. Note that text you are assigning to a string variable must be within quotation marks.

GETTING NUMERIC AND TEXT INPUT

The GetNumber command is used to allow the user to input a numeric value. It displays a dialog box with a text box for the number, as well as OK and Cancel buttons. The command pauses the macro until OK or Cancel are selected. An error message appears if a nonnumeric entry is made in the text box. The syntax for the command is

GetNumber(*Var* ;"*Prompt* ";"*Box-Title*")

For example, the command

GetNumber(Principal;"Enter the amount of the loan:";"Mortgage Calculation")

displays the dialog box shown in Figure 9.1. The number entered in the dialog box will be assigned to the variable Principal.

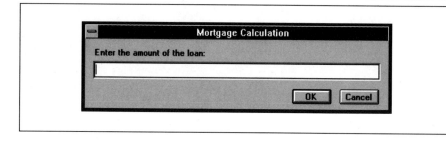

FIGURE 9.1:

Dialog box created with the GetNumber command

The GetUnits command works in a similar way to allow the entry of a number and a measurement unit, such as " or i (inches), c (centimeters), or p (points). If you do not enter a unit, WordPerfect assumes the value is in the default unit type, which can be set by using the DefaultUnits command, as in

DefaultUnits(Inches)

To display a dialog box for the input of a character string, use the GetString command. Like the GetNumber and GetUnits commands, GetString displays a dialog box and pauses until the user selects OK or Cancel. The syntax for the command is

GetString(*Var*;Length=*Numeric-Expression*;*"Prompt"*,*"Box-Title"*)

The Length parameter limits the number of characters that can be entered. For example, the command

GetString(Name;Length=20;"Enter your name";"Log On Sequence")

displays a dialog box titled Log On Sequence, the prompt *Enter your name*, and a text box that will accept up to 20 characters.

If you omit the Length parameter, a string of up to 64,000 characters is allowed. To accept only single-character entries, such as Y or N for Yes or No, use Length=1.

DISPLAYING MENUS

When you want the user to be able to select from several options, create a menu with the Menu command. This command displays a menu with the options you specify. The syntax is

Menu(*Var*;*Type*;*Horizontal-Position*;*Vertical-Position*; {*"Option-1"*;*"Option-2"*...*"Option-N"*})

If you are using a version of Word-Perfect 5.1 for Windows dated after April 1992, refer to Appendix C for more information on this feature.

Var is the variable that will hold the number of the selected menu item. *Type* specifies how the options are numbered in the list. It can be either LETTER or DIGIT. If you use LETTER, you can have up to 26 options and each is preceded with a letter, labeled consecutively from A to Z. Select DIGIT if you want up to 9 options numbered from 1 to 9.

The *Horizontal-Position* and *Vertical-Position* settings determine the menu's position on the screen, referenced from the top and left side of the screen in pixels. If you omit a position, the box will be centered on the screen; however, you must still insert the semicolons as placeholders. The menu options follow the other parameters. Note that all the parameters are enclosed within the parentheses, but the menu options are also enclosed within braces.

For example, the command

Menu(Result;Letter;;;{"Memo"; "Letter"; "Invoice"})

displays the menu shown in Figure 9.2 centered on the screen.

A Memo
B Letter
C Invoice

Menu created with the Menu command

To select an option from the menu, click on the choice or press the number or letter preceding it. You do not have to press ↵ after your selection. With both types (LETTER and DIGIT), the variable returned is a number. If you select A or 1, the resulting variable is 1. If you select B or 2, the variable is 2, and so on. You could then use the variable to perform some action, such as opening the selected file.

PROMPTING FOR INPUT

The Prompt command displays a dialog box with a message and the OK and Cancel buttons. The user can select OK to continue the macro or Cancel to stop it. The syntax is

Prompt("*Box-Title*";"*Prompt*";*Icon*;*Horizontal-Position*;*Vertical-Position*)

Icon is a number that represents the type of symbol that appears in the box: 0 (or omitted) is no icon, 1 is a stop sign, 2 is a question mark, 3 is an exclamation point, and 4 is an information icon.

The Prompt dialog box remains on the screen until you select one of its command buttons, until the macro ends, or until the EndPrompt command is encountered.

For example, the series of commands

Prompt("WARNING";"You have made an illegal entry";3;;)
Pause
EndPrompt

displays the dialog box shown in Figure 9.3, centered on the screen.

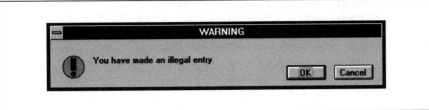

FIGURE 9.3:

Dialog box created with Prompt command

PAUSING FOR RESPONSE

The Prompt command will not pause the macro by itself. Use the Pause command to stop the macro and give the user time to select an option. The user then can continue the macro by selecting one of the command buttons, by pressing ↵ or Esc, or by selecting Macro ➤ Pause.

You can have a macro stop until a specific key is pressed by using the PauseKey command. The syntax is

PauseKey(Key:*Key-Code*;Character:"*Key-To-Press*")

The *Key-Code* determines which key you must press to continue the macro: Enter! or 0 for a ↵ keypress, Cancel! or 1 for an Esc keypress, Close! or 2 for a Ctrl-F4 keypress, or Character! or 3 for the character specified by *Key-To-Press*. For example, the command

PauseKey(Key:Cancel!)

pauses the macro until Esc is pressed. The command

PauseKey(Key:3;Character:"X")

pauses the macro until the uppercase letter X is pressed.

You can combine Prompt and PauseKey commands to create prompts for specific keypresses. For example, the commands

Prompt("Continue?";"Press Enter to continue";4;;)
PauseKey(Key:Enter!)

display the prompt

Press Enter to continue

PROGRAMMING CONDITIONS FOR DECISION MAKING

The If command is called a *conditional* because it makes a determination regarding which instructions are to be executed while the macro is running. It is the same as the IF THEN instruction in BASIC. The syntax is

If(*Condition*)
    Instructions...
EndIf

This structure means "If the condition is true, then perform the following instructions. If the condition is not true, skip all instructions up to the EndIf command."

    Another syntax for the command is

If(*Condition*)
    Instructions...
Else
    Alternate-Instructions...
EndIf

This structure means "If the condition is true, then perform the instructions up to the Else command. If the condition is not true, perform the instructions between the Else and EndIf commands."

    Using either syntax, you must include an EndIf command for each If command.

    The *Condition* can include any one of the following operators:

=	Equal to (do not use the assign operator :=)
<	Less than
>	Greater than
<>	Not equal to
>=	Greater than or equal to
<=	Less than or equal to

If you use string variables in an If condition, values must be enclosed in quotation marks, as in

If(Company="SYBEX")

The value of the variable must match the case exactly. For example, if Company had been assigned the value Sybex, the If condition would be false.

The If command is useful for programming menus. For example, here is a macro that displays a menu and executes a task depending on the user's selection from that menu:

```
Application(WP;WPWP;Default;"WPWPUS.WCD")
Menu(Result;Letter;;;{"Memo"; "Letter"; "Invoice"})
If(Result = 1)
   FileOpen(Filename:"Memo")
Else
   If(Result=2)
   FileOpen(Filename:"Letter")
Else
      If(Result=3)
      FileOpen(Filename:"Invoice")
      EndIf
   EndIf
EndIf
```

This macro displays a menu with three items. If the user selects the first item, which places the value 1 in the variable Result, WordPerfect will open the document called Memo. FileOpen( ) is the Product command that opens the file specified in parentheses.

If the user does not select the first item, the macro performs the second If command to determine if the user selected the second item. If so, it opens the Letter document. If the third item is selected, the Invoice document opens.

GETTING WORDPERFECT'S STATUS

The GetWPData command returns a variable that indicates a status condition of WordPerfect. The syntax is

GetWPData(MacroVariable: *Var*;SystemVariable:*Code*)

The system variable *Code* can be a variable name or its numeric equivalent. It indicates which status condition is returned to the macro variable. For example, the macro

```
GetWPData(MacroVariable:DOC;SystemVariable:Name!)
If(DOC<>"INVOICE")
```

```
    FileOpen("Invoice")
EndIf
```

opens the document named Invoice if it is not already the active document. It does this by placing the contents of the system variable Name!, which represents the name of the active document, into the variable DOC. Name! always returns the document name in all uppercase letters, so it must be in uppercase in the If condition. However, the parameter of the FileOpen command is not case sensitive.

Chapter 10 includes a list of common system variables. For a complete list of status conditions that can be tested, order the *Macro Manual* from Word-Perfect. You can also open the WPWPUS.WCD file in the WPC directory and look up the syntax for the GetWPData command.

REPEATING MACRO COMMANDS

In a program, a *loop* is a series of commands that are repeated. When programming loops, you must be sure to include some way of stopping the repetitions. Otherwise, you can be caught in an endless loop, in which the macro continuously repeats until you press Esc to stop the macro or you turn off your computer.

REPEATING IN STEPS

The For command is used to perform a loop a specific number of times. The syntax is

```
For(Var;Start;Condition;Step)
EndFor
```

The command performs the repetition in sequence, counting from the *Start*, which can be a number, variable, or mathematical expression. It continues, in steps, until the *Condition* is false. *Step* represents the amount by which to increment the variable.

For example, these commands print the numbers 1 to 50 down the left side of the page:

```
PosLineBegin()
For(Count;1;Count<=50;Count+1)
NumStr(Num;1;Count)
Type(Num)
```

```
HardReturn()
EndFor
```

The PosLineBegin( ) command moves the insertion point to the left margin. The command

```
For(Count;1;Count<=50;Count+1)
```

starts the For loop using the variable Count, initializes Count at 1 (the starting value), sets the loop to repeat as long as Count is less than or equal to 50, and increments the value of Count by 1 with each repetition. The loop will stop when Count is greater than 50.

The next command

```
NumStr(Num;0;Count)
```

is necessary because the Type command can print only strings. This command converts the numeric variable Count into the string variable Num with no decimal places.

The Type(Num) command inserts the number into the document, and then HardReturn( ) performs a carriage return. Finally, the EndFor command stops the loop after the condition Count<=50 is no longer true.

If you wanted to print all odd numbers, from 1 to 49, you would use the command

```
For(Count;1;Count<=50;Count+2)
```

To count down, start with a larger initial value and use a negative step value, as in

```
For(Count;50;Count>=1;Count–1)
```

You can also nest multiple For loops to create interesting effects. There must be an EndFor command for each For command. For example, this macro includes nested For commands:

```
Application(WP;WPWP;Default;"WPWPUS.WCD")
PosLineBegin()
For(Row;1;Row<=10;Row+1)
For(Col;1;Col<=Row;Col+1)
   Type("*")
EndFor
```

```
HardReturn()
EndFor
```

It creates this design:

```
*
**
***
****
*****
******
*******
********
*********
**********
```

The first For loop sets up 10 rows of lines. For each of these lines, the second For loop prints as many asterisks as the row number. The HardReturn( ) command between the EndFor commands causes each row of asterisks to print on a separate line.

The same design could be created using the ForEach command, which is a variation of the For command. Replace the first For command in the previous example with

```
ForEach(Row;{1;2;3;4;5;6;7;8;9;10})
```

With this loop, the variable is assigned each of the specified values in turn rather than using a sequential value. During the first repetition, the variable is assigned the first value in the list, during the second repetition the second value, and so on.

For loops can also be used to rearrange items, as in the following example (the lines are numbered for reference; do not enter line numbers as part of the macro):

```
1 Application(WP;WPWP;Default;"WPWPUS.WCD")
2 GetString(Name;Length=15;"Please enter your name";"Backwards
   Printing")
3 StrLen(Times;Name)
4 For(Char;Times;Char>0;Char-1)
5 SubStr(Let;Char;1;Name)
6 Type(Let)
7 EndFor
```

This program accepts a name, then prints the name backward.

The commands work as follows:

◆ Line 2: The GetString command displays a dialog box for entry of a name up to 15 characters long.

◆ Line 3: The StrLen (string length) command assigns the number of characters in the name to the variable Times.

◆ Line 4: Begins the For loop, assigning to the variable Char the initial value of the length of the name. The condition will repeat the loop as long as the variable Char is greater than 0. The step reduces the value by one for each repetition.

◆ Line 5: The SubStr (substring) command assigns a portion (number of characters) of the Name variable, starting at the specified position, to the Char variable. It uses the syntax

SubStr(*Var;Position;Number-of-Characters;String-Variable*)

For example, when the loop starts, the position is set at the number of characters in the string, so the variable is assigned one character of the name, starting at the last character. The next time the loop repeats, Char has been reduced by one, so the starting position is the next to the last character. The loop repeats, taking the next character to the left with each repetition.

◆ Line 6: Inserts each character returned by line 5 into the document.

◆ Line 7: Repeats the loop until the condition Char>0 is no longer true.

Another use for loops is to number items. For example, this macro allows you to enumerate a specific number of existing lines in a document:

```
1 Application(WP;WPWP;Default;"WPWPUS.WCD")
2 GetNumber (Result;"Enter the number of lines:";"Line Numbering")
3 InsertTypeover(Off!)
4 PosDocTop()
5 For(Count;1;Count<=Result;Count+1)
6 NumStr(Num;1;Count)
7 PosLineBegin()
8 Type(Num)
9 Tab()
10 PosLineDown()
11 EndFor
```

Here is a description of each line:

◆ Line 2: Requests the number of lines you want to number.

◆ Line 3: Ensures that Insert is on by turning off Typeover mode. In Typeover mode, the line numbers would replace the first letter in each line.

◆ Line 4: Moves the insertion point to the start of the document.

◆ Line 5: Begins the For loop.

◆ Line 6: Converts the variable Count into a string.

◆ Line 7: Moves the insertion point to the left margin.

◆ Line 8: Enters the number.

◆ Line 9: Inserts a tab.

◆ Line 10: Moves the insertion point to the next line.

◆ Line 11: Ends the loop when the condition is no longer true.

A routine like this could be used to automatically number a macro program so you could print a reference copy. However, the While command provides a more efficient way to perform the same function.

CONDITIONAL REPEATING

The While command repeats a series of instructions as long as a condition is true. The loop ends when the condition is false. The syntax is

```
While(Condition)
    Instructions...
EndWhile
```

This structure means "While the condition is true, repeat all the following instructions up to the EndWhile command." You must make sure that the instruction inside the loop will eventually make the test condition false to end the repetition.

If the *Condition* is false to begin with, the instructions will not be performed at all. If you want the instructions to be executed at least once, use the Repeat command.

For example, the following program inserts line numbers in front of each paragraph in a document.

```
1 Application(WP;WPWP;Default;"WPWPUS.WCD")
2 GetWPData(MacroVariable:Blank;
SystemVariable:DocumentBlank!)
3 If(Blank=True)
4 Quit
5 EndIf
6 InsertTypeover(Off!)
7 Num:= 1
8 Test:=" "
9 PosDocBottom()
10 Type("~")
11 PosDocVeryTop()
12 While(Test<>"~")
13 PosLineBegin()
14 NumStr(Line;1;Num)
15 Type(Line)
16 Tab()
17 Num:=Num+1
18 PosParagraphNext()
19 GetWPData(MacroVariable:Test;SystemVariable:LeftChar!)
20 EndWhile
21 DeleteCharPrevious()
```

This program works as follows:

◆ Line 2: The GetWPData command tests to see if the document is blank (an empty document).

◆ Line 3: The If command tests if it is a blank document.

◆ Line 4: Ends the macro if the document is blank (there is nothing to number). If you want to ensure that a macro cannot be executed when there is text on the screen, change the If command to If(Blank=False).

◆ Line 5: The EndIf command ends the If condition.

◆ Line 6: Ensures that Typeover mode is off.

◆ Line 7: Assigns the variable Num the value 1.

◆ Line 8: Assigns the variable Test a space. Num will be used to increment the line number; Test will be used to determine when the end of the program has been reached.

◆ Line 9: Moves the insertion point to the end of the document.

◆ Line 10: Inserts the tilde character. The tilde will be used to indicate when the macro has numbered the last line. If the tilde is used in the document you want to number, replace it here and in line 12 with some character that is not used.

◆ Line 11: Returns the insertion point to the start of the document.

◆ Line 12: Sets the While loop to continue as long as the variable Test is not equal to the tilde. Before using the variable for the first time, you must make sure it contains some character value that is not a tilde; this is the purpose of the assignment in line 8.

◆ Line 13: Moves the insertion point to the beginning of the line.

◆ Line 14: Converts the variable Num to a string.

◆ Line 15: Inserts the number.

◆ Line 16: Inserts a tab for spacing.

◆ Line 17: Increments the line number.

◆ Line 18: Moves the insertion point to the next paragraph. If there is no other paragraph, the insertion point will be moved to the end of the document.

◆ Line 19: Inserts the character to the left of the insertion point into the variable Test. The character will be a tilde only if the insertion point is at the end of the document.

◆ Line 20: Continues the loop as long as the condition is met (the character in Test is not a tilde).

◆ Line 21: When the character is a tilde, deletes the character to the left of the insertion point (the tilde that was inserted to mark the end of the document).

REPEATING UNTIL A CONDITION IS TRUE

The Repeat command performs a loop as long as a condition is false. It ends when the condition becomes true. The syntax is

```
Repeat
    Instructions...
    Until(Condition)
```

This command means "Repeat the following instructions until the next condition is met." The next condition is performed after the instructions, so the instructions will be performed at least one time.

You could substitute the Repeat structure for the For command in the line-numbering program shown in the previous section. Replace line 12 with the command Repeat and line 20 with the command Until(Test="~").

PROGRAMMING WITH SUBROUTINES

A subroutine is a series of instructions that can be performed as a unit. A subroutine is a program within a program. To perform the instructions in the subroutine, no matter where you are in the macro, you *branch* (move to) to the subroutine.

What occurs after you perform the subroutine depends on how you branch to it. If you use the Go or Case command, the macro continues on from the subroutine. If you use the Call or Case Call command, the program will return to the instructions that branched to the subroutine.

BEGINNING A SUBROUTINE

The Label command marks the beginning of a subroutine. The syntax is

Label(*Subroutine-Name@*)

The @ symbol is required after all label names.

The compiler will report a warning if you have a label that is not referenced or that is used by a Go, Call, Case, or other command. This warning will not affect the macro if everything else is correct, so you can continue the compiling process.

CONTINUING AT THE SUBROUTINE

The Go command continues the macro at the named subroutine. The syntax is

Go(*Subroutine-Name@*)

When the macro encounters this command, it moves to the subroutine indicated by the label. After performing the subroutine, it continues from that point on, without returning to the original location.

For example, a subroutine could use this structure:

```
Application (WP;WPWP;Default;"WPWPUS.WCD")
Instructions…
Go(Report@)
Instructions…
Label(Report@)
  Instructions
```

The instructions following the Application command are performed, then the Go command sends the macro to the subroutine called Report. The instructions following the Label are performed, and then the macro ends. The instructions between the Go and the Label commands are never executed.

Here is a slight modification of the same macro structure:

```
Application (WP;WPWP;Default;"WPWPUS.WCD")
Instructions…
Go(Report@)
Instructions…
Label(Report@)
  Instructions
Label(Invoice@)
  Instructions
```

In this case, three sets of instructions will be performed. After the program completes the instructions in Report, it continues with the instructions in Invoice. The instructions following the Go(Report@) command are never performed.

You could modify the macro to perform either Report or Invoice (not both), but this sequence would *not* work:

```
Application (WP;WPWP;Default;"WPWPUS.WCD")
Instructions…
If(Condition) Go(Report@) Else Go(Invoice@) Endlf
Instructions…
Label(Report@)
  Instructions
Label(Invoice@)
  Instructions
```

When the If command sends the program to Report, its instructions are executed. But the program then continues through the Invoice subroutine as well. To correct the problem, you could use this structure:

```
Application (WP;WPWP;Default;"WPWPUS.WCD")
Instructions...
If(Condition) Go(Report@) Else Go(Invoice@) EndIf
Instructions...
Label(Report@)
   Instructions
   Go(End@)
Label(Invoice@)
   Instructions
Label(End@)
```

With this structure, after completing the Report subroutine, the program branches to the End subroutine and stops. The End subroutine does not need to have any instructions.

RETURNING TO THE PROGRAM FROM THE SUBROUTINE

The Call command also branches to a subroutine. However, when the program encounters a Return command, it returns to the line following the Call command. The syntax is

```
Call(Subroutine-Name@)
```

Here is an example of a macro structure using the Call command:

```
Application (WP;WPWP;Default;"WPWPUS.WCD")
Instructions...
Call(Report@)
Instructions...
Go(End@)
Label(Report@)
   Instructions
Return
Label(Invoice@)
   Instructions
Label(End@)
```

This program performs the instructions following the Application command, then executes those in the Report subroutine. The Return command sends the program back to perform the instructions following the Call command. The instructions in Invoice are never performed.

If you call a subroutine later in the program, make sure the program will not perform the routine again accidentally. If you deleted the Go(End@) command in the program, for example, the macro would perform the Report routine twice: once because of the Call and a second time as it continued down from the line following the Call.

You can branch to subroutines anywhere in the program. The subroutine does not have to be after the Go or Call command. In fact, some programmers place all their subroutines at the start of the program in a structure such as this:

```
Application (WP;WPWP;Default;"WPWPUS.WCD")
Go(Main@)
Label(Report@)
   Instructions
Return
Label(Invoice@)
   Instructions
Return
Label(Main@)
   Instructions
   Call(Report@)
   Instructions
   Call(Invoice@)
```

The Go command begins executing the instructions in the routine called Main. When the subroutine Report or Invoice is needed, it is called from the main program. The Return commands ensure that only the called routine is performed.

BRANCHING BY VARIABLE VALUES

The Case structure directs the program to perform one of selected subroutines based on the value of a variable. The syntax is

Case(*Var*;{*Value-1*;*Routine-1*@*;*Value-2*;*Routine-2*@*;...Value-N*;*Routine-N*@} Default@)

If the variable has the value indicated by *Value-1*, the program branches to *Routine-1*. If the variable is *Value-2*, the program branches to *Routine-2*, and so on. If the variable has none of the values listed, the default routine will be performed.

For example, in the program shown in Figure 9.4, the menu selection determines whether an additional closing line is added to a letter. If you select either Nice, Warm, or Hostile from the menu, a line is added before the signature block. If you select None, the value of Result is 4, and only the default signature block is used.

Notice that the Go(End@) command is not needed at the end of the Hostile command because the program will perform the End subroutine anyway.

```
Application(WP;WPWP;Default;"WPWPUS.WCD")
Menu(Result;Letter;;;("Nice"; "Warm"; "Hostile";"None"))
Case(Result;{1;Nice@;2;Warm@;3;Hostile@};End@)

Label(Nice@)
     Type("We appreciate your business and support.")
Go(End@)

Label(Warm@)
     Type("You have been a true friend and supporter.")
Go(End@)

Label(Hostile@)
     Type("Our attorney will be contacting you.")

Label(End@)
     HardReturn()
     HardReturn()
     Type("Sincerely")
     HardReturn()
     HardReturn()
     HardReturn()
     Type("Alvin A. Aardvark")
```

FIGURE 9.4:

Menu selection program using Case command

BRANCHING BY VARIABLE AND RETURNING

The Case Call command is the same as the Case command, except that the subroutines are called, so program execution returns to the line following Case Call. The syntax is

Case Call(*Var*;{*Value-1*;*Routine-1@*;*Value-2*;*Routine-2@*;...*Value-N*; *Routine-N@*} *Default@*)

OTHER PROGRAMMING COMMANDS

WordPerfect provides many additional Programming commands that you can use in your own macros. The commands that have not been described in detail here are listed in Table 9.1.

COMMAND	FUNCTION
AssertCancel	Performs as if the Esc key were pressed.
AssertError	Performs as if an error has been encountered.
AssertNotFound	Performs as if a search has failed.
Beep	Sounds a beep tone.
ByteLen	Returns the length of a string in bytes.
BytePos	Returns the position of a byte in a string.
CancelOff	Causes Cancel commands to be ignored.
CancelOn	Allows Cancel commands to be accepted following a CancelOff command.
Chain	Waits until the macro is completed then executes another macro.
DefaultUnits	Specifies the unit of measurement.
ErrorOff	Causes error conditions to be ignored.
ErrorOn	Causes error conditions to be recognized following an ErrorOff.
Fraction	Assigns the decimal portion of a number to a variable.
OnError	Determines the Label subroutine to be performed when an error condition occurs.
OnError Call	Allows return from a Label subroutine when an error condition occurs.
ReturnCancel	Ends the execution of a Label subroutine and returns a cancel condition.
ReturnError	Ends the execution of a Label subroutine and returns an error condition.
ReturnNotFound	Ends the execution of a Label subroutine and returns a not found condition.
Run	Executes another macro immediately.
Speed	Controls the speed at which macro instructions are executed.
StrNum	Converts a string that consists of numeric characters into a numeric variable.

TABLE 9.1:

More WordPerfect Programming Commands

COMMAND	FUNCTION
SubByte	Assigns a portion of a string to a variable in bytes.
Wait	Pauses the macro for a specified amount of time, in tenths of seconds.

TABLE 9.1:

More WordPerfect Programming Commands (continued)

SPECIAL MACRO APPLICATIONS

You can automate filling out forms by using macros, merge commands, or combinations of the two methods. Depending on the speed of your computer system, a purely macro solution may not be as efficient as using merge techniques. You can compare the macro presented here with the merge procedures covered in Chapter 11. Macros are also useful for printing multiple copies of special documents, such as tickets and raffles.

USING MACROS TO AUTOMATE DATA ENTRY

When you use a table to set up a form that requires calculations, you can automate the entry of totals and other formula results (see Chapter 7). By using macros, you can take the automation even further.

Figure 9.5 shows a macro that completes the invoice form described in Chapter 7 and shown in Figure 7.15. The macro prompts the user for the client name and address, and inserts the date. It then accepts the details for each order until all 16 lines have been completed, or until the user selects Cancel or presses Esc.

After the Application command, the macro uses the OnCancel(End@) command, which controls where the macro goes if Esc is pressed. There is also an OnCancel Call command, which allows a subroutine to return to the location where Esc was pressed in the program.

The PosDocBottom( ) and PosDocTop( ) commands ensure that the entire table appears on the screen before the GetString command is executed. The PosLineDown( ) commands position the text on the form. If you use this macro, you must adjust the number of PosLineDown( ) commands to match the spacing of your invoice.

The TableCalculate( ) command recalculates the table after each item has been entered. This displays the total for the item and maintains a running total, but can dramatically slow the macro's speed. To calculate the amounts and totals only at the end of the invoice, move the command under the Label(End@) line in the last section of the macro.

```
Application(WP;WPWP;Default;"WPWPUS.WCD")
OnCancel(End@)
Title:="Aardvark Company Invoice"
Item:=1
Label(Start@)
FileOpen("Invoice")
PosDocBottom()
PosDocTop()
Display(On!)
For(Count;1;Count<=9;Count+1)
    PosLineDown()
EndFor
GetString(Name;Length=20;"Enter Client name:";Title)
Tab()
Type(Name)
PosLineDown()

GetString(Add;Length=20;"Enter address:";Title)
Tab()
Type(Add)
PosLineDown()

GetString(Address2;Length=20;"Enter second address:";Title)
Tab()
Type(Address2)
PosLineDown()

GetString(Address3;Length=20;"Enter third address:";Title)
Tab()
Type(Address3)
PosLineDown()
PosLineDown()
PosLineEnd()
Type("  ")
DateText()
PosLineDown()
PosLineDown()
PosLineDown()

Repeat

    GetString(Num;Length=6;"Enter item number:";Title)
    Type(Num)
    PosCellNext()

    GetString(Desc;Length=25;"Enter item name:";Title)
    Type(Desc)
    PosCellNext()
    GetNumber(Qnty;"Enter Quantity:";Title)
    NumStr(Sqnty;2;Qnty)
    Type(Sqnty)
    PosCellNext()
    GetNumber(Cost;"Enter price:";Title)
    NumStr(Scost;2;Cost)
    Type(Scost)

    TableCalculate()

    Item:=Item+1
    PosCellNext()
    PosCellNext()
```

FIGURE 9.5:

*Macro for automating
the invoice table*

FIGURE 9.5:

*Macro for automating
the invoice table
(continued)*

```
Until(Item=17)

Label(End@)

Menu(Result;Letter;;; ("Print"; "Do Not Print"))
If(Result=1) PrintDlg() EndIf
Menu(Result;Letter;;; ("Another Form"; "Quit"))
CloseNoSave(No!)
Close(No!)
Case(Result;(1;Start@;2;Quit@);Quit@)

Label(Quit@)
```

The commands

```
CloseNoSave(No!)
Close(No!)
```

clear the window containing the table, then close the window without any prompt, returning the screen to its condition before the macro was played.

The macro does not protect against some data-entry errors, although the GetNumber command will display an error message when a nonnumeric character is entered. It will not display a warning when a fraction is entered for a quantity, or a zero or negative number is entered for an amount. To ensure that only positive numbers are entered, modify the parts of the macro that accept the quantity and price. For example, replace the four lines that accept the quantity (beginning with the GetNumber line) with the following:

```
Label(Qty@)
GetNumber(Qnty;"Enter Quantity:";Title)
Integer(Qnty; Qnty)
NumStr(Sqnty;2;Qnty)
Type(Sqnty)
If(Qnty=>1)
    PosCellNext()
    Else
    Prompt(Title;"You must enter a positive number";1;;)
    PauseKey(Enter!)
    SelectCell()
    DeleteCharNext()
    Go(Qty@)
EndIf
```

The Integer command converts the quantity entry into a whole number. This ensures that a decimal number cannot be entered by accident. If a quantity of one or more is entered, the insertion point moves to the next cell and the macro continues. If the quantity is less than one, the prompt appears. When the user presses ↵, the entry in the cell is deleted, and the routine is repeated for another try.

NUMBERING AND ARRANGING TICKETS

When you create tickets or other small-size documents using a label form, you must copy the ticket from label to label (see Chapter 3). After printing the tickets, you need to manually arrange them in consecutive order.

The macro shown in Figure 9.6 will automate the process for you. Select the ticket form with two columns and five rows, create the first ticket, press Ctrl-↵, then run the macro. It requests how many pages of tickets you want, and then copies the ticket to fill the pages. It then turns on page numbering.

```
Application(WP;WPWP;Default;"WPWPUS.WCD")
GetNumber(Pages;"How many pages of tickets you want";"Ticket
        System")
PosDocVeryTop()
PageNumbering(Where:BottomCenter!)
PosDocTop()
SelectScreenDown()
EditCopy()
Count:=Pages*10-1
For(Start;1;Start<=Count;Start+1)
        EditPaste()
EndFor
PosDocBottom()
DeleteCharPrevious()
PosDocTop()
Count:=100+Pages
For(Start;101;Start<=Count;Start+1)
        Page:=Start
        For(Num;1;Num<=10;num+1)
                PageNumbering
                (
                        NewNumber:Page
                )
                Page:=Page+Pages
                PosPageNext()
        EndFor
EndFor
```

FIGURE 9.6:

Macro for copying and numbering tickets

Rather than number the tickets consecutively on each page, the macro staggers the numbers in a special way. When you stack the printed pages on top of each other, the tickets are numbered consecutively in stacks. For example, ticket number 1 on the first page of tickets will be directly over ticket number 2 on the second page. Cut each stack separately, then place the stacks together for consecutively numbered tickets.

PERFORMING MATH WITH MACROS

WordPerfect tables can perform only basic addition, subtraction, multiplication, and division. However, you can incorporate more complex math by performing the operations in a macro, then using the NumStr and Type commands to insert the results into a cell.

For example, the table shown in Figure 9.7 requires the input of a loan amount, interest rate, and length of the mortgage. The formula for calculating mortgage payments requires exponential math. In order to calculate and insert the mortgage amount, the form was automated by the macro shown in Figure 9.8.

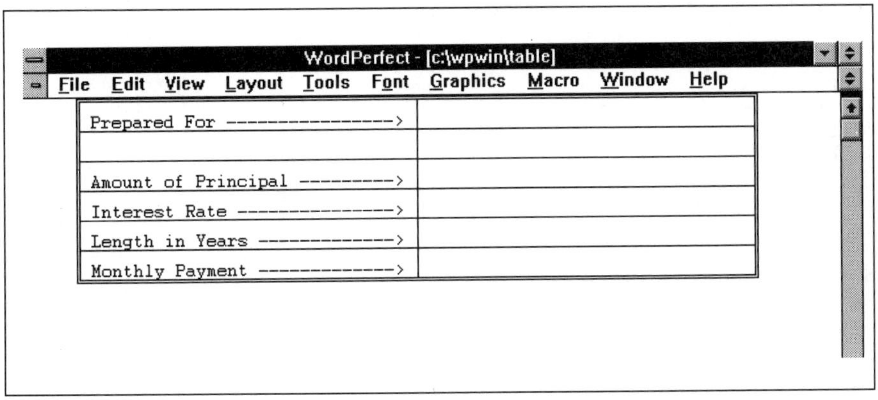

FIGURE 9.7:

Table that requires complex math

The If commands in the subroutines Amount, Percent, and Time ensure that a valid entry has been made. If not, the routine is performed again. Another If command checks whether the interest rate has been entered as a whole number or as a decimal (such as .07 for seven percent). If it is entered as a decimal, it is converted into a whole number for use later in the macro.

The task of taking a value to the Nth power is performed in a For loop. Initial values are set before the loop, then the amount is multiplied with each repetition. This loop can take some time, so a prompt with the Please Wait message is displayed during the computation. Note that if the user clears the screen without printing the completed table, the table will be gone.

```
Application(WP;WPWP;Default;"WPWPUS.WCD")
OnCancel(End@)
Title:="Mortgage Payment Estimate"
Prompt(Title;"Press Enter when ready";3;;)
PauseKey(Enter!)
EndPrompt
Principal:=0
Years:=0
Rate:=0
Label(Start@)
//The file Table must exist
FileOpen("Table")
PosDocBottom()
PosDocTop()
Display(On!)
PosCharNext()
Tab()
GetString(Name;Length=20;"Enter the client's name:";Title)
Type(Name)
PosCellDown()
PosCellDown()

Label(Amount@)
GetNumber(Principal;"Enter the amount of the loan:";Title)
If(Principal<=0) Go(Amount@) EndIf
NumStr(Amt;2;Principal)
Type(Amt)
PosCellDown()

Label(Percent@)
GetNumber(Rate;"Enter the interest rate:";Title)
If(Rate<=0) Go(Percent@)
     Else If(Rate<1) Rate:=Rate*100 EndIf EndIf
NumStr(Rte;2;Rate)
Type(Rte)
PosCellDown()

Label(Time@)
GetNumber(Years;"Enter the length in years:";Title)
If(Years<=0) Go(Time@) EndIf
NumStr(Yrs;0;Years)
Type(Yrs)
PosCellDown()

//The next series of lines calculates the payment while
//displaying a message on the screen

Prompt(Title;"Please Wait";3;;)
J:=0
Rate:=Rate / 1200
N:= Years * 12
Inc:= 1 + Rate X:=Inc
For(Var;1;Var<=N;Var+1)
     X:=X * Inc
EndFor

Temp:=1 * (Rate / (1 - (1 / X)))
Payment:= Temp * (Principal + J * 2000)
NumStr(Monthly;2;Payment)
EndPrompt
Type(Monthly)
```

```
Menu(Result;Letter;;; ("Print"; "Do Not Print"))
If(Result=1)  PrintFull() EndIf

Label(End@)
Menu(Result;Letter;;; ("Another Form"; "Quit"))
CloseNoSave(No!)
Close(No!)
Case(Result;{1;Start@;2;Quit@};Quit@)

Label(Quit@)
```

FIGURE 9.8:

*Macro for performing
the calculations
(continued)*

CHAPTER 10

Converting WordPerfect for DOS Macros

! n order to use macros designed for the DOS version of WordPerfect in WordPerfect for Windows, you must first convert them. WordPerfect for Windows includes a utility called the Macro Facility, which will convert macros for you. However, the utility cannot convert every WordPerfect for DOS command. This chapter explains how to use the Macro Facility to convert your macros, and how to manually convert the macro commands that the utility cannot handle.

RUNNING THE MACRO FACILITY

The Macro Facility uses the WPWIN\MACROS subdirectory as the default. To save time, copy your macros to this directory.

Whenever you play or record a macro from within WordPerfect for Windows, the Macro Facility opens in the background. It closes when you exit WordPerfect. When the Macro Facility is open, you can use the Windows Task List to switch to it while running WordPerfect. You can quickly open the facility in the background by selecting Macro ➤ Play (Alt-F10) ➤ Cancel. Press Ctrl-Esc to display the Task List, and then double-click on WordPerfect Macro Facility (or select it, then Switch). You can also run the facility by using WordPerfect's File Manager (see Chapter 15).

When you want to convert a series of long macros, run the Macro Facility on its own, without first starting WordPerfect. This gives the facility access to more memory and speeds up the conversion process. If you are not in Word-Perfect for Windows, run the Macro Facility from the Windows Program Manager: choose Run from the File menu, type MWFWIN.EXE, and press ↵. If you see a message indicating that the file cannot be found, enter \WPC\MFWIN.EXE in the Run dialog box.

CONVERTING A MACRO

The WordPerfect Macro Facility window has three pull-down menus: File, Macro, and Help. The Macro menu contains the commands for converting and compiling macros.

To convert a macro, select Convert from the Macro menu. In the Convert Macro dialog box, select the directory that contains the macro you want to convert to see a list of files with the .WPM extension. Select the macro that you want to convert, then select Convert. When the macro has been converted to WordPerfect for Windows format, you will see a dialog box similar to the one shown in Figure 10.1.

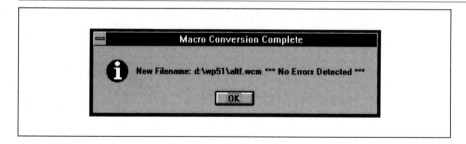

FIGURE 10.1:

Macro Conversion Complete dialog box

The converted macro will have the same name as the original file but with the .WCM extension. If you want to use a macro that was assigned to an Alt-key combination in the DOS version, you must rename it using CTRL and CTRLSFT, followed by the keystroke and the .WCM extension. For example, the conversion program will rename ALTH.WPM to ALTH.WCM. To execute it from the keyboard in the Windows version, rename it CTRLH.WCM or CTRLSFTH.WCM.

If the macro could not be completely converted, the dialog box will include the message

Macro Needs Editing

This means that the macro included commands that could not be converted by the program. You must edit that macro before it can be played in WordPerfect for Windows.

When you select OK, the list of macro files reappears. Select another macro to convert, or select Cancel to return to the Macro Facility window.

In some rare instances, a Windows unrecoverable error message will appear when you try to convert a macro. This means that there is a problem in the macro file and it cannot be converted. When you select OK, the Program Manager window will appear.

COMPILING CONVERTED MACROS

The macros you create in WordPerfect for Windows are automatically compiled before they are played. Compiling translates the text of the macro into a code that can be executed more quickly than the text itself. The code is placed at the beginning of the macro file, but it will not be displayed when you open the macro as a document. If you edit the macro after it has been compiled, WordPerfect will automatically recompile it before it is played. However, after editing or writing a macro in WordPerfect, it is a good idea to compile it in the Macro Facility before playing it.

The conversion process translates the text of a DOS version macro to the Window's version syntax, but the macro still must be compiled. If the macro appears to have converted properly, you should compile it in the Macro Facility before running it in WordPerfect. Some macros that seemed to convert without any problems may generate compilation errors.

To compile a macro in the Macro Facility, select Compile Macro from the Macro menu, choose the directory and macro from the list of files, and select Compile. If the macro compiles without an error message, you can try it in WordPerfect. However, you may discover that the macro needs to be edited because it does not perform as it did in the DOS version.

If any error messages appear during the compilation, note the information, and then select Continue Compilation to detect any additional problem areas. The Location of Error text box shows the line number and text of the line where the error was detected. This does not necessarily mean that this line contains an error. A missing parenthesis, for example, may not be detected until the following line.

To find the line indicated by the error message in the macro, look for the text that was indicated in the error message or count down to the line number. WordPerfect numbers each blank line as well, but a command divided by word wrap is counted as one line, not two.

PLAYING AND RECORDING MACROS FROM THE MACRO FACILITY

When you are running WordPerfect at the same time as the Macro Facility, the other options on the facility's Macro menu are available:

◆ **Play:** Allows you to select and play a macro. The macro will automatically play in the WordPerfect application for which it was designed, as indicated by the first two characters in the Application command. The application must be open for the macro to play.

◆ **Record:** Returns to WordPerfect and turns on Macro Record mode.

◆ **Terminate:** Terminates a macro. If you run a macro that does not behave properly, try pressing the Esc key. If that does not stop the macro, switch to the Macro Facility and select Terminate from the Macro menu.

EDITING MACROS WITH CONVERSION PROBLEMS

WordPerfect for DOS macros that change formats usually will convert without difficulty. However, macros that include Programming commands are likely to need editing before they can be played.

In the DOS version of WordPerfect, the macro language uses the same command structure as the merge language. In the Windows version, the macro structure has changed, and the merge structure has remained the same as in the DOS version. This means that the conversion problems relate to converted macros, not to merge files.

VIEWING THE CONVERTED FILE

When codes in a macro cannot be converted, switch to or start WordPerfect and open the macro file. It will have a .WCM extension. The Application command will appear as

Application(WP;WPWP)

and all Product commands will be preceded by WP, as in

WP.Display(State:Off!)

The WP. prefix is necessary because the conversion routine does not add the Default parameter to the Application command. If you want to insert commands without typing WP. before each one, edit the Application command so it appears as

Application(WP;WPWP;Default)

You do not have to add WPWPUS.WCD.

Macro commands that could not be converted have been changed to comments, with the // characters in front of them. These are the commands that you must convert manually.

Edit the macro, save it, and then try to compile it again in the Macro Facility. Although WordPerfect will compile it when you play it, it is safer to compile complex macros as a separate step.

CONVERSION GUIDE

This section provides a guide to solving the most common problems that arise in converting WordPerfect for DOS macros.

Text Commands

Macro commands using the form

{TEXT}{VAR1}~Enter your name~

will not convert. Use a GetString command instead, such as

GetString(Name;Length=15;"Please enter your name";"Title")

Use the variable Name in place of each reference to Var1 in the macro.

Base Font Commands

Commands that change the base font or allow selection of a new base font will not convert. Instead of

{FONT}4

which displayed a list of fonts for selection of a base font, display the Font dialog box by using the Product command

FontDlg()

Exit Commands

The {EXIT} command will not convert. You can replace it with one of several Windows version commands.

Use the command

AppClose()

to exit WordPerfect and be prompted to save any edited documents.

Replace the Exit command with

Close()

to close the current document and display the next document window. Use the Yes! parameter to be prompted to save any changes. The No! parameter will discard the changes. However, if the macro created a new document or opened an existing one, you will be prompted to save the document regardless of the parameter. To always close a document without being prompted, use the commands

CloseNoSave(No!)
Close(No!)

Another alternative for Exit is

CloseNoSave()

which closes the current document but does not close the window. A blank editing window remains even if there are other document windows in the background. Use the No! parameter to close the document without being prompted to save changes, or the Yes! parameter to see a prompt.

The If Exists Command

The {IF EXISTS} command tests whether a named variable has been assigned a value, as in

```
{IF EXISTS}Heading~
   Instructions
```

This command cannot be used in a macro and will not convert. Instead, assign the variable a null value at the start of the macro, then check for a non-null, as in

```
Heading:=""
Instructions...
   If(Heading<>"")
      Instructions...
   Endif
```

Control Commands

WordPerfect for DOS cursor-positioning and attribute commands look something like

```
{^P}{^A}{^M}{^/}Press {^]}Enter{^/} when you are finished{^/}
```

The DOS version commands use codes with these functions:

CODE	FUNCTION
^P	Designates that the next two codes show the character and line position to place the cursor.
^A	Moves the cursor to character position 1 when preceded by ^P.
^M	Moves the cursor to line 13 when preceded by ^P.
^/	Turns off bold.
^]	Turns on bold.

These commands will not convert in the Windows version. Instead, rewrite the command with the Prompt command to accomplish the same task, as in

```
Prompt("WARNING";"Press Enter when done";3;5;200)
Pause
EndPrompt
```

You must convert the line and character positions of the DOS macro to their pixel equivalents for the Windows macro.

Prompt Lines and Menus

Commands that use the {CHAR} command to create prompt lines, as in

```
{CHAR}1~
{^]}1 M{^/)emo;
{^]}2 R{^/)eport;
{^]}3 I{^/)nvoice:~
```

will not convert.

In their place, use the Menu command, such as

```
Menu(Result;Digit;;; {"Memo"; "Letter"; "Invoice"})
```

State Commands

The WordPerfect for DOS {STATE} command cannot be converted. This command returns a value based on the condition of WordPerfect. For example, the command

```
{IF}{STATE}&512~
   Instructions...
{ENDIF}
```

tests if Reveal Codes mode is on. If it is on, the value returned by {STATE} is 512. This command says "If the value returned by State is 512, perform the following instructions."

Instead of testing State against the returned value, you must use GetWPData and check the Boolean condition of the returned variable. The equivalent Windows command would be

```
GetWPData(MacroVariable:CodesOn;SystemVariable:135)
   If(CodesOn=True)
     Instructions...
   EndIf
```

The system variable 135 (or RevealCodesActive!) will return a True if codes are revealed.

Table 10.1 shows the DOS State values and their Windows equivalents. Note that three DOS values do not have equivalents in Windows.

DOS VERSION STATE VALUE		WINDOWS VERSION SYSTEM VARIABLE		
VALUE RETURNED	**MEANING**	**NUMBER**	**NAME**	**RETURNS**
3	Current document	128	CurrentDocument!	Integer 1–9
4	Editing screen	129	AtMainEdit-Screen!	True/False
8	Other screen			
16	Macro define mode	130	MacroDefActive!	True/False
32	Macro execute	131	MacroExecute-Active!	True/False
64	Merge active	132	MergeActive!	True/False
128	Block active	133	SelectMode-Active!	True/False
256	Typeover active	134	TypeoverMode!	True/False
512	Reveal Codes mode	135	RevealCodes-Active!	True/False
1024	Yes/No question			
2048	In a list			

TABLE 10.1:

WordPerfect for DOS State Values and WordPerfect for Windows System Variable Equivalents

System Commands

The {SYSTEM} command is another DOS version command that cannot be converted. It is similar to the State command in that it returns a value based on some condition of WordPerfect. With a System command, however, you must designate which condition is being tested.

For example, condition 1 (or Attrib) returns a value based on the attribute of the character at the cursor position. This WordPerfect for DOS macro determines whether the character is bold:

```
{IF}({SYSTEM}1~=4096)~
   Bold is the attribute
{ENDIF}
```

If the value returned is 4096, then the attribute at the cursor position is bold.

With the Windows version, use the GetWPData command to return a value into a system variable. The Windows version to test for a bold character is

```
GetWPData(MacroVariable:BoldOn;SystemVariable:77)
If(BoldOn=True)
    Instructions...
EndIf
```

System variable 77 (or FontBold!) returns True if the current attribute is bold, False if it is not bold.

Table 10.2 shows the DOS system variables and their Windows equivalents. Use the Windows system variable in the GetWPData command and check the macro variable for the returned value.

DOS VERSION SYSTEM VARIABLE AND VALUE RETURNED	WINDOWS VERSION SYSTEM VARIABLE AND VALUE RETURNED
Attrib (1); Returns 0	FontNormal! (64); Returns True/False
Attrib (1); Returns 1	FontExtraLarge! (65); Returns True/False
Attrib (1); Returns 2	FontVeryLarge! (66); Returns True/False
Attrib (1); Returns 4	FontLarge! (67); Returns True/False
Attrib (1); Returns 8	FontSmall! (68); Returns True/False
Attrib (1); Returns 16	FontFine! (69); Returns True/False
Attrib (1); Returns 32	FontSuperscript! (70); Returns True/False
Attrib (1); Returns 64	FontSubscript! (71); Returns True/False
Attrib (1); Returns 128	FontOutline! (72); Returns True/False
Attrib (1); Returns 256	FontItalics! (73); Returns True/False
Attrib (1); Returns 512	FontShadow! (74); Returns True/False
Attrib (1); Returns 1024	FontRedline! (75); Returns True/False
Attrib (1); Returns 2048	FontDoubleUnderline! (76); Returns True/False
Attrib (1); Returns 4096	FontBold! (77); Returns True/False

TABLE 10.2:

WordPerfect for DOS System Variables and Their WordPerfect for Windows Equivalents (with the GetWPData Command)

DOS VERSION SYSTEM VARIABLE AND VALUE RETURNED	WINDOWS VERSION SYSTEM VARIABLE AND VALUE RETURNED
Attrib (1); Returns 8192	FontStrikeout! (78); Returns True/False
Attrib (1); Returns 16384	FontUnderline! (79); Returns True/False
Attrib (1); Returns 32768	FontSmallCaps! (80); Returns True/False
CellAttr (23); Returns 0	CellNormal! (81); Returns True/False
CellAttr (23); Returns 1	CellExtraLarge! (82); Returns True/False
CellAttr (23); Returns 2	CellVeryLarge! (83); Returns True/False
CellAttr (23); Returns 4	CellLarge! (84); Returns True/False
CellAttr (23); Returns 8	CellSmall! (85); Returns True/False
CellAttr (23); Returns 16	CellFine! (86); Returns True/False
CellAttr (23); Returns 32	CellSuperscript! (87); Returns True/False
CellAttr (23); Returns 64	CellSubscript! (88); Returns True/False
CellAttr (23); Returns 128	CellOutline! (89); Returns True/False
CellAttr (23); Returns 256	CellItalics! (90); Returns True/False
CellAttr (23); Returns 512	CellShadow! (91); Returns True/False
CellAttr (23); Returns 1024	CellRedline! (92); Returns True/False
CellAttr (23); Returns 2048	CellDoubleUnderline! (93); Returns True/False
CellAttr (23); Returns 4096	CellBold! (94); Returns True/False
CellAttr (23); Returns 8192	CellStrikeout! (95); Returns True/False
CellAttr (23); Returns 16384	CellUnderline! (96); Returns True/False
CellAttr (23); Returns 32768	CellSmallCaps! (97); Returns True/False
CellState (24); Returns 0	CellJustification (104); Returns 1 (Left)
CellState (24); Returns 1	CellJustification (104); Returns 2 (Full)
CellState (24); Returns 2	CellJustification (104); Returns 3 (Center)
CellState (24); Returns 3	CellJustification (104); Returns 0 (Right)

TABLE 10.2:

WordPerfect for DOS System Variables and Their WordPerfect for Windows Equivalents (with the GetWPData Command) (continued)

DOS VERSION SYSTEM VARIABLE AND VALUE RETURNED	WINDOWS VERSION SYSTEM VARIABLE AND VALUE RETURNED
CellState (24); Returns 4	CellJustification (104); Returns 4 (Decimal)
CellState (24) Mod of Value; Returns 1	JustifyCellSpecific! (105); Returns True/False
CellState (24) Mod of Value; Returns 2	AttributeCellSpecific! (106); Returns True/False
CellState (24) Mod of Value; Returns 4	CellBottomAligned! (107); Returns True/False
CellState (24) Mod of Value; Returns 8	CellCenterAligned! (108); Returns True/False
CellState (24) Mod of Value; Returns 16	CellIgnoredWhileCalculating! (109); Returns True/False
CellState (24) Mod of Value; Returns 32	CellContentIsFormula! (110); Returns True/False
CellState (24) Mod of Value; Returns 64	CellLocked! (111); Returns True/False
Document (4); Returns 1	DocumentModified! (98); Returns True/False
Document (4); Returns 4	DocumentNeedsGenerating! (99); Returns True/False
Document (4); Returns 256	DocumentBlank! (100); Returns True/False
Document (4); Returns 512	BetweenTableCodes! (101); Returns True/False
Document (4); Returns 1024	BetweenMathCodes! (102); Returns True/False
Document (4); Returns 2048	BetweenOutlineCodes! (103); Returns True/False
Document (4); Returns 4096	BetweenColumnCodes! (116); Returns True/False

TABLE 10.2:

WordPerfect for DOS System Variables and Their WordPerfect for Windows Equivalents (with the GetWPData Command) (continued)

DOS VERSION SYSTEM VARIABLE AND VALUE RETURNED	WINDOWS VERSION SYSTEM VARIABLE AND VALUE RETURNED
Cell (2); Returns cell number	Cell! (2); Returns cell number
Column (3); Returns column number	Column! (3); Returns column number
Endnote (5); Returns endnote number	Endnote! (5); Returns endnote number
Equation (6); Returns equation number	Equation! (6); Returns equation number
Figure (7); Returns figure number	Figure! (7); Returns figure number
Footnote (8); Returns footnote number	Footnote! (8); Returns footnote number
Left (9); Returns number representing code	LeftCode! (9); Returns number representing the code
	LeftChar! (112): Returns character
Line (10); Returns line number	Line! (10); Returns line number
Name (12); Returns document name	Name! (12); Returns document name
Page (14); Returns page number	Page! (14); Returns page number
Path (15); Returns DOS path to document	Path! (15); Returns DOS path to document
POS (16); Returns cursor position	Pos! (16); Returns insertion-point position
Right (18); Returns number representing code	RightCode! (18); Returns number representing the code
	RightChar! (113); Returns character
TableBox (19); Returns table number	TableBox! (19); Returns table number
TextBox (20); Returns text box number	TextBox! (20); Returns text box number

TABLE 10.2:

WordPerfect for DOS System Variables and Their WordPerfect for Windows Equivalents (with the GetWPData Command) (continued)

DOS VERSION SYSTEM VARIABLE AND VALUE RETURNED	WINDOWS VERSION SYSTEM VARIABLE AND VALUE RETURNED
UserBox (21); Returns user box number	UserBox! (21); Returns user box number
Row (22); Returns row number	Row! (22); Returns row number
Version (28); returns installed version of WordPerfect	MajorVersion! (136); Returns major installed version of WordPerfect for Windows
	MinorVersion! (137); Returns minor installed version of WordPerfect for Windows
	InterimRelease! (138); Returns interim release number of installed version of WordPerfect for Windows

TABLE 10.2:

WordPerfect for DOS System Variables and Their WordPerfect for Windows Equivalents (with the GetWPData Command) (continued)

The values returned for graphic box numbers must be converted to their actual numbers in the document by using integer division. Divide the value by 32; the integer portion of the quotient represents the first-level number. The remainder of the division, using a modulus operation, is the second-level number. For example, if the GetWPData command returns 67 after this program segment:

```
GetWPData(MacroVariable:Result;SystemVariable:TableBox!)
Integer(First;Result/32)
Second:=Result–(First*32)
NumStr(One;0;First)
NumStr(Two;0;Second)
Type(One)
Type(".")
Type(Two)
```

WordPerfect will display table number 2.3. The integer result of 67 divided by 32 yields the first-level number 2. The modulus operation returns the amount remaining after the integer division, 67 − 64, or the second-level number 3.

Table 10.3 shows WordPerfect for Windows System variables without DOS version equivalents.

FUNCTION	VALUE RETURNED
Macropath! (114)	Path of MACROS directory
AutoCodePlacement! (139)	True if automatic code placement is on
ConfirmationOnCodeDelete!(140)	True if confirm on deletion is on
ReadOnlyDoc! (141)	True if current document is read-only
DocSummaryPromptOnExit! (142)	True if create summary on exit is on
SelectedText! (143)	String of the selected text

TABLE 10.3:

WordPerfect for Windows System Variables without WordPerfect for DOS Equivalents

REPLACING MACROS WITH CONVERSION PROBLEMS

In some cases, it will not be possible to edit the converted macro so that it performs as it did in WordPerfect for DOS. The solution is to create equivalent macros in WordPerfect for Windows.

HANDLING CONFIRMED REPLACEMENT MACROS

DOS version macros that perform confirmed replacement of text will be converted without an error message. However, they will not perform properly in WordPerfect for Windows.

For example, a WordPerfect for DOS macro that replaces *Wrong* with *Right* with confirmation looks like this:

```
{REPLACE}yWrong{SEARCH}Right{SEARCH}
```

The converted macro will look like this:

```
Application(WP;WPWP)
WP.Display(State:Off!)
WP.SearchReplace(SearchString:"Wrong";SearchDirection:
    Forward!;ReplacementScope:DocOnly!;ReplacementString:
    "Right";ReplacementAction:ReplaceOne!)
//*** NO CONVERSION ERRORS DETECTED ***
```

When you run the macro, only the first occurrence of the match will be changed, not every occurrence in the document.

Unfortunately, you cannot record a macro that performs prompted replacements. The only alternative is to write a macro that performs the function. The macro shown in Figure 10.2 is one example of how this can be done. It accepts a search-and-replacement string (up to 20 characters), assigns the length of the search string to the variable Times, and then sets up error traps for a search that fails and a cancel request.

```
Application(WP;WPWP;Default;"WPWPUS.WCD")
Title:="Confirmed Replacement"
GetString(Old;Length=20;"Enter the search text.";Title)
GetString(New;Length=20;"Enter the replacement text.";Title)
StrLen(Times;Old)
Count:=0
InsertTypeover(Off!)
OnNotFound(End@)
OnCancel(End@)
Display(On!)
PosDocTop()
Label(FindAndReplace@)
SearchText(SearchString:Old;SearchDirection:Forward!;
           SearchScope:DocOnly!)
SelectMode(On!)
For(Char;1;Char<=Times;Char+1)
     PosCharPrevious()
EndFor
FontStrikeout(On!)
Menu(Result;Letter;10;10; {"Replace"; "Skip"; "Cancel"})
FontStrikeout(Off!)
If(Result=2)
     SelectMode(Off!)
     For(Char;1;Char<=Times;Char+1)
     PosCharNext()
     EndFor
     Go(FindAndReplace@)
Else
     If(Result=3)
     Go(End@)
     EndIf
EndIf

DeleteCharNext()
Type(New)
Count:=Count+1
Go(FindAndReplace@)

Label(End@)
SelectMode(Off!)
NumStr(Report;1;Count)
Prompt(Title;Report+" Replacements made";4;;)
Pause
Quit
```

FIGURE 10.2:

Search and Replace macro

The macro proceeds to search for the first occurrence of the string, and then selects and strikes out the text so you can see it on the screen. The commands for the display are

```
SelectMode(On!)
For(Char;1;Char<=Times;Char+1)
   PosCharPrevious()
EndFor
FontStrikeout(On!)
```

The macro next displays the menu. When you select an option from the menu, the strikeout is removed. If you select to skip the replacement, it turns off Select mode, places the insertion point after the text, and then loops to the start of the subroutine to search for the next occurrence. If you select Cancel, the macro jumps to the End subroutine; otherwise, it deletes the selected characters and inserts the new ones.

The accumulator

```
Count:=Count+1
```

keeps a running total of the number of replacements made, then the macro loops to find the next occurrence.

When the user selects Cancel from the menu (or presses Esc to end the macro), or if the search string cannot be found, the End subroutine is executed. This turns off Select mode (in case you pressed Esc when the mode was on) and reports the number of replacements made.

MODIFYING STRING-MANIPULATION MACROS

WordPerfect for DOS string-manipulation commands such as {NTOK} and {KTON} will not be converted in the Windows version. {NTOK} converts a number to the character represented by it in the ASCII character set. {KTON} converts an ASCII character to its number.

These commands are frequently used for changing the case of letters. For example, adding 32 to the ASCII code of an uppercase letter results in the ASCII code of its lowercase equivalent.

Since WordPerfect for Windows does not convert these codes, you must perform the same function in another way. One method is to use the StrPos command. For example, this macro section will convert a letter stored in the variable Character to its ASCII value:

```
Upper:="ABCDEFGHIJKLMNOPQRSTUVWXYZ"
Lower:="abcdefghijklmnopqrstuvwxyz"
StrPos(Pos;Character;Upper)
  If(Pos<>0)
    AsciiCode:=Pos+64
  Else
    StrPos(Pos;Character;Lower)
      If(Pos<>0)
        AsciiCode:=Pos+96
      Endlf
Endlf
```

The StrPos command returns the position of a character in a string. If the character is in the string, the variable Pos will be greater than 0. If the character is found in the string Upper, its ASCII code is the position in the string plus 64. If the character is not in Upper, the macro looks for it in Lower. If the character is found in Lower, the macro adds 96 to the position.

The macro checks both Upper and Lower because the character could be a punctuation mark, which you are not interested in, or a code or WordPerfect character that does not have an ASCII value.

Using a similar macro, you can convert a character's case without computing the ASCII number. For example, suppose you accidentally pressed Caps Lock and typed an entire paragraph in the wrong case. The macro shown in Figure 10.3 will convert the cases of all letters without affecting numbers, punctuation marks, or codes.

The series of GetWPData commands store the cursor position of the tilde. You are then told to place the cursor at the start of the block. The insertion-point position is stored and then compared to the ending position in a series of If commands. If the starting position is after the ending position, the macro goes to a subroutine where it displays a message and uses the Replace command to delete the inserted tilde character.

The While loop then gets each character in the block. If it is not a code (which returns a null, represented by two quotation marks with nothing between them), the macro performs the Reverse subroutine. This routine works by determining if the character is uppercase or lowercase by using the StrPos command, then assigning the converted character by using the SubStr command. For example, if the character is in the fifth position in Upper, its lowercase equivalent is in the fifth position in Lower.

```
Application(WP;WPWP;Default;"WPWPUS.WCD")
GetWPData(MacroVariable:Blank;SystemVariable:DocumentBlank!)
If(Blank=True)
        Quit
EndIf
OnNotFound(End@)
Upper:="ABCDEFGHIJKLMNOPQRSTUVWXYZ"
Lower:="abcdefghijklmnopqrstuvwxyz"
InsertTypeover(Off!)
Prompt("Number";"Place cursor at the end of the block and
        press Enter";1;;)
PauseKey(Key:0)
Type(" ")
GetWPData(MacroVariable:PageEnd;SystemVariable:Page!)
GetWPData(MacroVariable:LineEnd;SystemVariable:Line!)
GetWPData(MacroVariable:PosEnd;SystemVariable:Pos!)
Prompt("Number";"Place cursor at the start of the block and
        press Enter";1;;)
PauseKey(Key:0)
EndPrompt
GetWPData(MacroVariable:PageStart;SystemVariable:Page!)
GetWPData(MacroVariable:LineStart;SystemVariable:Line!)
GetWPData(MacroVariable:PosStart;SystemVariable:Pos!)
If(PageStart>PageEnd) Go(WEnd@) EndIf
If(LineStart>LineEnd)
     If(PageStart=PageEnd) Go(WEnd@)
      EndIf
      EndIf
If (PosStart>PosEnd)
     If(PageStart=PageEnd) Go(WEnd@)
      EndIf
      EndIf
If(PageStart=PageEnd)
     If(PosStart=PosEnd) Go(WEnd@)
      EndIf
      EndIf
RevealCodes(On!)
GetWPData(MacroVariable:Char;SystemVariable:RightChar!)
Prompt("Number";"Please be patient. This isn't C or
       Pascal.";0;;)
While(Char<>"˜")
     If(Char<>"")
          Call(Reverse@)
     Else
     PosCharNext()
     EndIf
     GetWPData(MacroVariable:Char;SystemVariable:RightChar!)
EndWhile
EndPrompt
DeleteCharNext()
RevealCodes(Off!)
Quit
Label(Reverse@)
Flag:=0
     StrPos(Pos;Char;Upper)
     If(Pos<>0)
          SubStr(New;Pos;1;Lower)
          Flag:=1
     Else
          StrPos(Pos;Char;Lower)
          If(Pos<>0)
          SubStr(New;Pos;1;Upper)
```

```
        Flag:=1
        EndIf
    EndIf
    If(Flag=1)
        DeleteCharNext()
        Type(New)
    Else
    PosCharNext()
    EndIf
Return

Label(End@)
    Quit
Label(WEnd@)
    Prompt("Error";"Starting position must be before ending
        position";1;;)
    Pause
    PosDocTop()
    SearchReplace(SearchString:"˜";SearchDirection:Forward!;
        ReplacementScope:DocOnly!;ReplacementString:"";
        ReplacementAction:ReplaceAll!)
```

FIGURE 10.3:

*Macro for converting
character case
(continued)*

The Flag variable is used to keep track of when a conversion is made. If a character is changed, the variable is assigned the value 1. The flag is used to determine whether the old character should be deleted and the new one inserted.

HANDLING MACROS THAT ADD PAGE *X* OF *Y* NUMBERS

In WordPerfect for DOS, there are several ways to create a macro that shows the page number and the total number of pages in a document, such as Page 1 of 23. Unfortunately, many macros of this type cannot be converted because of problems with the State and System commands.

Figure 10.4 shows a program for numbering pages this way. Notice that two HeaderFooter commands are necessary. The first command inserts a blank footer at the start of the document. The second command inserts footers that contain the page-numbering text.

Adding a footer reduces the amount of text on a page. A document that may be 20 pages without a footer could be 21 with it. If you do not insert the blank footer before counting the pages, the total may be off, and your last page may be numbered something like Page 21 of 22.

```
    Application(WP;WPWP;Default;"WPWPUS.WCD")
    PosDocTop()
    HeaderFooter(Operation:Create!;Item:FooterA!)
    Close(Save:Yes!)

    PosDocBottom()
    GetWPData(MacroVariable:Of;SystemVariable:Page!)
    PosDocTop()
    NumStr(TotalPages;1;Of)

    For(Count;1;Count<=Of;Count+1)
    HeaderFooter(Operation:Create!;Item:FooterA!)
    LineCenter()
    Type("Page ")
    PageNumberInsert(WithStyle:Yes!)
    Type(Text:" of ")
    Type(TotalPages)
    Close(Save:Yes!)
    PosPageNext()
    EndFor
    PosDocTop()
```

FIGURE 10.4:

*Macro for numbering
pages X of Y*

CHAPTER 11

Merging Form Documents with Databases

You know the typical uses of form documents: advertisements, account statements, invoices, and announcements. But there are many other applications that you may not have considered. How many project bids, requests for proposals, and contracts do you produce that have paragraphs in common? Are you a job-seeker answering classified ads in the newspaper or a student requesting college applications? Even if you only send one such document a week, you actually produce the same letter 52 times!

In order to produce form documents, you need to create a WordPerfect database that contains the information you want to merge. You can use your databases to produce form letters, envelopes, labels, and database reports.

CREATING A DATABASE

A *database* contains all the pertinent information about a group of items. It could be the name, address, and other information about clients or employees. It could be the company's inventory or price list. WordPerfect calls the database the *secondary file.*

The secondary file is an electronic version of an index card file. Every card, called a *record,* contains all the data about one item. Each record has several pieces of information, such as the name of the item, quantity on hand, supplier, and price. Each piece of information is called a *field.* To create a database, you first need to determine which fields are necessary.

Field names can be only one word, without spaces, hyphens, or underline characters. The first 15 characters of the field name are significant. This means that you can use field names that are longer than 15 characters, but the first 15 must be different for each field. For example, the fields DateOf-PreviousOrder and DateOfPreviousPayment are treated as separate fields; DateOfPreviousOrder and DateOfPreviousOperation are considered the same field.

INSERTING FIELD MERGE CODES

We will now create a database of client information for use in this and later chapters. We will need the following fields to store this information:

FIELD NAME	FIELD CONTENTS
Company	Company name
Contact	Contact person's full name
Salutation	Name for the salutation
Title	Contact person's title
Address	Street address
Location	Post office box, suite, or other location
City	City
State	State
Zip	Zip code
Telephone	Telephone number
Credit	Credit limit

FIELD NAME	FIELD CONTENTS
Due	Amount due
LastAmount	Amount of the last order
LastOrder	Date of the last order

Notice that we have two fields for the contact's name. One field will store the entire name for use in addresses. The other will store the greeting to use in the salutation of a letter.

When you use field names, the first line in the database must contain a list of the names, and the order of the names must correspond to the order of the information in each of the records. For example, if the Company field is first in the list of field names, the company's name must be the first item in each record. Each record must have the same number of fields.

Follow these steps to create the database:

1. Start WordPerfect for Windows or clear the screen by selecting File ➤ Close (Ctrl-F4).

2. Select Tools ➤ Merge (Ctrl-F12) ➤ Merge Codes to display the dialog box shown in Figure 11.1. The list box contains all the merge codes that you can use for your applications.

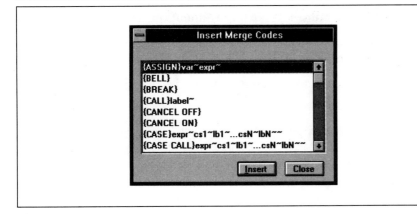

FIGURE 11.1:

Insert Merge Codes dialog box

3. Type **f**. A text box appears at the top of the list, and the list scrolls to highlight the first code that begins with the letter *f*, the {FIELD} command. As you type additional characters in the text box, the list scrolls to the codes that begin with those letters.

4. Scroll through the list box to highlight the code

{FIELD NAMES}name1~...nameN~~

5. Select Insert, or double-click on the code, to display the dialog box shown in Figure 11.2.

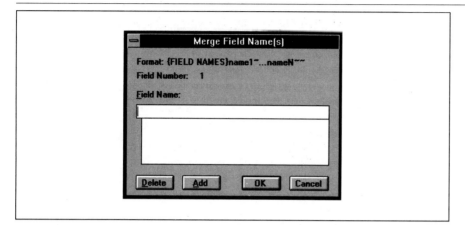

FIGURE 11.2:

Merge Field Names dialog box

6. Type **Company**, and then click once on Add. WordPerfect will increment the field number automatically as you add each field name.

7. Select the Field Name text box, type **Contact**, and select Add.

8. Select the Field Name text box, type **Salutation**, and select Add.

9. In the same way, add the 11 remaining fields for the database, as listed at the beginning of this section.

10. Select OK to return to the Insert Merge Codes dialog box, and then choose Close.

The list of field names appears in the document. The list is surrounded by the {FIELD NAMES} and {END RECORD} codes and followed by a hard page break. Each field name is followed by a tilde (~) and there is an extra tilde before the {END RECORD} code. WordPerfect uses the tilde to represent the end of codes that have parameters. The names of the fields are the parameters of the {FIELD NAMES} code. In addition to the tildes that represent the end of each field name, there must be another tilde to signify the end of the code. The {END RECORD} code has no parameters, so it does not require a closing tilde.

You can add, delete, and edit field names directly in the field name list. Just make sure that each name is followed by a tilde and that there are two tildes before {END RECORD}.

Note that the list of field names does not word wrap correctly on the screen. Because merge commands are codes, they do not take up any actual character space in the document. The position indicator in the status bar will not change when you move the insertion point from one side of a code to the other. For clarity, you can insert a carriage return before each field name to place each on its own line in the record.

Here are some important points to note about merge codes:

◆ Unlike WordPerfect macro commands, which you can type directly into the document, merge codes must be entered through the Merge menu, Insert Merge Codes dialog box, or special key combinations. You cannot type a merge code yourself.

◆ Every merge code is surrounded by braces.

◆ You can edit the text of a parameter but not the code within the braces. The code is treated as a single character; if you press Del to erase the beginning brace or press Backspace to erase the ending brace, the entire code will be deleted.

◆ Merge codes that are two words are separated by a space. For example, the merge code for ending an IF routine is {END IF}, unlike the macro command EndIf.

ENTERING DATA RECORDS

As you enter data into the fields to create records, you must designate the end of each field by inserting the {END FIELD} code. Mark the end of each record with the {END RECORD} code. Now we will type the information into our database fields.

1. Type **Comhype Computers** and press Alt-↵ to insert the {END FIELD} code followed by a carriage return. Alternatively, you can select Tools ➤ Merge ➤ End Field to add the code.

2. Type **Miss Elaine Cunningham** and press Alt-↵.

3. Type the following text in the fields, pressing Alt-↵ after each field entry. Do not press ↵, or you will get extra lines in your form documents. We are entering the date in the format *YY/MM/DD*, so we can later sort the file by date.

Elaine
President
431 Broad Street
Suite 120

Margate
NJ
08712
215-555-1765
1500
550
500
93/12/01

4. Select Tools ➤ Merge ➤ End Record (Alt-Shift-↵).

The {END RECORD} code is placed at the end of the record, and a hard page break is inserted, as shown in Figure 11.3. Do not press ↵ after inserting the code, or you will get an extra line at the beginning of the next record.

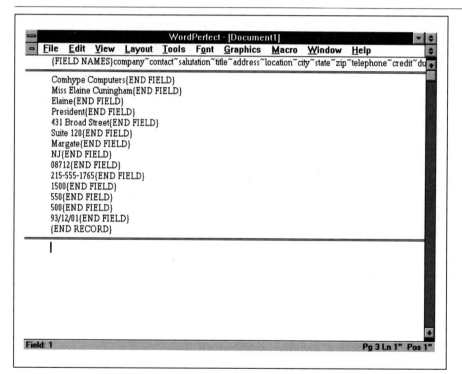

FIGURE 11.3:

First record added to the database

In the record you just created, you coded 14 fields. However, what if you had a record that did not have a second address line? Since each record must have the same number of fields, you have to insert an empty field—a line with the {END FIELD} code but no other information.

5. In the same manner, enter the information for the next three records, as shown in Figure 11.4. Notice that two records require empty fields because they do not have a second address line. Insert the {END RECORD} code after the last record. Each record, including the last, should end with a hard page break.

FIGURE 11.4:

Additional client records

```
DupliCopy Company{END FIELD}
Mr. Jackson H. Montgomery{END FIELD}
Jack{END FIELD}
President{END FIELD}
42 East Broad Street{END FIELD}
{END FIELD}
Reynoldstown{END FIELD}
PA{END FIELD}
19011{END FIELD}
215-295-0983{END FIELD}
1500{END FIELD}
600{END FIELD}
550{END FIELD}
92/11/16{END FIELD}
{END RECORD}
Chandler Scientific{END FIELD}
Mr. Adam Chandler{END FIELD}
Mr. Chandler{END FIELD}
President{END FIELD}
Osage and Wilson Avenues{END FIELD}
{END FIELD}
Dallas{END FIELD}
TX{END FIELD}
31223{END FIELD}
346-845-1987{END FIELD}
1500{END FIELD}
612{END FIELD}
150{END FIELD}
93/06/12{END FIELD}
{END RECORD}
Computers-R-Us{END FIELD}
Ms. Wilamini Boyle{END FIELD}
Ms. Boyle{END FIELD}
Vice President{END FIELD}
401 Ocean Ave.{END FIELD}
Box 12{END FIELD}
Northfield{END FIELD}
NJ{END FIELD}
01652{END FIELD}
609-567-0893{END FIELD}
1000{END FIELD}
235{END FIELD}
267{END FIELD}
93/02/01{END FIELD}
{END RECORD}
```

6. Select File ➤ Save (Ctrl-Shift-F3), type **Clients**, and select Save.

7. Select File ➤ Close (Ctrl-F4).

You can add or delete names as necessary. Just remember to maintain the proper format, with an {END FIELD} code after each field and an {END RECORD} code after each record. Also, be sure you have the same number of fields in the same order in each record.

Because a database is a WordPerfect document, you can use all the editing commands to maintain the information. It's easy to search for specific records, edit the text, move and copy data between records, and delete records.

USING FIELD NUMBERS INSTEAD OF NAMES

You can create a database where each field is associated with a field number rather than a field name. In our sample database, for example, field 1 is the name of the company, field 2 is the contact name, and so on.

If you do not want to use names at all, create the database without the {FIELD NAMES} code or the list of names; just start the file with the first record. The first field in each record is {FIELD}1~, the second {FIELD}2~, and so on. Keep in mind that when you use field numbers, you must remember which number represents each field to place the information in the correct location within the document.

WRITING FORM DOCUMENTS

Now that you have a database, you can create the *primary file*, which is the document that contains the form letter. When you come to a place where you want the variable information to appear, you enter a {FIELD} code to indicate the name or number of the field that you want inserted at that location. WordPerfect will insert the variable information during the merge process.

The fields can be used in any order in the form document; they do not have to be in the order they are in the database. You can also repeat the {FIELD} code within the document so that the same information will appear more than once.

Unlike other WordPerfect codes, merge codes are displayed on the screen along with other text. You do not have to select Reveal Codes to display them. As long as you merge the documents before printing, the variable information, not the codes, will be printed.

CREATING A PRIMARY FILE

Now we will create a form letter for all the clients in the database. The inside address will include a second line if it is available. However, if the address does not include a second line, we will use a command to prevent a blank line from appearing.

1. Enter your address and the date. You can use the Lethead macro that you created in Chapter 8.

2. Select Tools ➤ Merge (Ctrl-F12) ➤ Field to display the dialog box for inserting fields into a form letter.

3. Type **Contact** and select OK. The code {FIELD}Contact~ will appear in the text to represent the value in the Contact field. Each field you insert will appear this way.

4. Press ↵, select Tools ➤ Merge (Ctrl-F12) ➤ Field, type **Title**, and select OK.

5. Press ↵, select Tools ➤ Merge (Ctrl-F12) ➤ Field, type **Company**, select OK, and press ↵.

6. Select Tools ➤ Merge (Ctrl-F12) ➤ Field, type **Address**, select OK, and press ↵.

7. Select Tools ➤ Merge (Ctrl-F12) ➤ Field, type **Location?**, select OK, and press ↵.

To prevent a blank line from printing when there is no information in this field, you insert a question mark following the field name. The question mark tells WordPerfect to ignore any other text or codes on the line if the field is blank. In this case, it will ignore the hard carriage return at the end of the line, so a blank line will not appear.

8. Select Tools ➤ Merge (Ctrl-F12) ➤ Field, type **City**, and select OK.

9. Type a comma, and then press the spacebar.

10. Select Tools ➤ Merge (Ctrl-F12) ➤ Field, type **State**, and select OK.

11. Press the spacebar twice.

12. Select Tools ➤ Merge (Ctrl-F12) ➤ Field, type **Zip**, and select OK. The line will appear like this:

    {FIELD}City~, {FIELD}State~   {FIELD}Zip~

13. Press ↵ twice to insert a line space between the inside address and salutation.

14. Type **Dear** and press the spacebar.

15. Select Tools ➤ Merge (Ctrl-F12) ➤ Field, type **Salutation**, and select OK.

16. Type a colon (:), and then press ↵ twice to add a line space before the body of the letter.

17. Type the beginning of the first sentence (do not press ↵):

> **It has been ten years since we first opened for business, and we want to celebrate our anniversary with a special offer to one of our most valued customers,**

18. Press the spacebar, and then select Tools ➤ Merge (Ctrl-F12) ➤ Field. Type **Company** and select OK to insert the code for the company name.

19. Type a period (.) to end the sentence, and then press ↵ to start a new paragraph.

20. Type the remainder of the letter. The completed form letter is shown in Figure 11.5.

> **Please deduct 15% from the merchandise total of your next order. Sorry, we cannot offer a discount on shipping and handling charges. If you have any questions about this offer, contact your sales representative.**

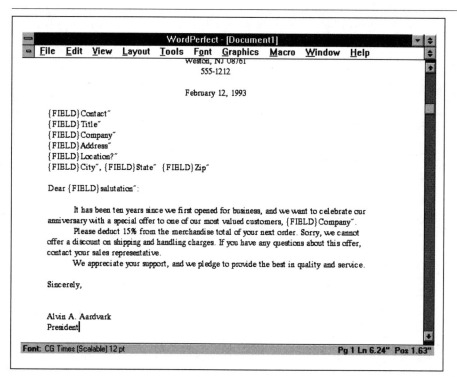

FIGURE 11.5:

Completed form document

We appreciate your support, and we pledge to provide the best in quality and service.

Sincerely,

**Alvin A. Aardvark
President**

21. Select File ➤ Save (Shift-F3), type **Discount,** and select Save.

22. Select File ➤ Close (Ctrl-F4) to clear the screen.

The merge codes and their effect on word wrap can be distracting. You can turn off their display by selecting File ➤ Preferences ➤ Display ➤ Display Merge Codes. When this option is turned off, you will not see merge codes surrounded by braces. However, tildes, field names, and variables will still appear. Repeat the process to turn on the display of merge codes.

Handling Blank Fields

When you use a question mark in the {FIELD} code, it causes any text or codes on the line following the blank field to be ignored. This works for printing inside addresses or envelopes because it ignores the carriage return and prevents a blank line. But within a paragraph, a question mark in the code will cause WordPerfect to ignore the rest of the text on the line—the rest of the text line will be missing.

Instead of using the question mark, use the {IF BLANK} command. Select this command from the Insert Merge Codes dialog box. It can be in one of the following forms:

{IF BLANK}*Field~ Instructions* {END IF}

{IF BLANK}*Field~ Instructions* {ELSE} *Instructions* {END IF}

{IF NOT BLANK}*Field~ Instructions* {END IF}

{IF NOT BLANK}*Field~ Instructions* {ELSE} *Instructions* {END IF}

For example, if field 6 in your secondary file contains locations, you could include the following line in the primary file:

We will deliver the package to {IF NOT BLANK}6~ {FIELD}6~ {ELSE}your office{END IF} when it arrives.

Then, when field 6 is not blank, the location will be inserted, as in

We will deliver the package to Suite 302 when it arrives.

If field 6 is blank (there is no location), the line will read

We will deliver the package to your office when it arrives.

MERGING PRIMARY AND SECONDARY FILES

After you have created the primary file (form document) and the secondary file (the database), you can merge them to produce the final documents. WordPerfect automatically sends the merged documents to the screen, but you can use merge commands to send them directly to the printer.

Merge your files from a clear document window. If the merge does not operate correctly, check for extra or missing tildes in the primary file. Also make sure that the secondary file is properly formatted, with the same number of fields in each record and the proper {END FIELD} and {END RECORD} codes. If you do not see any problems on the screen, reveal the codes and look for stray formatting instructions, which may be causing the problem.

MERGING TO THE SCREEN

To merge our database and form document, select Tools ➤ Merge (Ctrl-F12) ➤ Merge. In the Merge dialog box, type **Discount** in the Primary File text box, enter **Clients** in the Secondary File list box, and select OK.

As the letters are generated, the word Merging appears in the status bar. The letters will be displayed on the screen after all the records have been merged. Each letter is separated by a page break. You can edit any of the merged documents, then print them or save them on disk.

If you want to display the letters on screen as they are merged, add the {REWRITE} merge command at the end of the primary document. The

Discount document would end like this:

Alvin A. Aardvark
President
{REWRITE}

MERGING TO THE PRINTER

By adding the {PRINT} merge code to the primary file, you can direct the output to the printer instead of to the screen. Add the {PAGE OFF} code to prevent blank pages between the printed letters. Each letter is printed as it is generated without saving it on the disk. When you merge to the printer, no new document is created.

Merging to the printer is appropriate when you are generating many copies of the letter. If you merge them to the screen, you need enough disk space to hold all the documents, and you still must print them later.

We will edit the Discount file to add the codes to merge and print the letters at the same time.

1. Select File ➤ Close (Ctrl-F4) ➤ No to clear the document window without saving the merged letters on the screen.

2. Select File ➤ Open (F4), type **Discount**, and select Open.

3. Press Ctrl-End to reach the end of the document and select Tools ➤ Merge (Ctrl-F12) ➤ Page Off. This inserts the {PAGE OFF} code, which prevents extra form feeds (blank pages ejecting after each page).

4. Select Tools ➤ Merge (Ctrl-F12) ➤ Merge Codes, scroll through the list box, select to insert {PRINT}, and then select Close. The form document should now end with the codes

   {PAGE OFF}{PRINT}

5. Select File ➤ Save (Shift-F3) to save the edited form letter.

6. Select File ➤ Close (Ctrl-F4) to clear the document window.

7. Select Tools ➤ Merge (Ctrl-F12) ➤ Merge, type **Discount** in the Primary File box, type **Clients** in the Secondary File box, and select OK. The records will be merged into the form letters and printed.

8. Select File ➤ Exit (Alt-F4) to exit WordPerfect.

MERGING ENVELOPES AND LABELS

The records in a database can be merged with any primary file. To merge your records to print on envelopes or mailing labels, select the envelope or label form when you create the primary file. Enter the {FIELD} codes for the first envelope or label. For example, the first label in the primary file might look like this:

```
{FIELD}Contact~
{FIELD}Company~
{FIELD}Address~
{FIELD]Location?~
{FIELD}City~, {FIELD}State~    {FIELD}Zip~
```

Save the primary file, and then merge it with the secondary file that contains the mailing list. Each address will be inserted onto another label. When all the records have been merged, print the completed merged document on your label stock.

Note that you cannot merge labels directly to the printer. If you include the {PRINT} code in the primary file, only one label will print on each sheet.

You can also use the merge function to generate other types of documents you have created with label forms, such as place cards (see Chapter 3) or invitations (see Chapter 5). Instead of typing the name on each place card or invitation, insert the code

```
{FIELD}Name~
```

on the first label form, and then merge it with your database.

MERGING GRAPHICS

You can merge graphics into your form documents by inserting figure boxes as fields in the secondary file. For example, Figure 11.6 shows a database for creating a clip-art catalog.

The fields in the database include the name, height, width, and a sample from each clip-art file. The samples are graphic images inserted as character-anchored figure boxes, all scaled to the same size. The primary file for the clip-art catalog could be created on a label form.

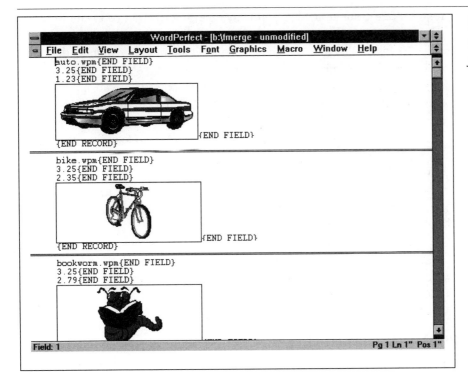

Secondary file containing figure boxes as fields

MERGING ASCII TEXT FILES

You can use a database created with a database program (such as dBASE) as a secondary file with WordPerfect if you save it as a delimited text file. In this type of file, the records and fields are separated by delimiters. Usually, each record ends with a carriage return and each field is separated by a comma or is enclosed in quotation marks.

To use the delimited file as a database, select Tools ➤ Merge (Ctrl-F12) ➤ Merge, and choose the ASCII Delimited Text (DOS) option in the Merge dialog box. When you select OK, a second dialog box will appear, prompting you to enter the characters or codes that surround each field and each record.

CREATING DATABASE REPORTS

Your WordPerfect database can also be used to create informative reports, such as price lists, student records, and sales reports. Create a primary file containing the {FIELD} codes for the variable information you want listed in the report. Place column headings and any other information you want to repeat on each page in a header.

To ensure that the columns in the report are properly aligned, define initial codes for the primary file. Delete all the tab stops and set new ones to position the columns. Using the default tab stops usually will not work because the {FIELD} code, field name, and closing tilde are not the same length as the inserted variable information. The columns in the merged document will not necessarily start at the position of the {FIELD} code in the primary file. If you set the tabs within the document rather than as an initial code, the entire tab-set formatting code will be repeated with each line of the report.

On screen, the text in the primary file may not appear to wrap correctly because of the merge codes. However, the lines will be printed properly in the merged document.

Since you do not want each line of the report printed on a separate page, you must suppress the hard page break that WordPerfect inserts after a record is merged. Do this by placing the {PAGE OFF} code at the end of the primary file.

MERGING A CLIENT LIST

Figure 11.7 shows a client contact list that was created by merging primary and secondary files. The document's initial codes were set to include tab stops only at the 2.5-inch and 5.25-inch positions. Then the report title, page number, date, and column headings were entered into a header.

The text of the document uses the following codes. When entering the commands, press Tab after the first two field names and press ↵ after the Telephone field.

{FIELD}Company~   {FIELD}Contact~   {FIELD}Telephone~
{PAGE OFF}

February 25, 1993	Client Contact List	
		Page 1
Company	Contact	Phone Number
Comhype Computers	Miss Elaine Cuningham	215-555-1765
DupliCopy Company	Mr. Jackson Montgomery	215-295-0983
Chandler Scientific	Mr. Adam Chandler	346-845-1987
Computers-R-Us	Ms Wilamini Boyle	609-567-0893

FIGURE 11.7:

Merged database report

Save the document under the name **Contacts.mrg.**

To print the report, select Tools ➤ Merge (Ctrl-F12) ➤ Merge, type **Contacts.mrg** in the Primary File box, and then type **Clients** in the Secondary File box. The records will be merged and displayed with each line following the next one on the same page. The header will not appear on the screen (except in Print Preview mode).

MERGING ORDER AND SALES LISTS

You can use similar techniques to produce other database reports. To print an order report, create the following primary file:

{FIELD}Company~   {FIELD}LastOrder~   {FIELD}LastAmount~
{PAGE OFF}

Save the file under the name **Orders.mrg**, and then close the document.

Next create a primary file to print a client contact sheet; do not include the {PAGE OFF} code in this document:

Client:	{FIELD}Company~
Name:	{FIELD}Contact~
Address:	{FIELD}Address~ {FIELD}Location~
	{FIELD}City~, {FIELD}State~ {FIELD}Zip~
Telephone:	{FIELD}Telephone~
Amount Due:	{FIELD}Due~
Last Order:	{FIELD}LastOrder~ for {FIELD}LastAmount~
Notes:	

Save the file under the name **Leads.mrg**, and then close the document window.

You can now create both of the database reports by merging these primary files with the Clients database.

BEYOND BASIC MERGING

Merging primary and secondary files to create form letters just touches on the power of WordPerfect's merge function. Primary files can include Programming commands, much like macro files. The syntax of the merge commands is different from that used in macros, but many of the commands perform the same functions. For example, you can use merge commands to accept user input, perform repetitions, and make decisions based on conditions.

Although merge commands are powerful, they do have certain limitations. They do not include insertion-point positioning functions, Product commands, or the GetWPData command (although the System command from the DOS version of WordPerfect has been retained). In addition, you cannot perform mathematic operations and numeric comparisons of fields with decimal numbers; merge commands work only with integer numbers. Fortunately, these limitations can be overcome by using both merge files and macros to perform a function, as you will learn in later chapters.

INSERTING MULTIPLE MERGE CODES

You enter all merge codes by using the Tools ➤ Merge menu or the Insert Merge Codes dialog box. If you have a mouse, you can leave the Insert Merge Codes dialog box on the screen so you can quickly move back and forth between it and the document. You can move the Insert Merge Codes dialog box to another location on the screen by dragging it by the title bar with the mouse.

Selecting some merge codes displays a dialog box prompting you for the code's parameters. You can either enter the parameters requested, or just select OK and then type the parameters directly in the document. For example, to begin a subroutine, select the {LABEL} command, and you will see a dialog box requesting the subroutine name. If you enter the name and select OK, the code will appear in the text in this format:

{LABEL}*Name~*

If you prefer, you can select OK in the dialog box and then type the name between the {LABEL} code and the tilde.

If the parameters include another merge command, you must enter them yourself rather than selecting from the dialog box (select OK to close the dialog box, return to the document, and then enter the parameters).

PROGRAMMING DERIVED COLUMNS

A *derived column* contains information that is calculated from the data in a database rather than stored in a database field. For example, suppose that you want to print a report listing the balance of available credit for each client. The balance is derived by subtracting the amount due from the credit limit. The following primary file will create the report:

```
{ASSIGN}Net~{FIELD}Credit~-{FIELD}Due~~{COMMENT}
~{FIELD}1~ {FIELD}11~ {FIELD}12~ {VARIABLE}Net~
{PAGE OFF}
```

For each record, this primary file assigns to the variable Net the difference between the credit limit and the amount due, and then prints a line in the report. Remember, merge commands will not work with decimal numbers; however, you can combine macro and merge commands to create this report, as explained in Chapter 13.

The {ASSIGN} command assigns a value to a variable, using the syntax

```
{ASSIGN} Var~ Value-or-Expression~
```

In the merge file, the expression

```
{FIELD}Credit~-{FIELD}Due~~
```

subtracts the fields. The difference between them is assigned to the variable Net. Notice that two tildes are required after the command (before the first comment): one ends the {FIELD}Due command, and the other ends the {ASSIGN} command.

The {COMMENT} command can be used to insert notes to yourself, such as

```
{COMMENT}This merge file prints the credit remaining~
```

since any text between the command and its closing tilde is ignored during the merge operation. It is also useful for spacing the merge program onto several lines, making the codes easier to read and understand. You cannot press ↵ within the primary file to end lines, because any carriage returns that are not between a merge code and its closing tilde will be inserted into the merged document.

For example, if you typed the primary file without the {COMMENT} command

```
{ASSIGN}Net~{FIELD}Credit~-{FIELD}Due~~
{FIELD}1~ {FIELD}4~ {FIELD}5~ {VARIABLE}Net~
{PAGE OFF}
```

after the {ASSIGN} command was executed, a carriage return would be inserted into the document. Then the line containing the fields and variable Net would print, and another carriage return would be added to move to the next line. This sequence would be repeated for every record, so the report would appear double spaced. With the {COMMENT} command at the end of one line and its closing tilde at the start of the next line, the carriage return between them is considered a part of the comment and ignored.

The next step is to insert the contents of the variable. In a merge program, the variable name must be a parameter of the {VARIABLE} command, using the syntax

{VARIABLE} *Variable-Name~*

If the variable named in the parameter has not been assigned a value, it will be treated as a null. You can determine whether the variable has a value by using the {IF EXISTS} command, with the syntax

{IF EXISTS} *Var~*
    Instructions
{END IF}

or

{IF EXISTS) *Var~*
    Instructions
{ELSE}
    Instructions
{END IF}

For clarity, the syntax is illustrated on several lines. You must use the {COMMENT} command to enter them this way without inserting extra lines in your document.

Programming Record Selection

You might not want to merge all the records in your secondary file with the primary file. For example, you may want to send form letters only to clients who have exceeded their credit limit. You can select those records if your database contains integer values in the Credit and Due fields. Start the primary file with this command:

{LABEL}Go~{IF}{FIELD}Due~<{FIELD}Credit~~{NEXT RECORD}{COMMENT}

~{GO}Go~{END IF}{COMMENT}
~

If you do not want a blank line inserted at the start of the document, enter the first line of text (such as your address) on the same line, after the closing tilde.

The {LABEL} command serves the same purpose as the macro Label command, naming a subroutine for the program to branch to (see Chapter 9). It uses the syntax

{LABEL}*Subroutine-Name~*

The {GO} command causes the program to continue execution at the designated subroutine.

WordPerfect uses a pointer to keep track of the next record to merge. The pointer moves to the next record when it reaches the end of the primary file. But in this primary file, after the first line is merged, the {GO} command returns to the start of the subroutine. The end of the primary file has not been reached, so the pointer does not move to the next record. The {NEXT RECORD} command forces WordPerfect to move the pointer to the next record so it can be retrieved in the next repetition of the loop.

The record selection is performed by the {IF} and {NEXT RECORD} commands. The syntax of the {IF} command is

{IF}*Condition~*
  Instructions
{END IF}

or

{IF}*Condition~*
  Instructions
{ELSE}
  Instructions
{END IF}

In this case, if the value in the Due field is less than the value in the Credit field, the next record is retrieved and the loop is repeated. When the amount in the Due field is higher than the amount in the Credit field, the document is merged. You must include a tilde at the end of the condition. Since the condition ends with a {FIELD} command, two tildes are required.

To test for a not-equal-to condition, use the operator !=, as in

{IF}"{FIELD}Name~"!="{FIELD}Contact~"~{NEXT RECORD}{COMMENT}

When comparing fields or variables that contain text, enclose the entire reference in quotation marks, as in

{IF}"{FIELD}Contact~"="Alvin Aardvark"~

or

{IF}"{FIELD}Company~"!="{FIELD}Contact~"~

Figure 11.8 shows three examples of how the {IF} command can be used to create database reports. The first example prints a listing of clients who have credit remaining. Note that there is no {COMMENT} command after the field list. This causes a carriage return to be inserted in the document whenever a line of the report is printed. The {END IF} command is on the next line so the carriage return will be inserted only when the {IF} condition is true.

```
{IF}{FIELD}Due~<{FIELD}Credit~~{COMMENT}
~{FIELD}Company~{FIELD}Due~{FIELD}Credit~
{END IF}{COMMENT}
~{PAGE OFF}

{IF}{FIELD}Due~<{FIELD}Credit~~{COMMENT}
~{FIELD}1~{FIELD}4~{FIELD}5~
{ELSE}{FIELD}1~ No Credit Remaining
{END IF}{COMMENT}
~{PAGE OFF}

{ASSIGN}Net~{FIELD}Due~+100~{COMMENT}
~{IF}{FIELD}Credit~>{VARIABLE}Net~~{COMMENT}
~{FIELD}1~ {FIELD}4~ {FIELD}5~
{END IF}{COMMENT}
~{PAGE OFF}
```

FIGURE 11.8:

Examples of the {IF} command

The second example in Figure 11.8 uses an {ELSE} command to print an alternate line of text for clients who have exceeded their credit. The final example prints a list of clients who have more than $100 credit remaining. It assigns the value in the Due field plus 100 to the variable Net and then compares this variable to the Credit field.

PROGRAMMING FOR USER INPUT

The {INPUT} command allows the user to enter information into the document at the location of the command. The syntax is

{INPUT}*Prompt~*

It displays a dialog box with your prompt, as shown in the example in Figure 11.9. The user presses Alt-↵ to end data entry and continue the merge.

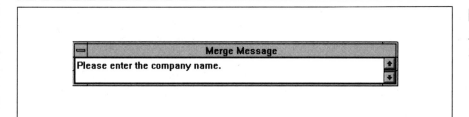

FIGURE 11.9:

Dialog box displayed by the {INPUT} command

By combining {INPUT} commands with other merge codes, you can mass produce form documents while customizing them at the time they are created. For example, this portion of a primary file lets you personalize letters by entering a suitable salutation depending on the recipient and tone of the letter:

{FIELD}Contact~
{FIELD}Company~
{FIELD}Address~
{FIELD]Location?~
{FIELD}City~, {FIELD}State~   {FIELD}Zip~

Dear {INPUT}Enter Salutation then press Alt-Enter~:

The primary file shown in Figure 11.10 automates the preparation of memos. It is the Memo template we created in Chapter 2, modified to include {INPUT} commands. With the original template, the user must move the insertion point to the end of each heading line (To, From, and Subject) before typing the text. The revised template places the text automatically.

To create the template, open the Memo.tmp document. Place the insertion point after the tab stop on each of the heading lines and enter the {INPUT} merge commands. Replace the date with the {DATE} merge code.

To use the template to create a memo, choose to merge the primary file, but do not enter the name of a secondary file; in this case, all the variable

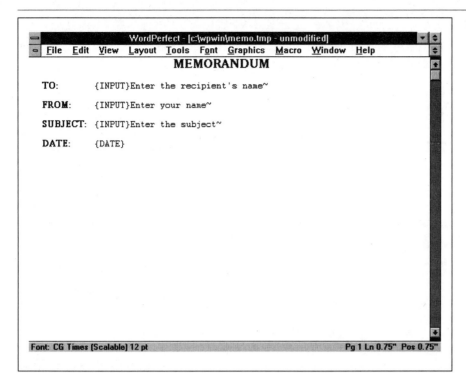

information is entered from the keyboard. WordPerfect will start the merge and place the insertion point at the location of the first {INPUT} command. Enter the information desired, then press Alt-⏎ to continue the merge. The merge will end after the final merge command.

Inputting Variable Values

The {TEXT} command also pauses the merge operation and displays a prompt. However, the text is inserted into a variable instead of into the document itself. The syntax is

{TEXT}*Var~Message~*

Press ⏎ to continue the merge.

For example, this primary file allows you to print a list of clients in a specific city and their telephone numbers:

{TEXT}Area~Enter the city~{COMMENT}
~{LABEL}Go~{COMMENT}

```
~{IF}"{FIELD}City~"="{VARIABLE}Area~"~{COMMENT}
~{FIELD}Company~  {FIELD}Contact~  {FIELD}Telephone~
{END IF}{COMMENT}
~{PAGE OFF}{NEXT RECORD}{GO}Go~
```

During the merge operation, the {TEXT} command is executed so that you can enter the name of a city. The Go subroutine is then repeated until the end of the secondary file. Each value in the City field is compared with the contents of the Area variable. If they are the same, the name, contact, and telephone number are printed. If you did not use a subroutine, the {TEXT} command would be executed for each record.

A variable is treated as a string or a number depending on the operation. This primary file allows you to increase the credit limit selectively for a special mailing:

```
{TEXT}More~Enter additional credit~{COMMENT}
~{ASSIGN}New~{FIELD}Credit~+{Variable}More~{COMMENT}
~Your new credit limit is {VARIABLE}New~
```

Pausing without a Prompt

The {KEYBOARD} command pauses the merge operation so the user can enter text into the document. No prompt appears. The syntax is simply {KEYBOARD}. Press Alt-↵ to continue the merge. For example, this line pauses the merge operation for entry of a salutation:

```
Dear {KEYBOARD}:
```

Prompting without Pausing

The {PROMPT} command displays a message but does not pause the merge. The syntax is

```
{PROMPT}Message~
```

The command is usually used with the {KEYBOARD} command, as in

```
{PROMPT}Please enter the salutation~
{KEYBOARD}
```

Inputting a Single Character

The {CHAR} command pauses the merge operation, displays a message, and allows the input of just a single character into a variable. The syntax is

{CHAR}Var~*Message~*

Entering the character continues the merge.

For example, you could request a single-digit entry to continue or stop the merge operation with these commands:

{CHAR}Result~Enter 1 to continue or 2 to stop~
{IF}{VARIABLE}Result~=1~{STOP}{END IF}

Inputting without Pausing

The {LOOK} command detects whether a key is pressed and inserts the character into a variable, without pausing the merge. The syntax is

{LOOK}*Var~*

Because this command does not pause the merge, it is normally used in loops to detect keyboard activity. For example, this merge program prints consecutive numbers down the page:

{PROMPT}Press e to end numbering~{COMMENT}
~{ASSIGN}Num~1~{COMMENT}
~{LABEL}Number~{COMMENT}
~{VARIABLE}Num~
{REWRITE}{COMMENT}
~{ASSIGN}Num~{VARIABLE}Num~+1~{COMMENT}
~{LOOK}Key~{COMMENT}
~{IF}"{VARIABLE}Key~"!="e"~{GO}Number~{END IF}

Instead of merging information from a database, this merge program performs a complete function, similar to macro programs (see Chapter 9).

USING WORDPERFECT FOR DOS MERGE FILES

In most cases, merge programs from WordPerfect 5.1 do not have to be modified to work in WordPerfect for Windows. However, you should test complex merge files, which contain many Programming commands, before using them.

You must convert merge files created with earlier versions of Word-Perfect. Open the merge file in WordPerfect for Windows, and then select Tools ➤ Merge (Ctrl-F12) ➤ Convert. Save the converted file and try merging it with sample data. If it does not work as you intended, edit the merge file in WordPerfect for Windows.

CHAPTER 12

Managing WordPerfect Databases

lthough you can manage your WordPerfect databases by using standard text-editing techniques, macros and merge files provide a much more efficient approach. In this chapter, you will learn how to automate many standard tasks, such as adding and deleting records and creating invoices.

The chapter also describes database sorting and selection techniques. You will find some useful macros for interactive sorting and selecting of records. The database macros guide the user and prevent errors.

WORKING WITH LARGE DATABASES

As you add fields and records to a database, it requires more and more time to open and save the file. Large databases are also more difficult to manipulate in other ways. To make a large database easier to work with, divide the secondary file into sections. Then you can merge the sections as if they were one large file by using the {CHAIN SECONDARY} command. This command tells WordPerfect to use the named file after it reaches the end of the current file. If you use field names, each file must contain a field name record.

Enter the {CHAIN SECONDARY} command after the {FIELD NAMES} command, as in

{FIELD NAMES}Company~Address~*Other-Fields*~~{COMMENT}
~{PROCESS}{CHAIN SECONDARY}*Filename*~{PROCESS}{COMMENT}
~{END RECORD}

The {PROCESS} commands tell WordPerfect to complete the current file.

If you do not use field names, insert the commands at the start of the first record, like this:

{PROCESS}{CHAIN SECONDARY}*Filename*~{PROCESS}{COMMENT}
~

Start the first record on the same line as the tilde.

AUTOMATING DATABASE FUNCTIONS

By combining macro and merge file techniques, you can automate common database-management functions. The following sections describe how to streamline adding records, deleting records, and locating duplicate records.

The macros and merge commands shown in this chapter assume your macros are stored in the MACROS subdirectory, and that your merge files and other documents are in the WPWIN directory. If you store your files elsewhere, be sure to designate the complete, correct path in the appropriate commands.

AUTOMATING NEW RECORD ENTRY

A combination of two macros and a merge file automates the addition of new records to your database. The merge file inserts the {END FIELD} and {END RECORD} codes and prompts the user to enter data for each field.

Creating the Macros

Create the first macro, which opens the Clients database, places the insertion point at the end of the file, and begins the merge file:

```
Application(WP;WPWP;Default;"WPWPUS.WCD")
Display(On!)
FileOpen("c:\wpwin\clients")
PosDocBottom()
MergeExecute("add.mrg")
```

Save the macro under the name **Append.wcm** in the MACROS subdirectory. Now create the second macro, which saves the file after record entry:

```
Application(WP;WPWP;Default;"WPWPUS.WCD")
FileSave()
Close()
```

Save the macro under the name **Save.wcm** in the MACROS subdirectory

Creating the Merge File

Finally, create the merge file, shown in Figure 12.1. Follow this procedure to enter the merge commands properly:

◆ Use the Tools ➤ Merge menu and Insert Merge Codes dialog box to insert all the merge codes.

◆ Let WordPerfect word wrap the {INPUT} command lines for you. Press ⤶ only after the {MRG CMD} code following {END FIELD}.

◆ Press Ctrl-⤶ to insert a page break after the {MRG CMND}{END RECORD}{MRG CMND} command line.

◆ Do not press ⤶ after the last line.

◆ You can use hard returns between a {COMMENT} and its closing tilde to make your merge programs easier to read.

Save the completed merge file under the name **Add.mrg**.

The merge file begins by assigning the character Y to the variable Flag. This variable is used to indicate when the user is finished adding records. Assigning this initial value ensures that at least one record can be added to the database.

Next is a {WHILE} repetition that contains a series of {INPUT} commands. Each {INPUT} command requests another field, which is inserted into the document. When the user presses Alt-⤶ after entering field data, the commands

{MRG CMND}{END FIELD}{MRG CMND}

insert the {END FIELD} code and a carriage return, and then the file continues with the next {INPUT} command. After the user presses Alt-⤶ for the last field, the {END RECORD} code and a hard page break are inserted.

The {CHAR} command displays a dialog box with a message and pauses until you enter a single character. Because the {WHILE} condition tests for an

```
{ASSIGN}Flag~Y~{COMMENT}
~{WHILE}"{VARIABLE}Flag~"!="N"~{COMMENT}
~{INPUT}Enter the company name, then press Alt-Enter~{MRG
   CMND}{END FIELD}{MRG CMND}
{INPUT}Enter the contact person, then press Alt-Enter~{MRG
   CMND}{END FIELD}{MRG CMND}
{INPUT}Enter the salutation (Dear...), then press Alt-Enter
   ~{MRG CMND}{END FIELD}{MRG CMND}
{INPUT}Enter contact's title, then press Alt-Enter~
   {MRG CMND}{END FIELD}{MRG CMND}
{INPUT}Enter the street address, then press Alt-Enter {MRG
   CMND}{END FIELD}{MRG CMND}
{INPUT}Enter any second address, then press Alt-Enter~{MRG
   CMND}{END FIELD}{MRG CMND}
{INPUT}Enter the city, then press Alt-Enter~{MRG CMND}{END
   FIELD}{MRG CMND}
{INPUT}Enter the state, then press Alt-Enter ~{MRG CMND}{END
   FIELD}{MRG CMND}
{INPUT}Enter the zip code, then press Alt-Enter~{MRG
   CMND}{END FIELD}{MRG CMND}
{INPUT}Enter the phone number, then press Alt-Enter~{MRG
   CMND}{END FIELD}{MRG CMND}
{INPUT}Enter the credit limit, then press Alt-Enter~{MRG
   CMND}{END FIELD}{MRG CMND}
{INPUT}Enter the amount outstanding, then press Alt-
   Enter~{MRG CMND}{END FIELD}{MRG CMND}
{INPUT}Enter the last order amount, then press Alt-
   Enter~{MRG CMND}{END FIELD}{MRG CMND}
{INPUT}Enter the last order date (YY/MM/DD), then press Alt-
   Enter~{MRG CMND}{END FIELD}{MRG CMND}
{MRG CMND}{END RECORD}{MRG CMND}

{CHAR}Flag~Add another record? Y/N~{COMMENT}
~{IF}"{VARIABLE}Flag~"="n"~{ASSIGN}Flag~N~{END IF}{COMMENT}
~{END WHILE}{CHAIN MACRO}c:\wpwin\macros\save~
```

uppercase *N*, the command

{IF}"{VARIABLE}Flag~"="n"~{ASSIGN}Flag~N~{END IF}

converts a lowercase *n*, if it was entered, into uppercase, so either an uppercase or lowercase *n* will stop the record-entry process.

When the {WHILE} condition is false, the {CHAIN MACRO} command plays the Save macro. This command designates a macro that should be played when the merge file ends, no matter where the command is placed in the merge file. The chained macro is executed when the merge ends normally, without being canceled or stopped by a {QUIT} or {STOP} merge code. (WordPerfect's {NEST MACRO} command executes a macro at the command's location in the file, and then returns to the merge file.) The Save macro saves the database and closes the document window.

Adding Records

The macros and merge file streamline new record entry. To see how the system works, use it now to add a record to the Clients database.

Select to play the Append macro. The macro will be compiled, and then the database will open. The insertion point moves to the end of the file, and a dialog box prompts you to enter the company name.

Enter the following information for each field of the new record. (Don't worry about the extra merge codes that appear in the document window—they will be erased automatically when you enter data.) Press Alt-↵ after each field entry. The {END FIELD} code will be inserted into the text, and the {INPUT} message for the next field will appear. If you press ↵ instead of Alt-↵, an extra line will be inserted in the record. To correct it, press Backspace, then Alt-↵.

> **Watson ComputerWorld   William Watson   Bill   President**
> **3647 Wilson Avenue   P.O. Box 692**
> **Ventnor   NJ   08063   555-9823**
> **1000   350   129   93/1/5**

When you press Alt-↵ after the last field, a dialog box will appear asking if you have any other records to add. Type **n**, and the Save macro will save and close the Clients database.

If any extra characters, spaces, or lines appear within new records, check your merge file carefully. Look for extra tildes, spaces, or missing {COMMENT} commands. Correct the merge file, delete the extra characters from the database, and then try adding another record.

AUTOMATING RECORD DELETION

Another common database-management task is deleting records. It is time-consuming to open a large database, scroll through the list to locate the record you want to delete, select the record, and then press Del. The macro shown in Figure 12.2 automates the deletion of records. Type the macro and save it under the name **Del.wcm** (the name Delete is already used by one of WordPerfect's built-in macros) in the MACROS subdirectory.

The first section creates two variables: Title for use in prompts and dialog boxes, and Count as an accumulator for reporting the number of deleted records. The GetString command requests the name of the company to delete. Next, Typeover mode is turned off, and then the OnNotFound and OnCancel commands end the process if WordPerfect cannot find the file or the user

```
//Delete record macro
Application(WP;WPWP;Default;"WPWPUS.WCD")
Title:="Delete Merge Record"
Count:=0
GetString(Delete;Length=20;"Enter the company name.";Title)
InsertTypeover(Off!)
OnNotFound(End@)
OnCancel(End@)
Display(On!)
FileOpen("c:\wpwin\clients")
PosDocTop()

Label(FindAndReplace@)
SearchText(SearchString:Delete;SearchDirection:Forward!;
           SearchScope:DocOnly!)
Menu(Result;Letter;10;10; ("Delete"; "Skip"; "Cancel"})
If(Result=2)
     Go(FindAndReplace@)
Else
     If(Result=3)
     Go(End@)
     EndIf
EndIf
PosLineBegin()
PosPageNext()
SelectMode(On!)
PosPagePrevious()
DeleteCharNext()
SelectMode(Off!)
Count:=Count+1
Go(FindAndReplace@)

Label(End@)
     SelectMode(Off!)
     NumStr(Report;1;Count)
     Prompt(Title;Report+" Deletions made";4;;)
     Pause

Quit
```

chooses Cancel. The next three command lines turn on the display, open the database, and ensure that the insertion point is at the start of the document.

The FindAndReplace subroutine performs the bulk of the macro. The SearchText command searches for the first occurrence of the text you entered. Although the GetString prompt requests the company name, the command will actually locate any occurrence of the characters in any field. The user can enter part of the company name, the contact's name, or information in any of the fields. This way, you can delete multiple records that have some field information in common. For example, to delete several clients in Philadelphia, enter Philadelphia at the company name prompt. However, be sure to enter enough search text information so that WordPerfect doesn't stop too often.

WordPerfect will place the insertion point at the end of the first occurrence of the text and display a menu with the options Delete, Skip, and Cancel.

The If conditions take care of the Skip and Cancel choices. Selecting Skip loops the macro back to the start of the subroutine, and the next occurrence of the string is located. Selecting Cancel executes the End subroutine.

The next command lines select the record and delete it after Delete is chosen:

◆ Move the insertion point to the start of the line (since it could be in any field).

◆ Move the insertion point to the beginning of the next record.

◆ Turn on Select mode.

◆ Move the insertion point back to the start of the record.

◆ Delete the record.

◆ Turn off Select mode.

◆ Increment the variable Count.

◆ Loop back to the start of the subroutine to look for the next occurrence of the text.

This process is repeated until Cancel is selected or the search text is not found. The End subroutine ensures that Select mode is off, reports the number of deletions, and then pauses until the user presses ↵ or selects OK.

The macro leaves the database open on the screen. This is added insurance against deleting records by accident. If you do not want to delete the records, close the document without saving it. To ensure that the modified database cannot be saved by accident, you can have the macro retrieve the database rather than open it, as explained later in this chapter.

FINDING DUPLICATE RECORDS

Have you ever received two of the same magazines or advertisements? Duplicated records in a database can be an expensive proposition. Before sending out a mailing, you should make sure that no one is listed twice.

The macro shown in Figure 12.3 scans the database and strikes out possible duplicate records. A duplicate record is defined as one that has the same company name as another record in the database. The macro does not save the file, but leaves it on the screen so that the user can confirm that the records are duplicates before deleting them from the file. Type the macro and save it under the name **Dup.wcm** in the MACROS subdirectory.

```
//Duplicate record macro
Application(WP;WPWP;Default;"WPWPUS.WCD")
Title:="Duplicate Record Macro"
Count:=0
InsertTypeover(Off!)
OnNotFound(End@)
OnCancel(End@)
OnError(End@)
FileOpen("c:\wpwin\clients")
PosDocTop()
Sort
(
    RecordType:MergeRec!;
    SortOrder:Ascending!;
    Selection:"";
    Key1Type:Alpha!;
    Key1Level1:1;
    Key1Level2:1;
    Key1Level3:1
)
SelectMode(On!)
PosLineEnd()
GetWPData(MacroVariable:Selected;SystemVariable:
         SelectedText!)
SelectMode(Off!)
PosPageNext()
Label(Loops@)
SelectMode(On!)
PosLineEnd()
GetWPData(MacroVariable:Match;SystemVariable:SelectedText!)
SelectMode(Off!)
If(Selected=Match)
     PosLineBegin()
     SelectMode(On!)
     PosPageNext()
     FontStrikeout(On!)
     SelectMode(Off!)
     Count:=Count+1
Else
     PosPageNext()
EndIf
Selected:=Match
Go(Loops@)

Label(End@)
     SelectMode(Off!)
     NumStr(Report;1;Count)
     Prompt(Title;Report+" Possible Duplicates";4;;)
     Pause
     PosDocTop()
Quit
```

After opening the Clients database, the macro sorts it by the company name (database sorting is described later in the chapter). This places records that have common company names in consecutive order.

The macro selects the company name, then uses the GetWPData command to insert the name into the variable Selected. If the file contains a field name record, it will be used for the first comparison. It will not match the first client record, so the macro will just move on to the next actual client record. It then turns off Select mode, moves to the next record, and begins the Loops subroutine.

Loops selects the company name of the record and inserts it into the variable Match. The If command compares Selected (the previous record) with Match (the current record). If they are the same, it strikes out the record, then counts it as a possible duplicate. Before the subroutine is repeated for the next record, the command

Selected:=Match

assigns the name of the current record to the variable Selected. When the next record is read, its name is assigned to Match. This process continues until the end of the database. When the entire database has been searched, a dialog box reports the number of possible duplicates.

This macro does not turn on the display because there is no need to see what is happening, and leaving the display off makes the macro run a little faster. Also, turning on the display can cause some strange characters to appear while the macro is running. They do not affect the results but can be distracting. You could add the command Display (On!) to see the effects on your system.

You can also customize the macro to check for duplicates in more than one field. For example, suppose you deal with several departments of a large corporation. The company name is the same but you have a different contact with each department. Since each department is treated as a separate client, you want to keep them both in the database. In this case, combine the Company and Contact fields in the selected strings by modifying the sections of the macro that select the string:

```
SelectMode(On!)
PosLineDown()
PosLineEnd()
GetWPData(MacroVariable:Selected;SystemVariable:SelectedText!)
SelectMode(Off!)

SelectMode(On!)
PosLineDown()
PosLineEnd()
GetWPData(MacroVariable:Match;SystemVariable:SelectedText!)
SelectMode(Off!)
```

Both the Company and Contact fields will be selected and stored in the variables Selected and Match for comparison.

If you want to delete all the duplicated records, use this macro:

```
Application(WP;WPWP;Default;"WPWPUS.WCD")
DocCompareRemove(KeepRedline:No!)
```

When you run this macro, all text formatted as strikeout will be deleted.

DESIGNING AN INVOICE-ENTRY SYSTEM

In Chapter 7, you learned how to create an invoice form as a table (Figure 7.14). Chapter 9 presented a macro for filling out the invoice (Figure 9.5). Using this system, the user still must type the client's name on the invoice, even though it is already in the database. In addition, the macro runs very slowly, and it must be changed if you delete or insert lines in the invoice form. You can create a more efficient system by combining macro and merge techniques. You will find that the merge codes operate much faster than the macro you created in Chapter 9.

CREATING THE INVOICE MACRO

The first macro saves the client's record into a temporary database (called Temp). The fields in this secondary file will be inserted into the client's invoice with merge commands so the information does not have to be typed. This macro is shown in Figure 12.4. Enter the macro and save it under the name **Invoice.wcm** in the MACROS subdirectory.

Once you create the invoice, you no longer need the temporary file. You could try to delete the file by inserting the FileDelete code at the end of the macro. You could also create a separate macro that deletes the file and execute it with the command {NEST MACRO} in the merge file. However, in both cases the command would be executed at the same time the file was being used by the merge, so WordPerfect would display an error message.

The solution is to leave the file on the disk, then delete it before you begin the next invoice. This is accomplished with these lines:

```
OnError(Start@)
FileDelete(Secondary)
Label(Start@)
```

```
//Invoice macro
Application(WP;WPWP;Default;"WPWPUS.WCD")
Title:="Invoice"
Primary:="Invoice"
Secondary:="Temp"
OnError(Start@)
FileDelete(Secondary)
Label(Start@)
OnError(End@)
OnNotFound(End@)
OnCancel(End@)
Go(Main@)
Label(End@)
     Quit
Label(Main@)
GetString(Client;LENGTH=20;"Enter the company name";Title)
InsertTypeover(Off!)
Display(On!)
FileOpen("c:\wpwin\clients")
PosDocTop()

Label(Search@)
SearchText(SearchString:Client;SearchDirection:Forward!;
          SearchScope:DocOnly!)
Menu(Action;Letter;;;{"Merge"; "Search Again"; "Cancel"})
Case(Action;{1;Merge@;2;Search@;3;End@};End@)

Label(Merge@)
PosLineBegin()
PosPageNext()
SelectMode(On!)
PosPagePrevious()
FileSave(Secondary)
SelectMode(Off!)
CloseNoSave(No!)
Close()
MergeExecute(PrimaryFile:Primary;SecondaryFile:Secondary)
```

FIGURE 12.4:

Macro to select a record and merge the invoice primary file

The OnError command sets up an error trap that would pass control to the subroutine Start, and then the FileDelete command is executed. Once the file is deleted, the Start subroutine is executed. If the file doesn't exist (this is the first time the macro was run or the temporary file was already deleted), the File-Delete command generates an error, and the macro continues at the Start subroutine.

The Start subroutine contains commands to end the process if there is an error, the file is not found, or Cancel is selected (the FileDelete command has already been bypassed or successfully executed). Control is then passed to the Main subroutine, which prompts the user to enter the company name for the invoice and then opens the database.

The Search subroutine is similar to the one used to locate records in the record-deletion macro. However, the options are Merge, Search Again, and Cancel, and a Case structure is used rather than If statements. If the user selects

Search Again (because the record is not the correct one), the macro loops back to search for the next occurrence of the text. Selecting Cancel executes the End subroutine, ending the process. When Merge is chosen, the record is selected and saved under the name Temp. The file is closed, and then the invoice is merged with the Temp file containing the single record.

CREATING THE CALCULATING MACRO

The other macro for the invoice-entry system calculates the formulas in the invoice when the merge operation is complete. Enter this short macro and save it under the name **Calc.wcm** in the MACROS subdirectory:

```
Application(WP;WPWP;Default;"WPWPUS.WCD")
PosLineUp()
TableCalculate()
```

A command in the merge file will run this macro. The PosLineUp( ) command places the insertion point inside the table before the calculation is performed.

PROGRAMMING THE INVOICE MERGE

The primary merge file for the invoice system is created with the invoice form, as shown in Figure 12.5. This merge file will insert the client's name and address and the date, and then prompt the user for the item number, description, quantity, and cost. After the last item is entered, it runs the Calc macro to compute the totals.

Type the following merge commands above the form as shown in Figure 12.5:

```
{ASSIGN}Count~0~{CHAIN MACRO}C:\WPWIN\MACROS\CALC~{COM-
MENT}
~Sold To:          {FIELD}1~
                   {FIELD}5~
{IF NOT BLANK}6~{FIELD}6~
{END IF}          {FIELD}7~, {FIELD}8~   {FIELD}9~
Date: {DATE}
```

The file begins by assigning the value 0 to the variable Count, which is used to keep track of the number of items entered (so the page length is not exceeded). The {CHAIN MACRO} command tells WordPerfect to execute the Calc macro (with its full path) when the merge file ends normally.

FIGURE 12.5:

Merge commands for automating the invoice form

The {FIELD} codes insert the name and address of the client from the secondary file. The codes must use field numbers instead of names because the field names record has not been moved to the Temp file along with the actual client record. The {DATE} command inserts the current date.

Now type the {INPUT} commands, one in each column across the top row. Note that in Figure 12.5, the column widths were adjusted to show the entire commands.

{LABEL}Go~{INPUT}Item #~

```
{INPUT}Description~
{INPUT}Quantity~
{INPUT}Cost~
```

In the second row under Item #, enter this command:

```
{CALL}Stop~{GO}Go~
```

The first two rows of the table contain the subroutine Go, which is repeated for each item. The {INPUT} commands prompt for the item, description, number of items, and price. If possible, keep the prompts short to fit the commands in the table cells.

Type the following commands, one above the *Thanks for the order!* block and one below it (see Figure 12.5):

```
{LABEL}End~
{GO}End1~
```

Enter a hard page break after the {GO}End1~ command, and then type the remainder of the file:

```
{LABEL}Stop~{ASSIGN}Count~{VARIABLE}Count~ + 1 ~{COMMENT}
~{IF}{VARIABLE}Count~=16~{GO}End~{END IF}{COMMENT}
~{CHAR}Flag~Another item? Y/N~{COMMENT}
~{IF}"{VARIABLE}Flag~"="n"~{ASSIGN}Flag~N~{END IF}{COMMENT}
~{IF}"{VARIABLE}Flag~"="N"~{GO}End~{END IF}{RETURN}
{LABEL}End1~
```

Save the completed merge file under the name **Invoice.mrg**.

After each line is entered, the subroutine Stop is called to increment the variable Count. When Count is 16, meaning that 16 records have been entered, control is passed to the subroutine End. This subroutine displays the remainder of the invoice, and then the Calc macro is executed.

If Count is less than 16, a dialog box appears, asking whether the user wants to enter another item. If the user enters N or n, the End subroutine is performed; otherwise, the {RETURN} command repeats the Go subroutine.

The End subroutine continues the merge to display the bottom section of the invoice. Control is then passed to subroutine End1, skipping over the remaining merge instructions so they do not appear in the completed invoice and ending the merge file normally to execute the Calc macro.

When the user is finished entering records, the final invoice will include only the table rows for each item entered and one blank row.

SORTING DATABASE RECORDS

For some applications, it is more efficient to sort the records in your database before merging them with a primary file. Here are some reasons for sorting records:

◆ You are planning a mass mailing. You can take advantage of lower postage rates by printing mailing labels sorted by zip code.

◆ Your cash flow is slowing down. You can print a report of clients sorted by the amount they owe, and then contact those at the top of the list.

To sort a database, use the Tools ➤ Sort (Ctrl-Shift-F12) command. This displays the Sort dialog box, shown in Figure 12.6.

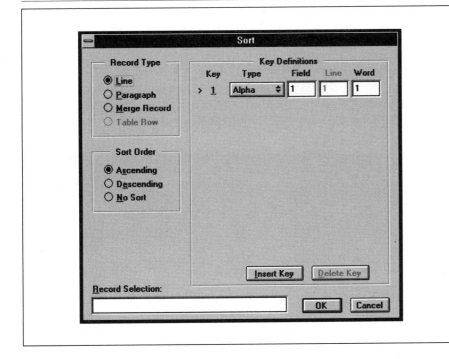

FIGURE 12.6:

Sort dialog box

DESIGNATING THE RECORD TYPE AND SORT ORDER

You can use this dialog box to sort records in a database as well as text in lines, paragraphs, and table rows. Choose one of the following in the Record Type section of the Sort dialog box:

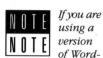

If you are using a version of Word-Perfect 5.1 for Windows dated after April 1992, refer to Appendix C for more information on this feature.

◆ **Line:** Sorts lines that end in a hard or soft carriage return. Use it for sorting lists and tabular columns.

◆ **Paragraph:** Sorts paragraphs that end in two or more hard carriage returns.

◆ **Merge Record:** Sorts records in a secondary file. A field name record will remain at the start of the database.

◆ **Table Row:** Sorts the rows of a table. It is available when the insertion point is in a table.

You can sort your records in ascending or descending order. You can also choose not to sort the records if you just want to select records, as explained later in this chapter.

DESIGNATING KEYS

The Tools ➤ Sort command arranges your records based on the value of one to nine key fields. For example, to sort the database by zip code, designate the Zip field as the key. Each key can be sorted in either alphanumeric (alpha) or numeric order, depending on the contents of the field. Numeric fields can contain decimal places.

For example, you could sort telephone numbers as an alpha or as a numeric field:

ORIGINAL ORDER	ALPHA SORT	NUMERIC SORT
676-9851	555-5412	WA7-1111
WA7-1111	555-9861	NE7-7700
555-9861	676-9851	555-5412
555-5412	NE7-7700	555-9861
NE7-7700	WA7-1111	676-9851

In an alpha sort, WordPerfect places telephone numbers starting with numbers before those starting with letters—in standard ASCII sequence.

Depending on the type of record you are sorting, you have several other key field options. For all types, you can sort the key field by word (the first, second, and so on). All records but tables can be sorted by field (the field number, not field name). For all types except Line, you can sort by the line within the key field. Additionally, you can sort table fields by cell.

For example, suppose your database contains the complete address in field 5:

2021 Challenger Drive
Alameda, CA 94501{END FIELD}

The zip code is contained in the fifth field, second line, third word. So to sort the file by the zip code, you would designate the key field with Type: Numeric, Field: 5, Line: 2, and Word: 3.

Now suppose that you want to sort the Clients database by the name of the contact, which is the second field. The contact names are in first name, last name order. If you select the first word as the key, the list will be sorted by the formal title: Mr., Ms., Miss, or Mrs. You cannot use the third word in the field because one of the clients (Mr. Jackson H. Montgomery) has a middle initial as the third word.

The solution is to use the last word in the field, which will always be the last name. Because the names have a different number of words, you cannot count forward to arrive at the word number. Instead, work backward from the end of the field, using a minus sign, as in Type: Alpha, Field: 2, Line: 1, Word: −1.

Note that this technique cannot be used if some of the names have special endings, such as Jr., Sr., or III, unless you type them in a certain way. When entering names such as these in the database, insert a hard space between the last name and the ending by pressing Ctrl-spacebar rather than the spacebar alone. When sorting, WordPerfect will treat the last name and ending as one word.

SORTING BY MULTIPLE KEYS

Sorting by multiple keys allows you to group records together as well as sort them. For example, suppose you want to print a report listing clients by city. Within each group of cities, you want the clients listed by zip code. Clients with the same zip code should be sorted by the contact's last name. This sort

If you are using a version of Word-Perfect 5.1 for Windows dated after April 1992, refer to Appendix C for more information on this feature.

involves three keys. The first key, called the primary key, is the City field. The second and third keys are Zip and Contact.

You enter the keys in reverse order: third key, then the second key, then the primary key. You will see why as you follow the steps to perform the multiple-key sort:

1. Open the Clients database and select Tools ➤ Sort (Ctrl-Shift-F12).

2. In the Sort dialog box, select Merge Record.

3. Pull down the Type list box and select Alpha.

4. In the Field text box, type **2**, the number of the Contact field.

5. In the Word text box for the third key, type **−1.**

6. Select Insert Key to add another key to the list. The key you just defined will move down to the second position, and the new key will be inserted as key 1.

7. Select Numeric for this key's type. In the Field text box for the key, type **9**, the number of the Zip field.

8. Select Insert Key to add another key to the list.

9. In the Field text box for what now is the first key, type **7**, the number of the City field.

10. Select OK to sort the records. You will see a dialog box reporting the progress of the sort, and then the database will reappear in the order you specified.

11. Close the database file without saving the changes.

PROGRAMMING INTERACTIVE SORTING

If you want users to be able to sort records on any field without teaching them how to use the Sort dialog box, you can create a macro to guide them through the process. Figure 12.7 shows a macro for sorting the Clients database. Create it and save it under the name **Sort.wcm** in the MACROS subdirectory.

The macro opens the database and prompts the user to enter the field number, which is assigned to the variable Look. The variable is inserted into the Sort command. The macro then performs one of three routines based on the type of the field. A separate routine is used for the Contact field, with −1 word as the key. You could modify the macro to input the field name, then convert the name to the field number (for the sort) in a Case command.

```
//Sort macro
Application(WP;WPWP;Default;"WPWPUS.WCD")
OnCancel(End@)
OnError(End@)
Display(On!)
FileOpen("c:\wpwin\clients")
PosDocTop()
GetNumber(Look;"Enter field number";"Sort Records")
Case(Look;{1;Alpha@;2;Name@;3;Alpha@;4;Alpha@;5;Alpha@;6;
          Alpha@;7;Alpha@;8;Alpha@;9;Number@;10;Alpha@;11;
          Number@;12;Number@;13;Number@;14;Alpha@};End@)

Label(Alpha@)
Sort
(
    RecordType:MergeRec!;
    SortOrder:Ascending!;
    Selection:"";
    Key1Type:Alpha!;
    Key1Level1:Look;
    Key1Level2:1;
    Key1Level3:1
)
Go(End@)

Label(Name@)
Sort
(
    RecordType:MergeRec!;
    SortOrder:Ascending!;
    Selection:"";
    Key1Type:Alpha!;
    Key1Level1:Look;
    Key1Level2:1;
    Key1Level3:-1
)
Go(End@)

Label(Number@)
Sort
(
    RecordType:MergeRec!;
    SortOrder:Ascending!;
    Selection:"";
    Key1Type:Numeric!;
    Key1Level1:Look;
    Key1Level2:1;
    Key1Level3:1
)
Label(End@)
```

SELECTING RECORDS FOR QUICK MERGING

You can select records from a database by creating a secondary database with specific records that meet a condition. If you have a large database, separating those you want to merge can be faster than selecting records as part of the merge program. Here are some reasons for using sorted and selected records:

◆ The sales manager is planning a trip to California. You can send letters to customers in that state to schedule visits.

◆ Business is slacking off. You can send a special mailing to customers who haven't ordered for some time.

◆ A new salesperson was hired to cover a territory of specific zip codes in the Detroit area. You can send letters to those customers to announce the personnel change.

To select records, you enter selection criteria in the Record Selection text box of the Sort dialog box. When the process is complete, the records not selected will be removed from the file. *Do not save the file under the same name unless you no longer need the records that were not selected!*

DEFINING SELECTION CRITERIA

Selection criteria can be simple, based on the value of one key, or complex, based on a number of keys. A simple selection is based on comparing a key with a specific value, either alphanumeric or numeric. The comparisons can include the following:

COMPARISON	SYMBOL	EXAMPLE
Equal	=	key1=500
Does not equal	<>	key1<>Chesin
Greater than	>	key1>200
Less than	<	key1<1000
Greater than or equal to	>=	key1>=500
Less than or equal to	<=	key1<=500

Don't add any spaces before or after any of the operator symbols. Alphanumeric values, such as Chesin in the example above, do not have to be enclosed in quotation marks. Numeric values and fields can contain decimal places.

Note the difference between < and >, and <= and >=. The number 500 is not greater than 500, but it is greater than or equal to (>=) 500. If you want to include records with that value, make sure that you include the equal sign in the selection criteria.

You can also use the global key, keyg, to select records containing a specified string of characters in any field. For example, the criteria

keyg=Watson

will select clients with the word *Watson* anywhere in the record.

Selection criteria cannot include direct key comparisons, such as

key1<key2

To perform a selection without sorting, select the No Sort button under Sort Order. This selects records but leaves them in their original order.

Complex selections compare the values of more than one key by using the + (OR) and * (AND) operators. For example, if you want to list clients who owe you more than $5,000 and live in Pennsylvania, the selection criteria would be

key1=PA * key2>5000

To find the clients who owe you more than $5,000 or who live in Pennsylvania (no matter how much they owe), the selection criteria would be

key1=PA + key2>5000

You can define more complex selection conditions by combining the AND and OR operators. For example, the following selection line selects clients with a credit rating of less than $1,000 and who owe more than $500, but also clients named Chesin no matter what they owe or what their credit is:

key1=Chesin + (key2>500 * key3<1000)

Since the conditions would normally be tested from left to right, the parentheses are needed to select the proper records. Without the parentheses, Word-Perfect would select clients either named Chesin or who owe more than $500, and all clients with credit ratings less than $1,000.

PROGRAMMING INTERACTIVE SELECTION

Suppose that you want users to be able to select records without teaching them how to define selection criteria. You also want to make sure that they do not accidentally save the resulting file under the same name as the original file, deleting the unselected records.

The macro shown in Figure 12.8 performs an interactive selection with one key of any field that must match the specified entry. Create the macro and save it under the name **Select.wcm** in the MACROS subdirectory.

```
//Select macro
Application(WP;WPWP;Default;"WPWPUS.WCD")
OnCancel(End@)
OnError(End@)
Display(On!)
FileNew()
Type( Text:" ")
FileRetrieve(Filename:"c:\wpwin\clients";AutoDetect:No!;
            InsertIntoDoc:Insert!)
DeleteCharPrevious()
GetNumber(Look;"Enter field number";"Sort Records")
GetString(Find;Length=20;"Enter select text";"Select
            Records")
Keys:="key1="+Find
Case(Look;(1;Alpha@;2;Name@;3;Alpha@;4;Alpha@;5;Alpha@;6;
            Alpha@;7;Alpha@;8;Alpha@;9;Number@;10;Alpha@;11;
            Number@;12;Number@;13;Number@;14;Alpha@);End@)

Label(Alpha@)
Sort(RecordType:MergeRec!;
    SortOrder:Ascending!;
    Selection:Keys;
    Key1Type:Alpha!;
    Key1Level1:Look;
    Key1Level2:1;
    Key1Level3:1)
Go(End@)

Label(Name@)
Sort(RecordType:MergeRec!;
    SortOrder:Ascending!;
    Selection:Keys;
    Key1Type:Alpha!;
    Key1Level1:Look;
    Key1Level2:1;
    Key1Level3:-1)
Go(End@)

Label(Number@)
Sort(RecordType:MergeRec!;
    SortOrder:Ascending!;
    Selection:Keys;
    Key1Type:Numeric!;
    Key1Level1:Look;
    Key1Level2:1;
    Key1Level3:1)

Label(End@)
```

FIGURE 12.8:

Macro to select records based on user entry

To avoid an accidental save of the database after record selection, the macro starts a new document, inserts a space, retrieves the database, and then deletes the space. This opens the document in an unnamed window. The

AutoDetect parameter is included in case a conversion message appears (if the database is not a WordPerfect file). The command

InsertIntoDoc:Insert!

prevents a dialog box from appearing to ask the user to confirm the insertion of the document into the current window.

The macro is very similar to the Sort macro presented earlier in the chapter. However, two user responses are required: one for the field number and another for the text to be compared with the key. The command

keys:="key1=" + Find

creates a variable in the correct format for insertion into the Sort command.

This chapter has shown how macros and merge files can be combined for sophisticated applications. In the next chapters, you will learn how to package your merge files and macros into a fully automated system.

CHAPTER 13

Assembling master documents
Programming interactive
document assembly
Using multiple secondary files

Automating Document Assembly

ordPerfect's merging functions provide the capability to combine files in a variety of ways. They can be used for managing databases, producing form documents, and inserting boilerplate files.

This chapter concentrates on techniques for document assembly. You will learn how to build complex documents from boilerplate files and from specially constructed secondary files. Our data-management and document-assembly system example combines WordPerfect's merging functions into a sophisticated, multitask application.

ASSEMBLING A MASTER DOCUMENT

The longer your document becomes, the more time it takes to open and save, or to move from the start and end. To save waiting time, you can write and edit the document in smaller sections, each a separate file, then create a master document to merge and format it for printing.

CREATING A MASTER DOCUMENT WITH LINKS

One way to create a master document is through the Tools ➤ Master Document submenu. The commands allow you to work with special codes, called *subdocument links,* which contain the names of documents on the disk that will be inserted into the master document.

To insert a subdocument link, place the insertion point where you want the document to appear in the master document, then select Tools ➤ Master Document ➤ Subdocument. This displays the Include Subdocument dialog box, shown in Figure 13.1. Type the name of the subdocument, and then select Include to add the link to the master document. The subdocument does not have to exist to be named in the link. This means that you can design the master document first, then create and save the subdocuments.

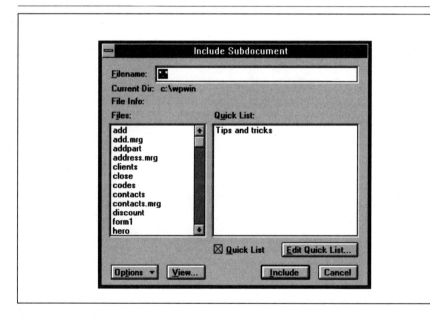

FIGURE 13.1:

Include Subdocument dialog box

When you want to print the master document or see how it will appear when completed, select Tools ➤ Master Document ➤ Expand Master. If the document contains a link with a subdocument that does not exist, Word-Perfect will display an error message, and then continue expanding the document. The subdocuments are recalled from the disk and inserted at the location of the link codes. They are surrounded by [Subdoc Start] and [Subdoc End] codes, which clearly show which parts of the expanded document are subdocuments.

You can edit the text of a subdocument in its own file before the master document has been expanded. When you expand the master, the most current version of the subdocument will be recalled. You can also edit the subdocument when it appears in the expanded master document. The edited version can then be saved automatically in its own file when you condense or save the master.

Keep in mind that the subdocuments will not print with the master document unless it has been expanded.

When you no longer need to see the text of the subdocuments, condense the master document to remove the subdocuments from the display (not remove the links). Select Tools ➤ Master Document ➤ Condense Master to display a dialog box with the message

Save All Subdocuments?

If you did not edit any of the subdocuments, select No. Otherwise, select Yes to display a dialog box with the message

Replace Existing File?
Part*X*
Prompt Before Replacing Subdocuments

Select Yes to replace the subdocument, No to retain the original version, or Cancel to stop the operation. If you want to replace all the subdocuments without being prompted, turn off the Prompt Before Replacing Subdocuments option.

Save a master document as you would any other document. If the master is expanded, a dialog box will appear asking if you want to condense it before saving. If you select No, the expanded document will be saved. If you select Yes, WordPerfect will condense it first.

The formatting and layout codes in the master document apply to all the subdocuments, just as if the documents were already combined. That is, a code remains in effect until WordPerfect encounters another code for the same format.

Include margin, header, footer, and page number codes in the master document to format each of the subdocuments. It is not necessary to include these codes in a subdocument unless you want it formatted differently. For example, suppose the last subdocument contains an index that you want numbered with small roman numerals. In the master document, turn on page numbering using the default numeric numbering. Then insert a hard page code at the beginning of the index document and select roman numeral numbering with a new page number set to 1. When the document is expanded, page numbering will run consecutively starting with the first page, but the index will start on a new page with its own numbering scheme.

CREATING A MASTER DOCUMENT WITH MERGE COMMANDS

Another way to create a master document is as a primary file containing {NEST PRIMARY} merge commands. For example, a Report.mrg file might look like this:

```
{NEST PRIMARY}Introduction~
{NEST PRIMARY}Hypothesis~
{NEST PRIMARY}Method~
{NEST PRIMARY}Results~
{NEST PRIMARY}Summary~
```

To assemble the master document, merge the primary file without naming a secondary file. The documents named in the {NEST PRIMARY} commands will be recalled from disk and assembled into a single document. For example, if you named the Report.mrg file shown above as the primary file, the Introduction, Hypothesis, Method, Results, and Summary files would be combined in the order in which they are listed.

DESIGNING AN INTERACTIVE DOCUMENT-ASSEMBLY SYSTEM

Using the merge command method, you can program interactive document assembly. This technique allows the user to select the files to be combined each time the master document is assembled. The system requires a primary file that creates another primary file based on user input, along with several macros to retrieve the files.

The document-assembly system described here builds a form letter from a series of boilerplate files on disk. The user selects the recipient's name, and the merge file inserts the name and address information from the database. Then each paragraph (boilerplate file) to be combined in the letter is chosen from a dialog box. Finally, the master document is merged with the temporary file to complete the form letter.

TRANSFERRING VARIABLES BETWEEN MACROS

One of the macros used in the assembly system is a generic subroutine that you can use in any application that requires the selection of a specific record in a database. The name of the database and the temporary file to store the record are passed to it by the calling macro. However, WordPerfect does not allow you to transfer the contents of a variable directly from one macro to another macro. Instead, you must pass them as merge variables

The MergeVariableSet command can transfer variables between a macro and a merge file, but we will use it to pass information from one macro to another. The syntax is

MergeVariableSet("*Var*";"*Value*")

It assigns a string value to a merge variable. Notice that both the variable name and the value must be in quotation marks.

The subroutine for retrieving the specified record uses the MergeVariableGet command to get the variable from the calling macro. It uses the syntax

MergeVariableGet(*Macro-Variable*;"*Merge-Variable*")

It assigns the contents of the merge variable to the named macro variable. The name of the merge variable must be in quotation marks.

CREATING THE ADDRESS FILE

Start by creating a merge file that contains the field information for the letter's address and salutation:

{DATE}

{FIELD}2~
{FIELD}1~
{FIELD}5~
{FIELD}6?~
{FIELD}7~, {FIELD}8~   {FIELD}9~

Dear {FIELD}3~:

Press ↵ twice, save the document under the name **Address.mrg**, and close the document window.

We used field numbers rather than names since the secondary file will contain just the client's record.

CREATING THE PRIMARY MERGE FILE

The body of the letter will be assembled from boilerplate files on the disk. Create the following short generic file, which can be used to assemble any number of documents. It accepts the names of the boilerplate files to be assembled and inserts the {NEST PRIMARY} commands. Do not press ↵ after the last line.

```
{ASSIGN}Flag~Y~{COMMENT}
~{WHILE}"{VARIABLE}Flag~"!="N"~{COMMENT}
~{PROMPT}Enter the name of a boilerplate, press Alt-Enter~{MRG
CMND}{NEST PRIMARY}{MRG CMND}{KEYBOARD}~
{CHAR}Flag~Another boilerplate? Y/N~{COMMENT}
~{IF}"{VARIABLE}Flag~"="n"~{ASSIGN}Flag~N~{END IF}{COMMENT}
~{END WHILE}{CHAIN MACRO}c:\wpwin\macros\primary~
```

Save the document under the name **Primary.mrg**, and then close the document window.

Notice the tilde after the {KEYBOARD} command. After the {PROMPT} command to request the name of the boilerplate file, the commands

```
{MRG CMND}{NEST PRIMARY}{MRG CMND}
```

insert the {NEST PRIMARY} code into the document. The {KEYBOARD} command allows the user to insert the name of the boilerplate file, and then the merge file inserts the tilde required after the file name in the {NEST PRIMARY} command.

WRITING THE LETTER MACRO

To make the system as easy to use as possible, create the following macro, which starts the entire process:

```
Application(WP;WPWP;Default;"WPWPUS.WCD")
Display(On!)
MergeExecute("primary.mrg")
```

Save the macro under the name **Letter.wcm** in the MACROS subdirectory, and then close the window.

WRITING THE PRIMARY MACRO

Next create the Primary macro, shown in Figure 13.2. This macro performs three functions:

◆ Retrieves the Address.mrg file and saves the newly assembled document on disk in a file called Letter.

◆ Runs the next macro we will write, Getname, which allows the user to select the letter's recipient.

◆ Merges the assembled primary file, Letter, with the temporary database, Temp, which contains the client's record.

```
Application(WP;WPWP;Default;"WPWPUS.WCD")
OnError(Start@)
FileDelete("Letter")
Label(Start@)
OnError(End@)
PosDocTop()
HardReturn()
HardReturn()
PosDocTop()
FileRetrieve(Filename:"c:\wpwin\address.mrg";AutoDetect:No!;
          InsertIntoDoc:Insert!)
PosDocTop()
SelectMode(On!)
PosDocBottom()
FileSave("Letter")
SelectMode(Off!)
CloseNoSave(No!)
MergeVariableSet("Secondary";"Temp")
MergeVariableSet("Database";"c:\wpwin\clients")
Run("c:\wpwin\macros\getname")
MergeExecute(PrimaryFile:"Letter";SecondaryFile:"Temp")
Label(End@)
```

FIGURE 13.2:

Primary macro that assembles the form document

Save the macro under the name **Primary.wcm** in the MACROS subdirectory, and then close the document window.

In the macro, the variables used with the MergeVariableSet commands are Secondary, which represents the name of the temporary file in which to place the record, and Database, which is for the name of the database to be opened. These are passed to the next macro we will create.

WRITING THE GETNAME MACRO

The final macro for the system allows the user to select the client's record and save it in the temporary database file. The Getname macro is shown in Figure 13.3. You can use this macro in any application that requires selecting a specific record from a specific database.

```
Application(WP;WPWP;Default;"WPWPUS.WCD")
Title:="Assemble Document"
OnError(Start@)
MergeVariableGet(Secondary;"Secondary")
MergeVariableGet(Database;"Database")

FileDelete(Secondary)
Label(Start@)
OnError(End@)
OnNotFound(GoTop@)
OnCancel(End@)
Go(Main@)
Label(End@)
    Quit
Label(Main@)
GetString(Find;Length=20;"Enter record name";Title)
InsertTypeover(Off!)
Display(On!)
FileOpen(Database)

Label(GoTop@)
PosDocTop()

Label(Search@)
SearchText(SearchString:Find;SearchDirection:Forward!;
            SearchScope :DocOnly!)
Menu(Action;Letter;;;("Merge"; "Search Again"; "Cancel"))
Case(Action;{1;Merge@;2;Search@;3;End@};End@)

Label(Merge@)
PosLineBegin()
PosPageNext()
SelectMode(On!)
PosPagePrevious()
FileSave(Secondary)
SelectMode(Off!)
CloseNoSave(No!)
Close()
```

FIGURE 13.3:

Getname macro to save the record in a temporary database

This macro is similar to the Invoice.wcm macro you created in Chapter 12. The differences are its use of the MergeVariableGet command (to get variables from the Primary macro) and its handling of the Not Found condition. The Invoice macro just stops if it reaches the end of the database without the user selecting a client record to merge. The Getname macro will return to the beginning of the database so that the user can scan it again for the correct client record. This is performed with the command

OnNotFound(GoTop@)

and the commands

Label(GoTop@)
PosDocTop()

Create the macro in Figure 13.3 and save the file under the name **Getname.wcm** in the MACROS subdirectory. To save time, you could recall and edit the Invoice.wcm file. If you do, check your work carefully before continuing and be sure to use the Save As command. If you use Save, you will delete the original file, which you may still want to use for completing invoices.

Note that because this macro needs the variables from the calling macro, it cannot be used by itself; it must always be executed from a macro that includes the assignments to the merge variables Secondary and Database.

CREATING THE BOILERPLATE FILES

Finally, create the six boilerplate files that can be merged into the assembled document:

◆ Enter the following paragraph, press ↵ twice, save the file under the name **Good**, and close the window:

You have been a valued customer, and I want to personally thank you for your support. We are all feeling the pinch of these economic times, so your continued support is greatly appreciated.

◆ Enter the following paragraph, press ↵ twice, save the file under the name **Overdue**, and close the window:

It has come to my attention that your account is now overdue. We have tried to be patient, but we are also experiencing cash flow problems.

◆ Enter the following paragraph, press ↵ twice, save the file under the name **Legal**, and close the window:

Unless you pay the total amount due in 30 days, we will be forced to take legal action.

◆ Enter the following paragraph, press ↵ twice, save the file under the name **Close1**, and close the window:

It has been a pleasure serving you in the past and we pledge to provide the best prices and service in the industry.

◆ Enter the following paragraph, press ↵ twice, save the file under the name **Close2**, and close the window:

Looking forward to hearing from you regarding this matter.

◆ Type the following closing, save the file under the name **Close**, and then close the window.

Sincerely yours,

Alvin Aardvark

COMPILING THE DOCUMENT-ASSEMBLY MACROS

When you execute a macro from the Play Macro dialog box, WordPerfect will compile the macro if necessary. Macros run directly from merge files will also be automatically compiled. However, a macro that is called from another macro with the Chain command must be compiled in the Macro Facility before it can be played. If the macro is not compiled, WordPerfect will display a warning dialog box.

Whenever you create a complex series of macros and merge files, such as the ones for our document-assembly system, you should compile all the macros first in the Macro Facility. Otherwise, you could waste time completing a merge operation only to have the system fail because of a macro error.

You should now run the Macro Facility and choose to compile the macros you have created: Letter.wcm, Primary.wcm, and Getname.wcm. Select Macro ➤ Play (Alt-F10) ➤ Cancel to ensure that the Macro Facility is running. Then press Ctrl-Esc to display the Task List and switch to the Word-Perfect Macro Facility. Select Macro ➤ Compile Macro to convert each macro. Finally, close the Macro Facility to return to WordPerfect. (See Chapter 10 for more details on using the Macro Facility.)

USING THE DOCUMENT-ASSEMBLY SYSTEM

Before running the document-assembly application, make sure you created and saved all the necessary files. Your disk should now contain the following files:

- Address.mrg
- Primary mrg
- Letter.wcm
- Primary.wcm
- Getname.wcm
- Good

- Overdue
- Legal
- Close
- Close1
- Close2

The macro files should all be stored in the MACROS subdirectory. The merge files and boilerplate text should be in the WPWIN directory.

Now let's use our system to create a customized letter.

1. Select Macro ➤ Play (Alt-F10), type **Letter**, and select Play. This plays the Letter macro, which runs the Primary file and displays a prompt for you to type the name of a boilerplate file.

2. Type **Overdue** and press Alt-↵.

3. Press **Y** to add another boilerplate paragraph.

4. Type **Legal**, press Alt-↵, and then press Y.

5. Type **Close2**, press Alt-↵, and then press Y.

6. Type **Close**, press Alt-↵, and then press N. The Primary macro is run. This inserts the Address.mrg file, saves the assembled file, then runs the Getname macro. A prompt appears asking you to enter the company name.

7. Type **Chandler** and press ↵. WordPerfect retrieves the Clients database, locates the record for Chandler, and displays the menu for merging.

8. Select A to merge the record. The client's record is saved in the Temp file, and the window closes. The macro continues by merging the primary and secondary files, completing the letter.

9. Select File ➤ Close (Ctrl-F4), then No to close the document window.

INCLUDING BOILERPLATE IN THE MASTER DOCUMENT

If you want to program just a few choices of boilerplate text to include in the merged document, you can accomplish this without creating individual disk files and macros. Instead, place the menus and boilerplate text directly in the merge file. Then the document can be assembled in a single merge operation.

For example, the portion of a merge file shown in Figure 13.4 displays a dialog box listing the paragraph choices. When you select an item from the list, the merge file inserts it into the document, then redisplays the dialog box.

```
(ASSIGN)Count˜1˜(COMMENT)
˜(ASSIGN)a˜ ˜(ASSIGN)b˜ ˜(ASSIGN)c˜ ˜(ASSIGN)d˜ ˜(ASSIGN)e˜
  ˜(COMMENT)
˜(Label)Selections˜(REWRITE)(CHAR)Pick˜
(VARIABLE)a˜  a Overdue
(VARIABLE)b˜  b Legal
(VARIABLE)c˜  c Nice
(VARIABLE)d˜  d Warm
(VARIABLE)e˜  e End
˜(COMMENT)
˜(CASE)(VARIABLE)Pick˜˜a˜Para1˜b˜Para2˜c˜Para3˜d˜Para4˜)
  (OTHERWISE)˜END˜

(LABEL)Para1˜(ASSIGN)a˜(Variable)Count˜˜
    It has come to my attention that your account is now
overdue. We have tried to be patient, but we are also
experiencing cash flow problems.
(ASSIGN)Count˜(VARIABLE)Count˜+1˜(COMMENT)
˜(IF)(VARIABLE)Count˜=5˜(GO)End˜(ELSE)(GO)Selections˜

(LABEL)Para2˜(ASSIGN)b˜(Variable)Count˜˜
    Unless you pay the total amount due in 30 days, we will be
forced to take legal action.
(ASSIGN)Count˜(VARIABLE)Count˜+1˜(COMMENT)
˜(IF)(VARIABLE)Count˜=5˜(GO)End˜(ELSE)(GO)Selections˜

(LABEL)Para3˜(ASSIGN)c˜(Variable)Count˜˜
    You have been a valued customer and I want to personally
thank you for your support. We are all feeling the pinch of these
economic times, so your continued support is greatly appreciated.
(ASSIGN)Count˜(VARIABLE)Count˜+1˜(COMMENT)
˜(IF)(VARIABLE)Count˜=5˜(GO)End˜(ELSE)(GO)Selections˜

(LABEL)Para4˜(ASSIGN)d˜(VARIABLE)Count˜˜
    It has been a pleasure serving you in the past and we pledge
to provide the best prices and service in the industry.
(ASSIGN)Count˜(VARIABLE)Count˜+1˜(COMMENT)
˜(IF)(VARIABLE)Count˜=5˜(GO)End˜(ELSE)(GO)Selections˜

(LABEL)End˜

Sincerely,


Alvin A. Aardvark
```

FIGURE 13.4:

Merge commands for selecting paragraphs from within a primary document

The variables place a number in front of the selected option, indicating its order in the document. For example, the dialog box in Figure 13.5 shows that the Overdue and Legal paragraphs were selected in that order.

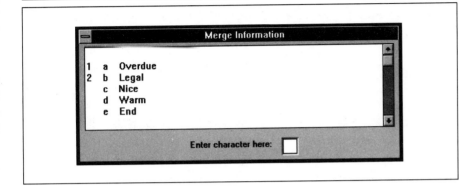

To end the merge file and complete the document, select the End option from the menu.

As an alternative to including the boilerplate text in the merge file, you could use merge commands to select external boilerplate files, as in

```
{LABEL}Para1~{ASSIGN}a~{Variable}Count~~
{NEST PRIMARY}Overdue~
{ASSIGN}Count~{VARIABLE}Count~+1~{COMMENT}
~{IF}{VARIABLE}Count~=5~{GO}End~{ELSE}{GO}Selections~
```

COMBINING DATABASE MANAGEMENT AND DOCUMENT ASSEMBLY

By combining macros and merge files, you can design an application that performs both database-management and document-assembly functions at the same time. For example, suppose that you have a database of prospective clients—companies that have requested information or applied for credit but who have not yet placed an order. You can create a system that performs both of these tasks:

◆ Adds a new record to the database

◆ Creates a form letter indicating the new client's credit limit and sales representative

To create this type of application, you need two new databases: one to store the address information for prospective clients and another to hold the names and telephone numbers of your sales representatives. Both databases are used to assemble the form letter.

SETTING UP THE DATABASES

Start by creating a database to store information on prospective clients. This merge file includes only the field name record:

{FIELD NAMES}Company~Contact~Salutation~Title~Address
~Location~City~State~Zip~Telephone~Credit~~{END RECORD}

Press Ctrl-⏎ to insert a page break, save the document under the name **Prospect**, and close the document window.

Now, create the database to store information about the sales representatives. We will include only names and telephone numbers. In your own applications, you can expand the database to store addresses, salaries, and commission information as well.

{FIELD NAMES}Name~Workphone~Homephone~~{END RECORD}

Wayne Newtown{END FIELD}
555-1872{END FIELD}
666-7354{END FIELD}
{END RECORD}

Samuel Shore{END FIELD}
555-1873{END FIELD}
661-9836{END FIELD}
{END RECORD}

Sarah Buchanan{END FIELD}
555-1874{END FIELD}
641-5661{END FIELD}
{END RECORD}

Save the document under the name **Reps**.

WRITING THE FORM LETTER

The output of this system will be a letter to the prospective client. It will be addressed to the client using field information from the Prospect database, and it will contain the name and phone numbers of the salesperson from the Reps database.

Type the following primary file:

{DATE}

{FIELD}2~
{FIELD}1~
{FIELD}5~
{FIELD}6?~
{FIELD}7~, {FIELD}8~　　{FIELD}9~

Dear {FIELD}3~:

Thank you for your interest in Aardvark Computers. We are processing your client information now.
{IF}{FIELD}11~<500~{COMMENT}
~ Please contact our accounting department to arrange for a line of credit. Until the process is complete, we will only be able to accept an order up to ${FIELD}11~.
{ELSE} {COMMENT}
~ We are pleased to provide you with a credit limit of ${FIELD}11~. If you would like an additional credit line, please contact our accounting department.
{END IF}{SUBST SECONDARY}Rtemp~{COMMENT}
~ Your sales representative is {FIELD}1~. The office number is {FIELD}2~ and the home number is {FIELD}3~. Please call your representative if you need any additional information.

{NEST PRIMARY}Close~

Save the primary file under the name **Prolet.mrg**, and then close the document window.

You will be merging this file with the Temp database, which is the temporary file that will store the address of the prospective client. To later include information about the sales representative, you must change to the secondary file by using the {SUBST SECONDARY} command. This tells WordPerfect to begin using the fields in the Rtemp database, which is a temporary file that holds the name and telephone numbers of the sales representative. The {NEST PRIMARY} command at the end of file merges the Close file, the standard closing you created for the document-assembly system.

Creating the Primary File for a Single Record

The application uses a merge file to input the data about prospective clients into the Prospect database. It is similar to the Add.mrg file for adding records, which you created in Chapter 12 (Figure 12.1), except that it allows the addition of just one record, which is then also used for the assembled form letter.

Create the merge file shown in Figure 13.6 and save it under the name **Pro.mrg**. To save time, you can retrieve the Add.mrg file and edit it.

```
{INPUT}Enter the company name, then Alt-Enter~{MRG
   CMND}{END FIELD}{MRG CMND}
{INPUT}Enter the contact person, then Alt-Enter~{MRG
   CMND}{END FIELD}{MRG CMND}
{INPUT}Enter the salutation (Dear...), then Alt-Enter~{MRG
   CMND}{END FIELD}{MRG CMND}
{INPUT}Enter contact's title, then Alt-Enter~{MRG CMND}
   {END FIELD}{MRG CMND}
{INPUT}Enter the street address, then Alt-Enter~{MRG CMND}
   {END FIELD}{MRG CMND}
{INPUT}Enter any second address, then Alt-Enter~{MRG CMND}
   {END FIELD}{MRG CMND}
{INPUT}Enter the city, then Alt-Enter~{MRG CMND}{END FIELD}
   {MRG CMND}
{INPUT}Enter the state, then Alt-Enter ~{MRG CMND}{END FIELD}
   {MRG CMND}
{INPUT}Enter the zip code, then Alt-Enter~{MRG CMND}{END
   FIELD}{MRG CMND}
{INPUT}Enter the phone number, then Alt-Enter~{MRG CMND}
   {END FIELD}{MRG CMND}
{INPUT}Enter the initial credit limit, then Alt-Enter~{MRG
   CMND}{END FIELD}{MRG CMND}
{MRG CMND}{END RECORD}{MRG CMND}
===========================================================
{CHAIN MACRO}c:\wpwin\macros\prosave~
```

FIGURE 13.6:

Primary document for inputting prospective client data

CREATING THE RECORD-ADDITION AND ASSEMBLY MACROS

Enter the first macro, which will begin the application:

```
Application(WP;WPWP;Default;"WPWPUS.WCD")
Display(On!)
FileOpen("c:\wpwin\prospect")
PosDocBottom()
MergeExecute("Pro.mrg")
```

Save it under the name **Proadd.wcm** in the MACROS subdirectory.

The Prosave macro, shown in Figure 13.7, performs the bulk of the application:

◆ Saves the entire Prospect database

◆ Saves the record of the new prospect in the Rtemp file

◆ Runs the next macro we will write, Getrep, which lets the user select a sales representative, then merges the Prolet file

Create the macro shown in Figure 13.7, and then save it under the name **Prosave.wcm** in the MACROS subdirectory.

```
Application(WP;WPWP;Default;"WPWPUS.WCD")
FileSave()
Second:="Temp"
OnError(Start@)
FileDelete(Second)
Label(Start@)
SelectMode(On!)
PosPagePrevious()
FileSave(Second)
SelectMode(Off!)
CloseNoSave(No!)
Close()
MergeVariableSet("Secondary";"Rtemp")
MergeVariableSet("Database";"c:\wpwin\reps")
Run("c:\wpwin\macros\getrep")
MergeExecute(PrimaryFile:"Prolet.mrg";SecondaryFile:Second)
```

FIGURE 13.7:

Macro for saving prospective client data and initiating remainder of the system

The Getrep macro, shown in Figure 13.8, is similar to the Getname macro you created earlier. It also uses the merge variables Secondary and Database to transfer variables between macros. However, this macro takes a slightly different approach to retrieving a record. Instead of asking the

```
Application(WP;WPWP;Default;"WPWPUS.WCD")
Title:="Assemble Document"
MergeVariableGet(Secondary;"Secondary")
MergeVariableGet(Database;"Database")
OnError(Start@)
FileDelete(Secondary)
Label(Start@)
OnError(End@)
OnCancel(End@)
Go(Main@)
Label(End@)
      Quit
Label(Main@)
InsertTypeover(Off!)
Display(On!)
FileOpen(Database)
PosDocTop()
Label(Search@)
GetWPData(LPage;Page!)
PosPageNext()
GetWPData(NPage;Page!)
If(Lpage=Npage)
      PosDocTop()
      PosPageNext()
EndIf

Menu(Action;Letter;;;("Assign"; "Next Rep"; "Cancel"))
Case(Action;{1;Merge@;2;Search@;3;End@};End@)

Label(Merge@)
PosLineBegin()
PosPageNext()
SelectMode(On!)
PosPagePrevious()
FileSave(Secondary)
SelectMode(Off!)
CloseNoSave(No!)
Close()
```

FIGURE 13.8:

Macro for obtaining sales representative data

user to enter the name, it displays each of the sales representatives in turn, allowing the user to choose one. The macro then saves the representative's record in the Rtemp file.

Create the macro shown in Figure 13.8 and save it as **Getrep.wcm** in the MACROS subdirectory.

If the user does not select a representative, the macro returns to the start of the database for another pass. Because the record selection does not involve a text string search, this is accomplished by comparing page numbers. When the macro moves the insertion point to the next record, it compares its page number (stored in the variable NPage) with the previous page number (stored in LPage). When the page numbers are the same, it means that the insertion point is at the end of the document and that the PosPageNext( ) command is having no effect. The insertion point is moved back to the start of the database, then past the field names record to the first prospective client record.

After you have created the Getrep.wcm, Proadd.wcm, and Prosave.wcm macros, compile them in the Macro Facility. Use the procedure outlined earlier in this chapter.

USING THE RECORD ADDITION AND FORM LETTER SYSTEM

To recap, the following files are necessary for the prospective client system:

- Prolet.mrg
- Getrep.wcm
- Pro.mrg
- Reps
- Proadd.wcm
- Prospect
- Prosave.wcm
- Close

Now, let's suppose that we just heard from a prospective client. We want to add the company to the Prospect database and assemble a form letter.

1. Select Macro ➤ Play (Alt-F10), type **Proadd**, and select Play. This runs the Pro.mrg file to enter the company information into the Prospect database.

2. Type **Adam Computer Warehouse** and press Alt-⏎.

3. In the same way, enter the following information, pressing Alt-⏎ after each field:

   Michael Adam
   Mr. Adam
   President
   647 Lock Road
   P.O. Box 337
   Philadelphia
   PA 19112
   676-4456
   300

When you press Alt-⏎ after the last field, the Prosave macro will be executed. This saves the Prospect database and saves the company information into the Temp file, then executes the Getrep macro. The name of the first sales representative in the database appears.

4. Press B to see the name of the next salesperson.

5. Press A to accept that salesperson, saving the name and telephone numbers in the Rtemp temporary file. The Prosave macro continues by merging the primary and secondary files. The completed letter is shown in Figure 13.9.

6. Select File ➤ Close (Ctrl-F4), then No to close the document window without saving the letter.

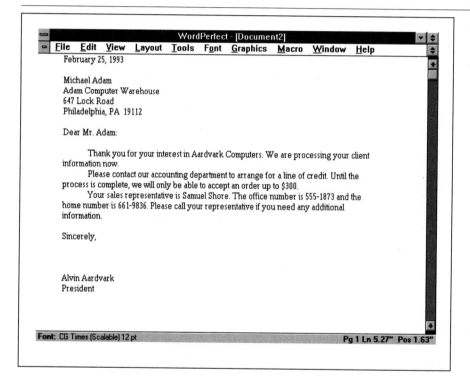

FIGURE 13.9:

Completed prospective client form letter

DEVELOPING YOUR OWN APPLICATIONS

The sample applications presented in this chapter were designed to serve as a starting point for creating your own applications. Begin by creating the database that will contain the information needed for the application. Then modify the sample merge files and macros to create your own files:

◆ A merge file for inputting information, such as Add.mrg to add multiple records or Pro.mrg to add an individual record

◆ A macro that executes the merge file, such as Proadd.wcm

◆ A macro for deleting records, such as Del.wcm

◆ A macro for marking duplicate records, such as Dup.wcm

◆ A macro for selecting a specific record, such as Getname.wcm or Getrep.wcm

◆ Merge files for creating the assembled document

Whenever possible, create general modules that you can use in more than one application, such as the Getname and Getrep macros shown in this chapter. After you have a library of such modules, you can develop applications quickly. The modules will serve as building blocks that require only calling macros and merge files.

For example, you can edit the Del and Dup macros to work with both the Clients and Prospect databases. Add a menu and If commands such as these to both files:

```
Menu(Result;Letter;10;10; {"Clients"; "Prospect"})
If(Result=2)
    Database:="c:\wpwin\clients"
Else
    Database:="c:\wpwin\prospect"
Endlf
```

Then edit the FileOpen command to read:

```
FileOpen(Database)
```

In Chapter 14, we will take this application even further by completely automating the invoicing process for both clients and prospective clients.

CHAPTER 14

Merging fields into tables
Performing decimal math in merges
Automating accounts receivable
Updating client records
Designing menus and applications

Creating Your Own Applications

The merge files and macros described in earlier chapters are the building blocks for a complete data-management system. However, they still require the user to merge files or play macros. This chapter describes how to organize the components into an application that allows users to perform functions by selecting menu options, so that they do not need to understand any of the technical details.

This chapter concentrates on the automation of functions that would otherwise require a great deal of work. For example, you will build an accounts receivables and client record system that would require hundreds, perhaps thousands, of programming instructions in a language such as C or Pascal.

MERGING DATA INTO TABLES

Suppose you want to create a table from information stored in one of your databases. Rather than manually entering the data into a table created with

WordPerfect's table feature, you can use a merge file and a macro to automate the process. For example, in preparation for a meeting with the sales staff, you could create a two-column table containing the names of clients and the amount each owes.

The primary file names the fields to be merged from the secondary file, and the macro converts the resulting document into a table. Create the merge file in the form of a database report, setting just the tabs you need for the columns (see Chapter 11). For example, this merge file creates a two-column list containing the client names and the amount they owe:

```
{CHAIN MACRO}c:\wpwin\macros\mergetab~{COMMENT}
~{FIELD}1~    {FIELD}12~
{PAGE OFF}
```

After the merge is completed, the insertion point will be in a blank line under the last line of text. The following macro (named Mergetab.wcm to work with the merge file shown above) deletes the blank line, selects the document, and then converts it into tabular columns:

```
Application(WP;WPWP;Default;"WPWPUS.WCD")
DeleteCharPrevious()
SelectMode(On!)
PosDocTop()
TableConvert(ConvertFrom:TabularColumns!)
```

PERFORMING CALCULATIONS WITH DECIMAL VALUES

Unlike the DOS version of WordPerfect, WordPerfect for Windows does not have a columnar math function for calculations that are not within a table. Using the {ASSIGN} command, you can perform some math in merge files, but it is limited to integer math. For example, you cannot use merge commands alone to calculate your sales totals because the fields contain decimal places. To automate calculations with dollars and cents and other decimal values, take advantage of the functions available for tables.

Create a merge file that contains the fields to be used in the calculations, and then write a macro that converts the data into a table and inserts the formulas. For example, suppose you want to total and average the values in the Due field of our Clients database to determine how much money is outstanding. This merge file creates a one-column document containing the values in that field:

```
{CHAIN MACRO}c:\wpwin\macros\tot~{FIELD}12~ {PAGE OFF}
```

The Tot.wcm macro, shown in Figure 14.1, totals the column, then uses the first three cells in the table to store and calculate the average. Only the final result will appear on the screen. Note that you need at least two clients for this macro, because it will automatically insert an extra blank row at the end of the table.

FIGURE 14.1:

Macro for calculating the total and average of field data

```
Application(WP;WPWP;Default;"WPWPUS.WCD")
SelectMode(On!)
PosDocTop()
TableConvert(ConvertFrom:TabularColumns!)
PosDocBottom()
PosLineUp()
GetWPData(NumRow;Row!)
NumRow:=NumRow-1
If(NumRow<2)
      Prompt("Math";"You need at least 2 clients";4;;)
      Pause
      Quit
EndIf
GetWPData(Cell1;Cell!)
TableFormula(Formula:"+")
SelectMode(State:On!)
PosLineEnd()
GetWPData(Total;SelectedText!)
SelectMode(State:Off!)
PosGoTo(Cell:"A1")
PosLineBegin()
SelectMode(On!)
PosLineEnd()
DeleteCharPrevious()
SelectMode(Off!)
PosGoTo(Cell:Cell1)
PosLineBegin()
SelectMode(On!)
PosLineEnd()
EditCopy()
SelectMode(Off!)
PosGoTo(Cell:"A1")
EditPaste()
PosGoTo(Cell:"A2")
PosLineBegin()
SelectMode(On!)
PosLineEnd()
DeleteCharPrevious()
SelectMode(Off!)
NumStr(DivBy;2;NumRow)
Type(DivBy)
PosGoTo(Cell:"A3")
TableFormula(Formula:"A1/A2")
SelectMode(On!)
PosLineEnd()
GetWPData(Average;SelectedText!)
SelectMode(State:Off!)
CloseNoSave(No!)
Close()
Type("The total is : ")
Type(Total)
HardReturn()
Type("The average is : ")
Type(Average)
```

This macro works as follows:

◆ Converts the list into a table but does not delete the blank line at the end. This line will be used to store the total.

◆ Moves the insertion point into the last cell.

◆ Inserts the row and cell number into variables.

◆ Subtracts 1 from the row number to obtain the number of records in the database. This will become the number to divide into the total to calculate the average.

◆ Adds the + function to the bottom cell as a formula. This totals the column and inserts the result.

◆ Selects the result and stores it in the variable Total.

◆ Deletes the value in cell A1, then copies and pastes the total in the last cell into cell A1.

◆ Deletes the contents of cell A2, converts to text the variable storing the number of rows, and inserts the resulting text in cell A2. You must convert the number to a string in order to use the Type command to insert it. When performing math, WordPerfect will still treat the cell contents as a number.

◆ Moves the insertion point to cell A3 and inserts the formula A1/A2.

◆ Selects the result in cell A3 and stores it in the variable Average.

◆ Closes the window without saving the document.

◆ Inserts the total and average with Type commands.

It might seem easier to select the total in the final cell, convert it to a number, and then divide it by the number of cells, as follows:

```
GetWPData(Total;SelectedText!)
SelectMode(Off!)
StrNum(Sum;Total)
Average:=Sum/NumRow
NumStr(Ave;2;Average)
Type("The average is   :")
Type(Ave)
```

Unfortunately, this will not work when the total is greater than 999.99. The reason is that results with thousands are inserted into cells with a comma as the thousands separator, and the StrNum command stops converting a string to a number at the first nonnumeric character (other than the decimal point). For example, the resulting string 3,456.12 would be inserted into the variable Sum as 3.

PRODUCING DERIVED COLUMNS

Derived columns created with merge commands have the same limitation as other math calculations: they can include only integer numbers. By using the techniques described above, you can produce derived columns with decimal numbers.

For example, in Chapter 11, you learned how to create a derived column that contained the difference between the client's credit limit and the amount due. To generate this same column with decimal numbers, start a new document, clear all the tab stops, and set new tab stops at 2 and 4 inches. Then create this merge file:

```
{FIELD}1~   {FIELD}11~   {FIELD}12~
{PAGE OFF}{CHAIN MACRO}c:\wpwin\macros\net~
```

Then write the following macro, named Net.wcm. This macro creates a table from the merged document, adds a fourth column, and then inserts the formula (B1–C1), which calculates the difference between the Credit and Due fields.

```
Application(WP;WPWP;Default;"WPWPUS.WCD")
DeleteCharPrevious()
SelectMode(On!)
PosDocTop()
TableConvert(ConvertFrom:TabularColumns!)
Tab()
Tab()
PosLineEnd()
TableOptions(Columns:4)
TableFormula(Formula:"B1–C1")
TableFormula(Copy:Down!;Count:100)
```

The final line of the macro copies the formula down as many as 100 times. Instead of using GetWPData to get and store the number of rows, the macro uses a number large enough to handle an average-size list. WordPerfect will not generate an error if the table has fewer than 100 rows (clients). If there are more than 100 rows in your database, increase the number in the Count parameter.

DESIGNING AN ACCOUNTS RECEIVABLE SYSTEM

In the previous chapters, we have developed a database of client information as well as an invoicing macro and merge file. In a fully automated system, the three fields that directly relate to invoices would be updated every time the client places an order. The amount of the invoice would be added to the Due field and inserted in the LastAmount field. The date of the order would be inserted in the LastOrder field.

We also have a database of prospective clients (developed in Chapter 13), which does not include the Due, LastAmount, and LastOrder fields. However, prospective clients become full-fledged clients when they place their first orders. An ideal system would automatically modify the prospective client record to include the three fields, place the record in the Clients database, and remove the record from the Prospect database. It would do all this without the user inputting whether the order is from a new or established client. The system should make the determination and perform the correct processing for either type of client.

A fully automated system would also keep a running total of orders and the amount of sales tax due for tax purposes. Although this sounds like too much to expect from a word processing program, WordPerfect can perform all these functions for you.

To program this automated accounts receivable system, modify the Invoice.wcm and Calc.wcm macros (from Chapter 12) and create two small auxiliary files. One file will store the running totals of sales and sales tax. The other file will store the extra fields to be added when a prospective client is transferred to the Clients database.

MODIFYING THE INVOICE MACRO

Retrieve the Invoice.wcm file and modify the macro so that it detects which database contains the client record. The modified Invoice macro is shown in Figure 14.2. After editing it, save the macro under the same name.

In the modified Invoice macro, the command

MergeVariableSet("Flag1";"N")

sets the variable Flag1, which will be used to indicate whether the invoice has been placed by a company in the Prospect database or the Clients database. (We call the variable Flag1 because the variable Flag is already used in the

```
Application(WP;WPWP;Default;"WPWPUS.WCD")
MergeVariableSet("Flag1";"N")
Title:="Invoice"
Primary:="Invoice"
Secondary:="Temp"
OnError(Start@)
FileDelete(Secondary)
Label(Start@)
OnError(End@)
OnNotFound(Pro@)
OnCancel(End@)
Go(Main@)

Label(End@)
     Prompt(Title;"You have canceled the procedure or an
            error has occurred.";1;;)
     Pause
     Quit

Label(NotFound@)
     Prompt(Title;"Customer name not found. Please check
            your records";1;;)
     Pause
     Quit

Label(Pro@)
     CloseNoSave(No!)
     Close()
     FileOpen("c:\wpwin\prospect")
     MergeVariableSet("Flag1";"Y")
     PosDocTop()
     OnNotFound(NotFound@)
     Go(Search@)

Label(Main@)
     GetString(Client;Length=20;"Enter the company
               name";Title)
     InsertTypeover(Off!)
     Display(On!)
     FileOpen("c:\wpwin\clients")
     PosDocTop()

Label(Search@)
     SearchText(SearchString:Client;SearchDirection:
               Forward!; SearchScope:DocOnly!)
     Menu(Action;Letter;;;{"Merge"; "Search Again";
          "Cancel"})
     Case(Action;{1;Merge@;2;Search@;3;End@};End@)

Label(Merge@)
     PosLineBegin()
     PosPageNext()
     PosPagePrevious()
     SelectMode(On!)
     PosPageNext()
     FileSave(Secondary)
     SelectMode(Off!)
     CloseNoSave(No!)
     Close()
     MergeExecute(PrimaryFile:Primary;SecondaryFile:
                  Secondary)
```

FIGURE 14.2:

*Invoice macro modified
to distinguish a client
from a prospective client*

Invoice merge file.) Since most invoices will come from current clients, the variable is set to indicate this condition at the start of the macro.

If the company name is not found in the Clients database, the command

```
OnNotFound(Pro@)
```

passes control to the Pro subroutine, which begins a search of the Prospect database:

```
Label(Pro@)
   CloseNoSave(No!)
   Close()
   FileOpen("c:\wpwin\prospect")
   MergeVariableSet("Flag1";"Y")
   PosDocTop()
   OnNotFound(NotFound@)
   Go(Search@)
```

The Pro subroutine closes the Clients database and opens the Prospect database. It then sets the variable Flag1 to Y, indicating that the order is from a prospective client and some additional processing must be performed at the end of the merge. It makes sure the insertion point is at the start of the database, and then begins the Search subroutine, which looks for the record matching the name.

When the client record is located, the user selects Merge from the menu. The record is then placed in the temporary secondary file and merged with the invoice.

CREATING THE AUXILIARY FILES

We need two additional files to make this system work:

◆ Close the document window and create the file to hold the running totals of sales and sales tax. Simply type **0**, press ↵, and type **0**. Save the file under the name **Tots**.

◆ Close the document window and create the file to store the extra fields required when transferring a record from the Prospect database to the Clients database. Press Alt-↵ three times to insert three {END FIELD} codes. Then press Backspace to delete the hard carriage return after the last code. Save the file under the name **Codes**, and close the document window.

REVISING THE CALC MACRO

The rest of the application will be performed by a new, lengthier version of the Calc macro. The macro is shown in Figures 14.3, 14.4, and 14.5. The sections of the macro are shown and described individually to clarify their purposes. When you create the macro, type the text in all three figures into a single file.

```
//Section 1
Application(WP;WPWP;Default;"WPWPUS.WCD")
Prompt("Invoice Program";"Don't touch that dial
    -- wait while records are updated";4;;)
PosLineUp()
TableCalculate()
PosCellNext()
PosCellNext()
PosCellDown()
SelectMode(On!)
PosLineEnd()
GetWPData(Tax;SelectedText!)
SelectMode(Off!)
PosCellDown()
SelectMode(On!)
PosLineEnd()
GetWPData(Tot;SelectedText!)
SelectMode(Off!)
FileOpen("Tots")
SelectMode(On!)
PosLineEnd()
GetWPData(Total;SelectedText!)
SelectMode(Off!)
PosLineDown()
PosLineBegin()
SelectMode(On!)
PosLineEnd()
GetWPData(TaxTot;SelectedText!)
SelectMode(Off!)
PosDocTop()
SelectMode(On!)
PosDocBottom()
DeleteCharPrevious()
SelectMode(Off!)
StrNum(A;Tot)
StrNum(B;Tax)
StrNum(C;Total)
StrNum(D;TaxTot)
D:=D+B
C:=C+A
NumStr(TaxTot;2;D)
NumStr(Total;2;C)
Type(Total)
HardReturn()
Type(TaxTot)
FileSave()
Close()

MergeVariableGet(Flag1;"Flag1")
If(Flag1="Y")
    Go(Proc)
EndIf
```

FIGURE 14.3:

Section of Calc macro that performs processing required for all invoices

```
//Section 2
    FileOpen("Temp")
    SelectMode(On!)
    PosLineEnd()
    GetWPData(Name;SelectedText!)
    SelectMode(Off!)
    PosDocBottom()
    PosLineUp()
    PosLineUp()
    PosLineUp()
    PosLineUp()
    PosLineEnd()
    PosCharPrevious()
    SelectMode(On!)
    PosLineBegin()
    GetWPData(Due;SelectedText!)
    DeleteCharNext()
    SelectMode(Off!)
    StrNum(A;Due)
    StrNum(B;Tot)
    C:=A+B
    NumStr(Due;2;C)
    Type(Due)
    PosLineDown()
    PosLineEnd()
    PosCharPrevious()
    SelectMode(On!)
    PosLineBegin()
    DeleteCharNext()
    SelectMode(Off!)
    Type(Tot)
    PosLineDown()
    PosLineEnd()
    PosCharPrevious()
    SelectMode(On!)
    PosLineBegin()
    DeleteCharNext()
    SelectMode(Off!)
    DateFormat("5/%2/%1")
    DateText()
    FileSave()
    Close()
    FileOpen("Clients")
SearchText(SearchString:Name;SearchDirection:Forward!;
        SearchScope:DocOnly!)
PosLineBegin()
SelectMode(On!)
PosPageNext()
DeleteCharPrevious()
SelectMode(Off!)
FileRetrieve(Filename:"c:\wpwin\temp";AutoDetect:No!;
            InsertIntoDoc:Insert!)
FileSave()
Close()
Quit
```

FIGURE 14.4:

Section of Calc macro that processes an invoice from a current client

Section of Calc macro that processes an invoice from a prospective client

```
//Section 3
Label(Pro@)

FileOpen("Clients")
PosDocBottom()
FileRetrieve(Filename:"c:\wpwin\temp";AutoDetect:No!;
            InsertIntoDoc:Insert!)
SelectMode(On!)
PosLineEnd()
GetWPData(Name;SelectedText!)
SelectMode(Off!)
PosDocBottom()
PosLineUp()
PosLineUp()
PosLineEnd()
HardReturn()
FileRetrieve(Filename:"c:\wpwin\codes";AutoDetect:No!;
            InsertIntoDoc:Insert!)
Type(Tot)
PosLineDown()
PosLineBegin()
Type(Tot)
PosLineDown()
PosLineBegin()
DateFormat("5/%2/%1")
DateText()
FileSave()
CloseNoSave(No!)
Close()
FileOpen("Prospect")
SearchText(SearchString:Name;SearchDirection:Forward!;
            SearchScope:DocOnly!)
PosLineBegin()
SelectMode(On!)
PosPageNext()
DeleteCharPrevious()
SelectMode(Off!)
FileSave()
Close()
```

Common Processing

The first section of the macro (Figure 14.3) performs tasks that are required regardless of the client. The first three lines are the same as the original Calc macro, with the addition of a prompt to let the user know that the process might take time (depending on the client). These place the insertion point in the table and then calculate the item totals, sales tax, and grand total.

The next lines position the insertion point in the cell containing the calculated sales tax, select it, and insert the amount into the variable Tax. Next, the macro moves the insertion point to the cell containing the grand total, selects the amount, and stores it in the variable Tot.

The macro opens the Tots file and stores the first and second lines of the file in the variables Total and TaxTot, respectively. The text in the Tots file is then selected and deleted.

Since the Selected! parameter deals with string characters, all the values must be converted to numbers before any calculations can be performed. This is accomplished by the lines

```
StrNum(A;Tot)
StrNum(B;Tax)
StrNum(C;Total)
StrNum(D;TaxTot)
```

The total and tax from the invoice are then added to the previous running totals in the lines

```
D:=D+B
C:=C+A
```

Before the values can be inserted into the document with the Type command, they are converted back to strings with the commands

```
NumStr(TaxTot;2;D)
NumStr(Total;2;C)
```

Then the macro enters the values on two separate lines and saves the file with the commands

```
Type(Total)
HardReturn()
Type(TaxTot)
FileSave()
Close()
```

The macro next accesses the variable Flag1. If Flag1 contains Y, the order was placed by a prospective client, and control is transferred to the subroutine in the third section of the macro. Otherwise, the commands in the second section are performed.

Client Processing

The second section of the Calc macro (Figure 14.4) is performed when the order is placed by a current client. The client's record in the Temp file is a duplicate of the record in the Clients database. The macro changes the record in Temp and then replaces the record in Clients with the updated one.

This section opens the temporary database, selects the first line (the company name), and places it in the variable Name. Later, the company name is used to search for the customer's record in the Clients database.

The macro then moves the insertion point to the first line that must be changed (the Due field). It stores the client's current amount due in the variable Due, then erases the current value in the field without deleting the {END FIELD} code, with the commands

```
PosLineEnd()
PosCharNext()
SelectMode(On!)
PosLineBegin()
GetWPData(Due;SelectedText!)
DeleteCharNext()
SelectMode(Off!)
```

It then converts the values to numbers, adds them together, and inserts the result back in the record as a string, using the commands

```
StrNum(A;Due)
StrNum(B;Tot)
C:=A+B
NumStr(Due;2;C)
Type(Due)
```

The next series of lines deletes the last-order amount and inserts the total of the current invoice. The macro then deletes the last-order date and inserts the current system date. Before inserting the date with the DateText( ) code, the command

```
DateFormat("5/%2/%1")
```

sets the format to match the way that dates have been entered: *YY/MM/DD*. The temporary file is saved and the window is closed.

Next the macro opens the Clients database and searches for the client's record. Since it stored the first line of the record in the variable Name, it will get an exact match through the SearchText command. The record is deleted, then the record in Temp is retrieved and inserted in its place. The modified Clients database is saved, and this section of the macro ends.

Prospective Client Processing

The final section of the macro (Figure 14.5) is performed when a prospective client places its first invoice. It works as follows:

◆ Opens the Clients database.

◆ Inserts the prospective client's record from Temp.

◆ Stores the client's name in the variable Name.

◆ Moves the insertion point to the line following the last field in the record and inserts a blank line.

◆ Retrieves the Codes file, which adds the {END FIELD} codes that we need for the Due, LastAmount, and LastOrder fields.

◆ Places the value of Tot, which is the total of the client's first invoice to date, in both the Due and LastAmount fields and inserts the date.

◆ Saves the Clients database.

◆ Opens the Prospect database.

◆ Searches for the prospective client record.

◆ Deletes the located record.

◆ Saves the modified Prospect database.

MANAGING FORM DOCUMENTS AND MACROS

Suppose that you have a number of database reports that you frequently print and several macros that perform database-maintenance functions. You can automate the report-creation and database-management processes so that they can be performed by someone who is not familiar with the technical aspects.

DESIGNING MENUS

One way to automate reports and maintenance functions is through a macro that displays a menu of available reports and data files. The user selects the desired files and then executes the merge operation.

Figure 14.6 shows a macro for selecting primary and secondary files. It assumes you have the three primary files Contacts.mrg, Orders.mrg, and Leads.mrg, as well as a secondary file named Vendors. The macro merges the

FIGURE 14.6:

Macro for merging files
from a menu

```
//Merge menu

Application(WP;WPWP;Default;"WPWPUS.WCD")
OnError(End@)
Title:="Merge Menu"
Prompt(Title;"Select the primary file to merge";2;0;0)
Menu(PFile;Letter;;; ("Contact list"; "Order list";
    "Lead sheet"))
EndPrompt
Prompt(Title;"Select the database file to merge";2;0;0)
Menu(SFile;Letter;;;("Clients"; "Vendors"))
EndPrompt
Case(PFile;(1;Contacts;2;Orders@;3;Leads@);End@)
Label(Memo@)
        Primary:="contacts.mrg"
Go(Sec@)

Label(Letter@)
        Primary:="orders.mrg"
Go(Sec@)

Label(Invoice@)
        Primary:="leads.mrg"

Label(Sec@)

Case(SFile;(1;Clients@;2;Vendors@);End@)
Label(Clients@)
        Secondary:="clients"
Go(Merge@)

Label(Vendors@)
        Secondary:="vendors"

Label(Merge@)
        MergeExecute(PrimaryFile:Primary;SecondaryFile:
                        Secondary)
        Prompt(Title;"Select the option";2;0;0)
        Menu(Action;Letter;;; ("Print"; "Save"; "Display"))
        EndPrompt
        Case(Action;(1;Print@;2;Save@;3;End@);End@)
        Label(Print@)
            PrintFull()
        Go(End@)

        Label(Save@)
            GetString(Name;Length=8;"Enter file name";Title)
            FileSave(Name)

Label(End@)
```

files, and then lets the user select to print the resulting document, save it to a disk file, or just display it on the screen. A prompt is used with the menu to explain that some action is necessary. Create this macro and save it under the name **Merge.wcm**.

You can further automate the process by designing a central menu that includes all database options. The macro shown in Figure 14.7 includes the

```
//Database options menu

Application(WP;WPWP;Default;"WPWPUS.WCD")
OnError(Quit@)
Title:="Main Menu"
Prompt(Title;"Select a function to perform:";2;0;0)
Menu(Main;Letter;;; ("Add clients"; "Delete clients";
    "Check for duplicates"; "Sort database"; "Select
    record"; "Add prospect"; "Merge records"; "Invoice";
    "Client letter"; "Quit"))
EndPrompt
Case(Main;{1;Append@;2;Delete@;3;Dups@;4;Sort@;5;Select@;6;
    Prospect@;7;Merge@;8;Invoice@;9;Letter@};Quit@)
Label(Append@)
    Chain("c:\wpwin\macros\Append")
Go(Quit@)

Label(Delete@)
    Chain("c:\wpwin\macros\Del")
Go(Quit@)

Label(Dups@)
    Chain("c:\wpwin\macros\Dup")
Go(Quit@)

Label(Sort@)
    Chain("c:\wpwin\macros\Sort")
Go(Quit@)

Label(Select@)
    Chain("c:\wpwin\macros\Select")
Go(Quit@)

Label(Prospect@)
    Chain("c:\wpwin\macros\Proadd")
Go(Quit@)

Label(Merge@)
    Chain("c:\wpwin\macros\Merge")
Go(Quit@)

Label(Invoice@)
    Chain("c:\wpwin\macros\Invoice")
Go(Quit@)

Label(Letter@)
    Chain("c:\wpwin\macros\Letter")

Label(Quit@)
```

options to add and delete records, check for duplicates, send a form letter to a prospective client, and print an invoice. It also includes an option for merging primary and secondary files.

The Chain command executes another macro when the current one ends. After a function is selected and performed, the macro ends. The macro must end normally for the Chain command to be performed.

To nest a macro, use the Run command, such as

```
Run("c:\wpwin\macros\append")
```

This executes the macro when the command is performed, without waiting until the macro ends. When the nested macro is completed, control returns to the calling macro.

The ideal application would always return to this central menu. However, because the menu options here perform a variety of macros and merge operations, it is not as simple as using the Run command in place of Chain and repeating the menu until the user selects Quit. In some cases, WordPerfect would return to the Main menu while a merge was still in progress and the screen would contain the merge output as well as the menu.

Another alternative is to chain back to the Main menu after each function. For example, edit the End subroutine in the Merge menu to appear as

```
Label(End@)
   Chain("c:\wpwin\macros\main")
```

Note that the Del, Dup, and Invoice macros leave the resulting file on the screen so that the user can decide whether to save the file. Add a subroutine to each macro that prompts the user to either save or abandon the changes before chaining back to the Main menu. The subroutine would appear like this:

```
Prompt(Title;"Select the option";2;0;0)
Menu(Action;Letter;;;{"Save"; "Abandon"})
EndPrompt
Case(Action;{1;Save@;2;Abandon@};Abandon@)

Label(Save@)
   GetString(Name;Length=8;"Enter file name";Title)
   FileSave(Name)

Label(Abandon@)
   CloseNoSave(No!)
   Close()
   Chain("c:/wpwin/macros/main")
```

If you use the /M- switch and name this macro in the command line when you start WordPerfect, the menu will appear automatically when WordPerfect is loaded (see Chapter 8).

ADDING DATABASE FUNCTIONS TO A BUTTON BAR

Another way to make your database-management and invoice macros easily accessible is to add them to a Button Bar. A Button Bar also provides a visual reminder of the functions and macros that are available. With the bar displayed, the user does not need to remember the macro name or scroll through the Play Macro dialog box to perform a function.

Create a Button Bar for database functions in the same way you add buttons for templates. See Chapter 8 for details.

DESIGNING DATABASE APPLICATIONS

Although WordPerfect cannot replace a dedicated database program, you can create some remarkably robust applications with macros and merge files. A WordPerfect-based application may require quite a bit of programming—work you might not have to perform in a database program—but it does have some advantages.

Because the application is based in WordPerfect, you can use all of WordPerfect's editing and formatting functions to create eye-catching and effective form documents and reports. You can combine your database with graphics, tables, outlines, and other document-oriented features not available in traditional database programs.

Before designing your own applications, make backup copies of any databases, documents, macros, and merge files that you may be editing or accessing. If you accidentally erase a file or make it inoperable, the original will still be available.

Always test your macros from a blank document window to avoid editing or closing a file that you want to maintain. Then test them again from a document containing sample text. Unless the macro is designed to edit or insert text into the current document, design your macros so that they open a new window, perform their functions, then close the window without affecting other windows or documents.

While you can create some useful applications, do not expect them to run with the speed you would expect from a database manager or from an application written in Pascal, BASIC, or some other computer language. Keep in mind that your macros are running on top of, or in addition to, WordPerfect itself.

CHAPTER 15

Setting up read-only files
Automatically naming and saving files
Creating a document-management
system

Managing Your Document Files

ave you ever searched for a disk file, given up, retyped it, and then later accidentally stumbled across the original? To avoid this and similar time-wasting and frustrating experiences, establish an efficient document-management system, consisting of standard procedures for naming, saving, and retaining documents.

This chapter describes a complete document-management application that uses WordPerfect macros. You will also learn how to record Windows macros to overcome the limitations of WordPerfect macros for file management.

RETAINING THE DEFAULT DIRECTORY

When you are working with files in several directories, you may want to maintain WPWIN as the default directory and just access other directories for specific documents. However, by default, the Change Default Dir option is selected in the Open and Save As dialog boxes.

With Change Default Dir turned on, when you select a new directory from the Directories list box, it becomes the default directory used in these dialog boxes during the remainder of your WordPerfect session. To list files in another directory, you must select it in the Directories list box. Turn this option off to keep WPWIN as the default directory.

MANAGING FILES WITH WORDPERFECT

WordPerfect for Windows provides a number of ways to manage your files. You can work with files directly from the File Open and File Retrieve dialog boxes, or you can use the more powerful File Manager for working with disks, directories, and files.

Many file-management functions are available through the Options drop-down list in the File Open and File Retrieve dialog boxes. Options include copying, deleting, moving, renaming, and finding files. This list provides a convenient way of managing files without running the Windows or WordPerfect File Manager. All the options, excluding finding files, can also be performed by using macro commands.

The WordPerfect File Manager is a powerful application. It provides all the capabilities of the Windows File Manager, as well as a viewer for displaying a file's contents.

PROTECTING A FILE BY MARKING IT READ-ONLY

To prevent templates, merge files, and other critical documents from being edited or deleted, use the WordPerfect File Manager to designate the file as Read-Only.

Select File ➤ File Manager, choose the file's drive and directory, and highlight its name. Then select File ➤ Change Attributes (Ctrl-A) to display the Change File Attributes dialog box. Select Read Only in the Attributes section, and then choose Change.

DEVELOPING A DOCUMENT-MANAGEMENT SYSTEM

You need to know two things to locate a document: its name and its location on the disk. Therefore, to develop a document-management system, you must design a method for naming files and placing them in an appropriate directory.

To ensure that files are stored where you can find them, create a separate directory for each category of your files. For example, suppose the three executives in your office have the last names Chesin, Nestle, and Smith. Create a directory named CHESIN to store Ms. Chesin's files, a directory called NESTLE to hold Mr. Nestle's documents, and a directory named SMITH for Ms. Smith's files. You would then know immediately which directory to look in to find a document written by a particular executive.

Selecting appropriate file names requires some thought. Some organizations number each file consecutively but keyed to the creator by initials. Ms. Smith's files are SM101, SM102, and so forth; Mr. Chesin's are CH101 and CH102. Unfortunately, this naming convention does not make a file easy to identify. Few persons could remember the contents of SM101 while working on SM305.

The alternative to a numbering system is to use distinctive file names. However, as your inventory of documents grows, it becomes difficult to think of a unique and meaningful name for each document. After a while, the file names become as cryptic as file numbers. A solution is to create a special index to help locate documents.

The document-management system we will develop here uses file numbers and an index to help locate documents. The system will perform the following tasks:

◆ Maintain a file containing the last numbers used for each executive.

◆ Automatically assign the next consecutive number to a file.

◆ Save the file in the proper directory.

◆ Maintain an index of files in each directory.

◆ Allow the user to select and open a file in a specific directory by matching a search string against the file name or description in the index.

◆ Allow the user to search all directories for a key word or phrase.

◆ Allow the user to select and open a file from the list displayed after a search of all directories.

◆ Allow the user to delete a file and its entry in the index.

◆ Display a dialog box with file-management options.

PREPARING FOR THE SYSTEM

You need several directories and files on your disk in order to enter and run the macros to see how the document-management system works. Use the

WordPerfect File Manager to create the sample directories:

1. Start WordPerfect and select File ➤ File Manager to run the File Manager program.

2. Select File ➤ Create Directory.

3. Type **C:\CHESIN**, and then select OK.

4. Use the same technique to create the **C:\NESTLE** and **C:\SMITH** directories.

5. Select File ➤ Exit to return to WordPerfect.

6. To create the file that will store the last file numbers for each of the three executives, type the following in a blank document window:

101
101
101

7. Save the file as **Docnum** and then close the file.

8. To create blank index files in each of the directories, start with a blank document window. Then select File ➤ Save As (F3) three separate times and save the empty file under the names **C:\CHESIN\CHFiles**, **C:\NESTLE\NEFiles**, and **C:\SMITH\SMFiles**.

9. Close the document window.

NAMING AND SAVING FILES

The macro shown in Figure 15.1 numbers and saves files, creates an index of files, and maintains the file numbers. Create the macro and save it under the name **Savefile.wcm** in the MACROS subdirectory.

This macro starts by displaying a menu with the names of the three executives and the option Cancel. If the user selects Cancel, the macro ends. Otherwise, it opens the file Docnum, which contains the document numbers of the last files saved under the system. The numbers are in the same order as the names in the menu; that is, the first number represents the last document saved for Chesin, the second number is the last document saved for Nestle, and the third number is the last document saved for Smith.

In the For loop, the PosLineDown command moves the insertion point to the appropriate number for the selected person. If the first person in the menu is selected, however, the insertion will already be on the appropriate

```
//Save file
Application(WP;WPWP;Default;"WPWPUS.WCD")
Display(Off!)
OnError(End@)
OnNotFound(End@)
Title:="File Save Program"
Menu(Person;Letter;;; {"Chesin"; "Nestle";"Smith"; "Cancel"})
If(Person=4)  Go(End@)  EndIf
FileOpen("DOCNUM")
Person:=Person-1
For(Lines;1;Lines<=Person;Lines+1)
     PosLineDown()
EndFor
SelectMode(On!)
PosLineEnd()
GetWPData(LastNum;SelectedText!)
DeleteCharPrevious()
SelectMode(Off!)
StrNum(NewNum;LastNum)
NewNum:=NewNum+1
NumStr(Name;2;NewNum)
Type(Name)
FileSave()
Close()
Person:=Person+1
If(Person=1) Dir:="c:\chesin\"
     Init:="CH"
     Else
     If(Person=2) Dir:="c:\nestle\"
     Init:="NE"
     Else
     If(Person=3) Dir:="c:\smith\"
     Init:="SM"
     EndIf
     EndIf
EndIf

FileName:=Dir+Init+Name
FileSave(FileName)
Close()

FileName:=Dir+Init+"Files"
FileOpen(FileName)
PosDocBottom()
GetString(Purpose;Length=30;"Enter the purpose";Title)
Type(Init)
Type(Name)
Tab()
Type(Purpose)
HardReturn()
FileSave()
Close()
Label(End@)
```

FIGURE 15.1:

Macro to name and save files and maintain a file index

line. To take care of this, the variable Person is reduced by 1, so the loop will execute 0 times if the first person in the menu is selected.

The macro selects the text on the line, converts it to a number, increments the value by 1, then converts it back to a string. The text must be a string in order to be written back into the document and used for later commands in the macro. The new number is written to the file in the same relative position, and then the file is saved and closed.

The variable Person is now incremented by 1. This allows the If commands that follow to be consistent with a similar series of commands in the macro to retrieve a file. Using similar modules in macros makes them easier to understand and change later.

The If commands determine the directory and the beginning initials of the file name. These are concatenated to the string storing the file number in the command

FileName:=Dir+Init+Name

Concatenation combines several strings into one. For example, if the user selects Chesin from the list, the variable Dir is assigned the string C:\CHESIN\ and Init is assigned CH. If the variable Name is 102, then Dir+Init+Name results in C:\CHESIN\CH102, the full path and name of the file. This is assigned to the variable FileName, which is then used in the FileSave command to write the file to the correct directory. The Save As dialog box appears with the Filename text box already completed. The user selects Save to continue the macro.

The variables Dir and Init are then concatenated with the word Files to create the path and name of the index file, such as C:\CHESIN\CHFiles. The macro opens the file and moves the insertion point to the end of the list.

The GetString command then requests the purpose of the file. The user should enter a description or date that helps identify the document, such as the entries shown in the sample index file in Figure 15.2.

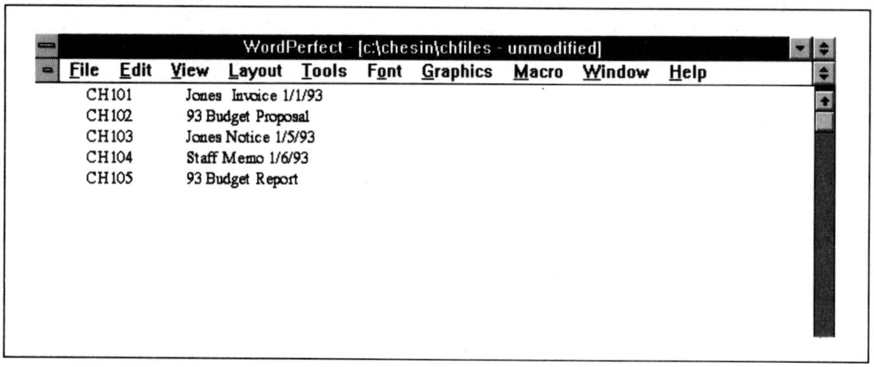

FIGURE 15.2:

Sample index file

```
WordPerfect - [c:\chesin\chfiles - unmodified]
File   Edit   View   Layout   Tools   Font   Graphics   Macro   Window   Help

CH101      Jones Invoice 1/1/93
CH102      93 Budget Proposal
CH103      Jones Notice 1/5/93
CH104      Staff Memo 1/6/93
CH105      93 Budget Report
```

Our macro limits the string to 30 characters. You can change the parameter to allow longer strings, but they must be short enough to ensure that the description does not word wrap to the next line. This is because it will be necessary to select the file number at the start of the line in another macro.

The macro enters the file number into the index, inserts a tab, and then adds the description. The carriage return moves the insertion point to the next line so that the file is ready for the next document entry, and then the index is saved and closed and the macro ends.

Printing File Names on Documents

You might want to add the file name to the end of the document so you can identify it later. You can do this in the Savefile.wcm macro by adding these commands just before the document is saved, before the FileSave(FileName) command:

```
PosDocBottom()
HardReturn()
Type(Name)
```

The carriage return ensures that the file number is not on the same line as the last line of text. If you want more space between the text and the file number, include several hard return commands. Unfortunately, the carriage returns could result in WordPerfect inserting a page break and printing the file name on its own page. Also, only the number of the file appears, with no initials indicating the author or directory in which the file is stored.

As an alternative, insert the complete file name, without the path, in a footer on the last page of the document. To do this, add these lines to the Savefile.wcm macro, just before the FileSave(FileName) command:

```
Note:=Init+Name
PosDocBottom()
PosPageTop()
HeaderFooter(Create!;FooterB!)
Type(Note)
Close(Save:Yes!)
Menu(Result;Letter;;; {"Print"; "Do Not Print"})
If(Result=1) PrintFull() EndIf
```

The user's initials are concatenated with the file number and stored in the variable Note. The insertion point is placed at the start of the last page, and then a footer is created with the file name. The macro also gives you the opportunity to print the document before it is saved.

OPENING INDEXED FILES

The macro shown in Figure 15.3 simplifies the process of opening a file. Type the macro and save it under the name **Getfile.wcm** in the MACROS subdirectory.

```
//Get file
Application(WP;WPWP;Default;"WPWPUS.WCD")
OnError(End@)
OnNotFound(End@)
OnCancel(End@)
Title:="File Get Program"

Menu(Person;Letter;;; ("Chesin"; "Nestle";"Smith"; "Cancel"))
If(Person=1) Dir:="c:\chesin\"
     Init:="CH"
     Else
     If(Person=2) Dir:="c:\nestle\"
     Init:="NE"
     Else
     If(Person=3) Dir:="c:\smith\"
     Init:="SM"
     Else
     If(Person=4) Go(End@)
     EndIf
     EndIf
     EndIf
EndIf
FileName:=Dir+Init+"Files"
FileOpen(FileName)
GetString(Find;Length=30;"Enter the string";Title)
InsertTypeover(Off!)
Display(On!)
PosDocTop()

Label(Search@)
SearchText(SearchString:Find;SearchDirection:Forward!;Search
          Scope:DocOnly!)
Menu(Action;Letter;;; ("Open"; "Search Again"; "Cancel"))
Case(Action;(1;Open@;2;Search@;3;End@);End@)

Label(Open@)
PosLineBegin()
SelectMode(On!)
PosWordNext()
GetWPData(Name;SelectedText!)
SelectMode(Off!)
CloseNoSave(No!)
Close()
Filename:=Dir+Name

FileOpen(FileName)

Label(End@)
```

FIGURE 15.3:

*Macro to open a file
listed in the index*

The macro lets you select the directory name, then determines the path and beginning initials of the files in the index. It next opens the appropriate index file and uses a GetString command for the input of a search string. The user can enter the file's number or a key word or phrase used in the description.

When each occurrence of the string is located by the Search command, a menu appears with the options Open, Search Again, and Cancel. When the user selects Open, the insertion point moves to the start of the line, and the first word—the file name—is selected and saved in the variable Name. The macro then closes the index, concatenates the variables Dir and Name, and opens the correct file.

SELECTING AN INDEXED FILE

If a match is not located by the Search command in the Getfile macro, the index will remain on the screen. To open one of the files in the list, use the macro shown in Figure 15.4. Type the macro and save it with the name **Pickfile.wcm** in the MACROS subdirectory.

```
//Get file from index shown on the screen by failed search

Application(WP;WPWP;Default;"WPWPUS.WCD")
OnError(End@)
OnNotFound(End@)
OnCancel(End@)
Title:="File Get Program"
GetWPData(Pathname;Path!)
Prompt(Title;"Place insertion point in file line and press
        Enter";1;;)
PauseKey(Enter!)
PosLineBegin()
SelectMode(On!)
PosWordNext()
GetWPData(Name;SelectedText!)
SelectMode(Off!)
FileName:=Pathname+Name
FileOpen(FileName)

Label(End@)
```

FIGURE 15.4:

Macro to open a file listed in the index after a failed search

The macro determines the file's directory by using the GetWPData command and the Path system variable. It then prompts the user to place the insertion point in the line of the file to open and press ↵. It saves the file's name in the variable Name, and then concatenates the path and name to open the file.

SEARCHING MULTIPLE FILES

In some instances, the user might not know the author of the document, or there may be documents in several directories that relate to the same client or subject. In these cases, the user will want to scan the index files in each of the directories and display a list of files containing the search phrase (such as a name or date). A macro for this purpose is shown in Figure 15.5. Enter the macro and save it under the name **Search.wcm** in the MACROS subdirectory.

The macro requests the input of a search string (the file number or any text in the description), and then sets up a Not Found error trap that passes control to the subroutine Next. The macro then opens a new file and inserts a sentence and two carriage returns into the clipboard. The sentence serves as a heading for the final output, showing the contents of the search string. This process also clears other text that may have been in the clipboard from a previous operation.

The macro assigns to the variable Filename the path and name of the first index file to be searched. The index file is opened, and control is passed to the subroutine Search.

The Search subroutine locates each occurrence of the search string in the index file and then appends the line containing the phrase to the clipboard. The EditAppend command adds selected text to the clipboard without deleting its existing contents. When the string is not found in the file, the OnNot-Found error trap takes effect, sending the macro to the Next subroutine. Here, the index file is closed and the Return command passes control back to the body of the macro, following the Call(Search@).

The entire process is repeated for the other directories. Note that before searching the final directory, the OnNotFound error trap is changed to send control to the End subroutine. No Call(Search@) command is needed after the final directory is named because the subroutine will be performed anyway. When the search string is not located in the last directory, the End subroutine closes the index file and then pastes the contents of the clipboard into the document window.

An example of the output of this macro is shown in Figure 15.6. In this case, all the index files were searched for references to Jones.

SELECTING FROM THE FILE LIST

The macro shown in Figure 15.7 opens one of the files listed by the Search macro. Type the macro and save it under the name **Fromlist.wcm** in the MACROS subdirectory.

```
//Search all directories

Application(WP;WPWP;Default;"WPWPUS.WCD")
OnError(End@)
OnCancel(Stop@)
Display(On!)
Title:="File Get Program"
GetString(Find;Length=30;"Enter the file name or search
          string";Title)
InsertTypeover(Off!)
OnNotFound(Next@)
FileNew()
Type("List of files relating to ")
Type(Find)
HardReturn()
HardReturn()
PosDocTop()
SelectMode(On!)
PosDocBottom()
EditCut()
SelectMode(Off!)
FileName:="c:\chesin\chfiles"
FileOpen(FileName)
Call(Search@)
FileName:="C:\nestle\nefiles"
FileOpen(FileName)
Call(Search@)
OnNotFound(End@)
FileName:="c:\smith\smfiles"
FileOpen(FileName)

Label(Search@)
SearchText(SearchString:Find;SearchDirection:Forward!;Search
          Scope:DocOnly!)
PosLineBegin()
PosLineBegin()
SelectMode(On!)
PosLineDown()
EditAppend()
SelectMode(Off!)
Go(Search@)

Label(End@)
     CloseNoSave(No!)
     Close()
     EditPaste()
     PosDocTop()
     Quit

Label(Next@)
     CloseNoSave(No!)
     Close()
     Return

Label(Stop@)
```

FIGURE 15.5:

*Macro to search all
index files for a
matching string*

This macro is similar to Pickfile.wcm, except that it determines the directory path. The initials in the file name are stored in the variable Init, and then the macro selects the path in a series of If statements. The path and file name are concatenated, and the file is opened.

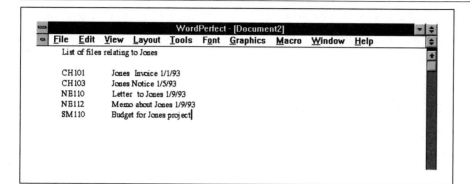

FIGURE 15.6:

*Sample report displayed
by Search macro*

```
//Get file from a search of all directories

Application(WP;WPWP;Default;"WPWPUS.WCD")
OnError(End@)
OnNotFound(End@)
OnCancel(End@)
Title:="File Get Program"
Prompt(Title;"Place insertion point in file line and press
     Enter";1;;)
PauseKey(Enter!)
PosLineBegin()
SelectMode(On!)
PosWordNext()
GetWPData(Name;SelectedText!)
SelectMode(Off!)
SubStr(Init;1;2;Name)
If(Init="CH") Dir:="c:\chesin\"
     Else
     If(Init="NE") Dir:="c:\nestle\"
     Else
     If(Init="SM") Dir:="c:\smith\"
     EndIf
     EndIf
EndIf
FileName:=Dir+Name
FileOpen(FileName)

Label(End@)
```

FIGURE 15.7:

*Macro to open a file
from the list displayed
by the Search macro*

DELETING AN INDEXED FILE

Deleting an indexed file involves removing the file itself, as well as deleting
its listing in the index (to prevent anyone from selecting it accidentally). The
macro to accomplish this task is similar to the Getfile.wcm macro.

First, make a copy of the Getfile macro. Select File ➤ Open, choose the MACROS directory, and highlight Getfile.wcm. Then pull down the Options list and select Copy to display the dialog box shown in Figure 15.8.

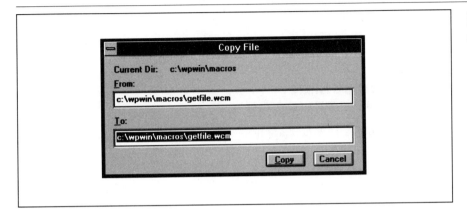

FIGURE 15.8:

Copy File dialog box

The file name in the To text box is already selected. Press → to remove the highlighting, and then press Backspace to delete the name Getfile.wcm (do not delete the backslash that precedes the file name). Type the name of the new macro, **Erase.wcm**, and select Copy or press ↵. Select Cancel to return to the document window.

Next open the Erase.wcm file in the MACROS directory. Edit the macro, from the Menu command to the end, to appear like this:

```
Menu(Action;Letter;;; {"Delete"; "Search Again"; "Cancel"})
Case(Action;{1;Delete@;2;Search@;3;End@};End@)

Label(Delete@)
PosLineBegin()
SelectMode(On!)
PosWordNext()
GetWPData(Name;SelectedText!)
SelectMode(Off!)
PosLineBegin()
SelectMode(On!)
PosLineDown()
DeleteCharPrevious()
SelectMode(Off!)
FileSave()
Close()
```

```
Filename:=Dir+Name
FileDelete(FileName)
Label(End@)
```

Save the edited macro and close the document window.

The macro will select and delete the index line, then save the edited index file before deleting the document itself.

USING THE DOCUMENT-MANAGEMENT APPLICATION

The document-management application includes the following files, stored in the MACROS subdirectory:

◆ Savefile.wcm

◆ Getfile.wcm

◆ Pickfile.wcm

◆ Search.wcm

◆ Fromlist.wcm

◆ Erase.wcm

RUNNING THE MACROS

One way to use the application is to run the appropriate macro:

◆ To save a file, run the Savefile macro, select the directory, and enter a brief description.

◆ To open a file in a known directory, run the Getfile macro. Select the directory and enter the file number or a key word or phrase used in the description. When the listing for that file appears, select Open from the menu. If a match isn't found, read over all the descriptions. If the file you want is listed, run the Pickfile macro, place the insertion point in the line, and then press ↵.

◆ To list files that have a key word or phrase in common, run the Search macro. Type the search string, and then wait until the list is displayed. To open a file from the displayed list, run the Fromlist macro. Place the insertion point in the listing for the file and press ↵.

◆ To delete a file, run the Erase macro. Select the directory and enter the file number or a key word or phrase used in the description. When the listing for that file appears, select Delete from the menu. Word-Perfect will delete the listing, save the index, and delete the file from the disk.

USING A BUTTON BAR OR KEYSTROKES

To make the document-management macros even more accessible, add them to a Button Bar (see Chapter 8). If you prefer using the keyboard (or do not have a mouse), you can copy each of the macros to a new file, giving them a Ctrl-Shift keystroke name. For example, to assign them to Ctrl-Shift-1 through Ctrl-Shift-5, give the macros the following file names:

MACRO	COPY TO
Savefile	Ctrlsft1.wcm
Getfile	Ctrlsft2.wcm
Pickfile	Ctrlsft3.wcm
Search	Ctrlsft4.wcm
Fromlist	Ctrlsft5.wcm
Erase	Ctrlsft6.wcm

You can copy the files from the DOS prompt or from the File Open dialog box. To run one of the macros, press Ctrl-Shift and the assigned key.

CREATING A FILE MANAGEMENT MENU

The macro shown in Figure 15.9 provides the menu of file-management options shown in Figure 15.10. It includes options for opening a file, printing a list of documents in a user's index file, and searching all the index files for a matching string. Create the macro and save it under the name **Docman.wcm**, or **Ctrlsftd.wcm** if you want to run it using a key combination.

Note the syntax of the FileDelete, FileCopy, and FileMove commands. FileMove can also be used to rename a file; give the New string variable a different name but the same path as the source file.

The Direct subroutine opens a user's index file, prints the variable Dir at the top of the page, and then gives the user the option of printing the directory.

```
//Document management
Application(WP;WPWP;Default;"WPWPUS.WCD")
Title:="Document Management"
Label(Main@)
Menu(Result;Letter;;;
     ("Open an indexed file";
     "Delete an indexed file";
     "Erase a non-indexed file";
     "Copy a file";
     "Rename or move a file";
     "Print an index";
     "Search for a subject";
     "Quit this menu"))

Case(Result;{1;Open@;2;Delete@;3;Erase@;4;Copy@;5;Move@;6;
     Direct@;7;Search@;8;End@};End@)

Label(Open@)
     Chain("c:\wpwin\macros\getfile")
Go(End@)

Label(Delete@)
     Chain("c:\wpwin\macros\erase")
Go(End@)

Label(Erase@)
     GetString(Name;Length=35;"Enter the file to delete";
               Title)
     FileDelete(Name)
Go(End@)

Label(Copy@)
     GetString(Source;Length=35;"Enter the file to copy";
               Title)
     GetString(New;Length=35;"Enter the new path and name";
               Title)
     FileCopy(Source;New)
Go(End@)

Label(Move@)
     GetString(Source;Length=35;"Enter the file to copy";
               Title)
     GetString(New;Length=35;"Enter the new path and name";
               Title)
     FileMove(Source;New)
Go(End@)

Label(Direct@)
Menu(Person;Letter;;; ("Chesin"; "Nestle";"Smith"; "Cancel"})
If(Person=1) Dir:="c:\chesin\CH"
     Else
     If(Person=2) Dir:="c:\nestle\NE"
     Else
     If(Person=3) Dir:="c:\smith\SM"
     Else
     If(Person=4) Go(Main@)
     EndIf
     EndIf
     EndIf
```

```
EndIf
FileName:=Dir+"Files"
FileOpen(FileName)
PosDocTop()
HardReturn()
HardReturn()
PosDocTop()
Type(Dir)
Display(On!)
PosDocBottom()
PosDocTop()
Menu(Result;Letter;;; ("Print"; "Do Not Print"))
If(Result=1)  PrintFull()  EndIf
Go(End@)

Label(Search@)
      Chain("c:\wpwin\macros\search")

Label(End@)
```

FIGURE 15.9:

*File management
macro (continued)*

```
A Open an indexed file
B Delete an indexed file
C Erase a non-indexed file
D Copy a file
E Rename or move a file
F Print an index
G Search for a subject
H Quit this menu
```

FIGURE 15.10:

File Management menu

The commands

HardReturn()
HardReturn()
PosDocTop()
Type(Dir)

insert two blank lines at the beginning of the document and enter the directory. Then the commands

Display(On!)
PosDocBottom()
PosDocTop()

ensure that the document is displayed on the screen before the menu appears, giving the user the option to print the index.

The third, fourth, and fifth menu options are designed for files not listed in the file indexes. For example, the Copy a File option will not change the copied file's index listing. If you want this capability, create a separate macro.

AUTOMATING OPERATIONS WITH WINDOWS MACROS

If you do not use a file-indexing system similar to the one illustrated in the Savefile and Getfile macros, you can still locate files with one of WordPerfect's Find options. Use the Options drop-down list in the File Open dialog box or the WordPerfect File Manager.

Unfortunately, you cannot use a WordPerfect macro to automate a Find operation or to perform any specific task from within File Manager. Word-Perfect does not have a Product command that executes the Find function in the Options list. Also, although the command

FileManager()

will start the File Manager from within WordPerfect, the macro will be suspended and will not continue until you return to the WordPerfect window.

If you want to automate a Find or File Manager operation, you must use a Windows macro—keystrokes and mouse actions recorded by Windows itself. A Windows macro is defined as part of the Windows environment.

RECORDING A WINDOWS MACRO

You create a Windows macro with the Recorder accessory in the Windows Accessories group. Windows macros can only be recorded; they cannot be written or edited. You can record mouse actions, but recorded keystrokes are more reliable.

Follow these steps to create a macro to find files:

1. Press Ctrl-Esc to display the Task List, select Program Manager, and then choose Switch To.

2. Open the Accessories group window and run the Recorder application.

3. Press Ctrl-Esc, select WordPerfect, then Switch To. Switching back to Word-Perfect allows you to return to it again directly from the Recorder.

4. Press Alt-Tab to switch back to the Recorder.

5. Select Macro ➤ Record to display the dialog box shown in Figure 15.11.

6. Type **Find** in the Record Macro Name text box, type **F2** in the Shortcut Key text box, and make sure the Ctrl check box is selected. Then select Start. By assigning this shortcut, you will be able to execute this macro by pressing Ctrl-F2. Windows minimizes the Recorder window, and the WordPerfect window appears.

7. Press Alt-F O to display the File Open dialog box.

8. Press Alt-T, then Alt-↓ F to select the Find option.

9. Press Alt-F to display the Find Files dialog box, shown in Figure 15.12.

10. Press Ctrl-Break to display the options Save Macro, Resume Recording, and Cancel Recording. Select Save Macro, then OK.

11. Select Cancel three times to return to the document window.

12. Press Alt-Tab to switch back to the Recorder. The Find macro is listed in the window.

13. Select File ➤ Save, type **WP**, and then press ↵ to save the macro file so it can be recalled later.

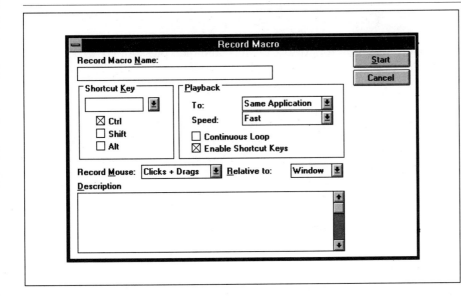

FIGURE 15.11:

Record Macro dialog box in the Windows Recorder

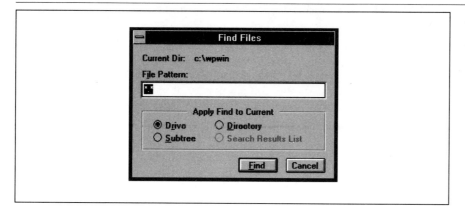

CREATING A WINDOWS MACRO FOR ADVANCED SEARCH FUNCTIONS

For more advanced file-finding operations, which include search parameter specifications, use the WordPerfect File Manager. Now create another Windows macro for complex file searches:

1. The Recorder window should still be open. Select Macro ➤ Record, type **Advanced File Search** as the macro name and **F2** as the shortcut key. Then select the Shift check box. This macro will be executed by pressing Ctrl-Shift-F2.

2. Select Start to return to WordPerfect, and then press Alt-F F to start the File Manager.

3. Press Alt-S A to initiate an advanced file search, and then press Ctrl-Break.

4. Select Save Macro, then OK.

5. Press Alt-F4 twice to return to WordPerfect, press Alt-Tab to switch back to the Recorder, and then select File ➤ Save.

6. Press Alt-Tab to switch back to WordPerfect.

RUNNING WINDOWS MACROS

As long as the Recorder application is open and the WordPerfect macro file is loaded, you can find files in WordPerfect by pressing Ctrl-F2 or Ctrl-Shift-F2. Each time you start Windows, however, you must load the macro file.

To load the macro file, run the Recorder accessory and select File ➤ Open. Select WP.REC from the list box that appears. You can minimize the Recorder or just switch to WordPerfect.

Because you assigned shortcut keys to your Windows macros, you can quickly execute them from within WordPerfect. Follow these steps to test the macros for finding files:

1. In WordPerfect, press Ctrl-F2 to find a file. When you want to locate a file, enter its name, and then press ↵. You can use the wildcards * and ? to locate groups of files.

2. Select Cancel twice to return to WordPerfect.

3. Press Ctrl-Shift-F2 to start File Manager and initiate an advanced file search. The options in the dialog box let you customize the search parameters, including selecting files based on their creation dates.

4. Press Alt-F4 twice to return to WordPerfect.

Use Windows macros to perform other operations that cannot be recorded or written in WordPerfect macros. For example, create a macro that switches to the Macro Facility and selects Macro Compile, or a macro that minimizes WordPerfect and runs another application such as Paintbrush.

APPENDIX A

WordPerfect for Lawyers

aw offices use a large number of forms, such as wills, pleadings, leases, and contracts. Because the forms include standard headings, layout, and boilerplate text, their production can easily be automated by using macros and merge files.

The level of automation depends on your office procedures. At a minimum, you should create a template for each form. The template should contain the document's initial codes and the standard heading. For additional control, add merge commands that position the insertion point and prompt the user for the desired input.

To include boilerplate paragraphs, use the master document techniques discussed in Chapter 13. Write a macro that lets the user select the paragraphs from disk.

TIME ACCOUNT BILLING

Law firm clients are typically billed for time spent on their case. To keep track of the amount of time spent writing and editing legal documents, create the macros shown in Figures A.1 and A.2.

```
//Start.wcm
Application(WP;WPWP;Default;"WPWPUS.WCD")
Title:="Assemble Document"
Menu(Person;Letter;;; ("Chesin";"Nestle";"Smith";"Cancel"))
If(Person=4) Go(End@)  EndIf
If(Person=1) Dir:="c:\chesin\"
    Else
    If(Person=2) Dir:="c:\nestle\"
    Else
    If(Person=3) Dir:="c:\smith\"
    EndIf
    EndIf
EndIf

FileName:=Dir+"CHARGES"
FileOpen(FileName)

PosDocBottom()
DateFormat("2/1/5  7:9")
DateText()
Tab()
FileNew()

Label(End@)
```

FIGURE A.1:

Macro for recording starting time of task

```
//End.wcm
Application(WP;WPWP;Default;"WPWPUS.WCD")
Title:="Ending Time"
DocNext()
DateFormat("2/1/5  7:9")
DateText()
GetString(Purpose;Length=20;"Enter the purpose";Title)
Type("  ")
Type(Purpose)
HardReturn()
FileSave()
Close()
```

FIGURE A.2:

Macro for recording ending time of task

The macro in Figure A.1, named Start.wcm, opens a document called Charges and inserts the date and time (in 24-hour format). It then opens a new window where you can write a document or retrieve and edit an existing one. The macro assumes that a file called Charges exists in each of the directories.

When you have completed your work, run the End.wcm macro shown in Figure A.2. This macro switches back to the Charges document window, inserts the current date and time, and then saves the file.

This time-keeping system works only if just two windows—Charges and the document you are working on—are open. Otherwise, the DocNext( ) command might switch to, insert the date into, and save the wrong document.

If you have a number of windows open, delete the command DocNext( ) from the End.wcm macro. When you are done working on a document, switch back to the Charges document before running End.wcm.

DESIGNING A DOCUMENT-ASSEMBLY AND TIME-ACCOUNTING SYSTEM

By modifying the Start.wcm and End.wcm macros, you can completely automate a document-assembly and time-accounting system. As an example, we will design a procedure for creating a common type of legal document. The process will also record the starting and ending times of the document assembly, and use the Savefile macro you wrote in Chapter 14 to add the document to the index.

CREATING THE MERGE TEMPLATE

The merge file shown in Figure A.3 is a template for completing notices of appeal and similar documents. The merge file begins by designating a chain to the macro Mend.wcm, which is a modified version of End.wcm. The merge file then inputs values for the attorney's name, identification number, two lines for the client's name, and a heading that specifies the type of document being assembled.

The heading will be recorded with the billing file using a MergeVariable-Get command in the Mend.wcm macro. If it were left blank during the merge, the macro would halt and report an error. So if you do not enter a heading, the {IF BLANK} command assigns a default value.

The top section of the document is filled in by {TEXT} commands and the contents of merge variables. Then {INPUT} commands are used to record the plaintiff, court division, term and year of the session, and docket number.

The title of the document is displayed as the contents of the variable Heading. Note that the entire variable command is underlined and in boldface. This will cause the contents of the variable to appear that way in the assembled document.

The {KEYBOARD} command allows you to enter the body of the notice. When you are finished, press Alt-↵ to continue the merge, which completes the signature block and executes the Mend.wcm macro.

```
{CHAIN MACRO}c:\wpwin\macros\Mend~{COMMENT}
~{TEXT}Attorney~Enter attorney's name~{COMMENT}
~{TEXT}IDNo.~Enter ID number~{COMMENT}
~{TEXT}Client~Enter client line 1~{COMMENT}
~{TEXT}Client2~Enter client line 2~{COMMENT}
~{TEXT}Heading~Enter type of notice~{COMMENT}
~{IF BLANK}Heading~{ASSIGN}Heading~NOTICE~{END IF}

HALOID, SENNA & COMEDO
By: {VARIABLE}Attorney~          Attorneys for Defendant
Identification No. {VARIABLE}IDNo.~      {VARIABLE}Client~
43 Cresol Avenue                         {VARIABLE}Client2~
Philadelphia, PA 19101
(215) 555-1297
```

{INPUT}Enter Plaintiff~	:	COURT OF COMMON PLEAS
	:	{INPUT}Enter the division~
VS	:	PHILADELPHIA COUNTY
	:	
{VARIABLE}Client~	:	{INPUT}Enter Term and Year~
{VARIABLE}Client2~	:	{INPUT}Enter Number~

{VARIABLE}Heading~

```
{KEYBOARD}




HALOID, SENNA & COMEDO


By:_____
      {VARIABLE}Attorney~

Attorneys for Defendant
{VARIABLE}Client~
{VARIABLE}Client2~
```

FIGURE A.3:

Merge file for automating legal notices

STARTING THE MERGE

Edit the Start.wcm macro to create the macro that begins the merge process. Add the command

MergeExecute("Notice.mrg")

on the line under the FileNew( ) command, then save the macro with the name **Mstart.wcm** in the MACROS subdirectory. This macro will insert the starting time in the Charges file, open a new document, and begin the merge.

COMPLETING THE DOCUMENT ASSEMBLY

When you have completed the notice, you need to add the ending time to the Charges file, then save the assembled document in the proper directory. Edit End.wcm so it appears as shown in Figure A.4, and then save it under the name **Mend.wcm** in the MACROS subdirectory. Finally, compile it in the Macro Facility.

```
//Mend.wcm
Application(WP;WPWP;Default;"WPWPUS.WCD")
Title:="Assemble Document"
DocNext()
DateFormat("2/1/5  7:9")
DateText()
MergeVariableGet(RE;"Heading")
Type("   ")
Type(RE)
HardReturn()
FileSave()
Close()
Run("c:\wpwin\macros\savefile")
```

FIGURE A.4:

Macro for inserting ending time of merge operation and document heading

Like End.wcm, this macro returns to the Charges document and inserts the ending time. However, instead of requesting the purpose of the document, it inserts the contents of the variable Heading. The macro then runs Savefile.wcm, which numbers and saves the assembled document, and updates the index file.

RUNNING THE APPLICATION

When you want to complete a notice, run the Mstart.wcm macro. It will insert the starting time in the Charges file and start the merge.

The merge file will display a series of five dialog boxes requesting information. Enter the data requested and press ↵ after each entry. Two lines are allowed for the client's name. This is to accommodate long names that might not fit in one line of the heading.

The remaining dialog boxes that appear are generated by {INPUT} commands. Enter the data requested and press Alt-↵ after each entry. The merge file will pause when it reaches the {KEYBOARD} command. Type the text of the notice, and then press Alt-↵.

The Mend.wcm macro adds the ending time and saves the Charges file, and then executes Savefile.wcm.

When the process is complete, the Docnum file, the index file, and the Charges file will be updated. The assembled document will be stored in the appropriate directory.

DEVELOPING YOUR OWN LEGAL APPLICATIONS

By using similar techniques, you can automate many tasks that involve routine and repetitive typing. Identify documents that can be automated, and then create templates and merge files for each.

Use macros like Start and End, and Mstart and Mend, to execute the merge and save the completed document. For an even more efficient system, try combining sections of the Savefile macro into the Mend macro, so that the Charges file also contains the path and name of the assembled document for cross reference.

In developing your own systems, don't limit yourself to document assembly. Consider other tedious typing chores that could be made easier. For example, the macro shown in Figure A.5 automates entering dates in the

```
//Date conversion
Application(WP;WPWP;Default;"WPWPUS.WCD")
Title:="Date"
GetString(Day;Length=2;"Enter day";Title)
GetString(Mnth;Length=2;"Enter month";Title)
GetString(Year;Length=4;"Enter year";Title)
TH:="th"
If(Day="1") TH:="st" EndIf
If(Day="21") TH:="st" EndIf
If(Day="31") TH:="st" EndIf

If(Day="2") TH:="nd" EndIf
If(Day="22") TH:="nd" EndIf

If(Mnth="1") Month:="January" EndIf
If(Mnth="2") Month:="February" EndIf
If(Mnth="3") Month:="March" EndIf
If(Mnth="4") Month:="April" EndIf
If(Mnth="5") Month:="May" EndIf
If(Mnth="6") Month:="June" EndIf
If(Mnth="7") Month:="July" EndIf
If(Mnth="8") Month:="August" EndIf
If(Mnth="9") Month:="September" EndIf
If(Mnth="10") Month:="October" EndIf
If(Mnth="11") Month:="November" EndIf
If(Mnth="12") Month:="December" EndIf
Date:=Day+TH+" day of "+Month+", "+Year
Type(Date)
```

FIGURE A.5:

Macro for inserting formatted date

format

27th day of March, 1993

After the macro inputs the day, month, and year, it determines the ending that must follow the day: *st* for the 1st, 21st, and 31st; *nd* for the 2nd and 22nd; and *th* for all others. The macro then determines the month and formats and prints the entire date. It is not a complicated macro, but it helps perform an everyday task.

APPENDIX B

Academic WordPerfect

ost academic institutions have specific layout requirements and strict rules for formatting footnotes, endnotes, bibliographies, outlines, and other document elements. Because you need to adhere to these formatting requirements consistently, macros and merge files can be of invaluable help in creating academic documents.

CREATING THE ACADEMIC TEMPLATE

Designing a complete template for academic documents can involve four areas:

◆ Page layout requirements specify the margins, page numbers, headers and footers, and chapter and section divisions.

◆ Text layout requirements specify the text font and size, justification, line spacing, spacing between paragraphs, and special formats for quotations and other specific elements.

◆ Heading requirements specify the size and format of headings and subheadings.

◆ Reference requirements specify the format and placement of footnotes, endnotes, bibliographic entries, tables, and figures.

Using the methods described in Chapter 2, create a template and styles for each layout element. Set the document initial codes for all the page and text layout requirements for standard text. Then create a series of styles.

Start with styles for page layouts that differ from the regular text pages. For example, some formats require that every chapter start on its own page with a special margin and chapter heading. Start the style with a page break, margin setting, and the word *Chapter* properly formatted. To start a new chapter, apply the style and then type the chapter number or title.

Next, create styles for special paragraph formats, such as for long quotations or in-text references. Some layouts, for instance, use single-spacing and extra-wide margins for long quotations.

Create a style for each heading level, including the font, size, character formatting, and spacing between the heading and the text.

In the document initial codes, set the footnote options to match the required style. Select Layout ➤ Footnote ➤ Options to display the Footnote Options dialog box. Then set the numbering method, the style for the text and notation reference number, the spacing within and between notes, a continuation message, a minimum note height, the position of the notes, and the format of the separator, if any, between the notes and the text. Select Layout ➤ Endnote ➤ Options and set the format for the endnotes.

Save the completed template, and then type a list of the style names for your reference.

WRITING A FOOTNOTE MACRO

Even with the footnote options set in the template, you still must format the text of your footnotes. Most colleges and universities provide or sell a stylebook that shows the required format. Many stylebooks show different formats for referencing books, articles, compilations, works of a series, newspapers, and other sources. In addition, each style may vary with the number of authors or other specifics about the reference.

A macro that handles all the possibilities would be rather long and complex. One alternative is to create a series of macros, one for each type of reference.

Figure B.1 shows an example of a macro that formats a standard footnote, referencing pages from a book. When you are ready to enter a footnote in the text, select Layout ➤ Footnote ➤ Create, and then run the macro.

```
Application(WP;WPWP;Default;"WPWPUS.WCD")
Title:="Footnote"
Author:=""
Work:=""
Place:=""
Pub:=""
Date:=""
Label(Author@)

GetString(Author;Length=20;"Enter primary author";Title)
If(Author="") Go(Author@) EndIf
Type(Author)
GetNumber(More;"How many additional authors?";Title)
If(More>2)
     Type (",")
     FontItalic(On!)
     Type(" et al, ")
     FontItalic(Off!)
EndIf
If(More=1)
     GetString(Author;Length=20;"Enter second
               author";Title)
     Type(" and ")
     Type(Author)
     Type(", ")
EndIf
If(More=2)
     GetString(Author;Length=20;"Enter second
               author";Title)
     Type(", ")
     Type(Author)
     Type(", and ")
     GetString(Author;Length=20;"Enter third author";Title)
     Type(Author)
     Type(", ")
EndIf
If(More=0)
     Type(", ")
EndIf

Label(Work@)
GetString(Work;Length=20;"Enter title";Title)
If(Work="") Go(Work@) EndIf
FontUnderline(On!)
Type(Work)
FontUnderline(Off!)

Label(Place@)
GetString(Place;Length=20;"Place of Publication";Title)
If(Place="") Go(Place@) EndIf
Type(" (")
Type(Place)
Type(": ")

Label(Pub@)
GetString(Pub;Length=20;"Enter publisher";Title)
If(Pub="") Go(Pub@) EndIf
Type(Pub)
Type(", ")
```

FIGURE B.1:

Macro for creating footnotes

```
Label(Date@)
GetString(Date;Length=4;"Enter year of publication";Title)
If(Date="") Go(Date@) EndIf
Type(Date)
Type(") ")

GetString(PP;Length=1;"Did you reference more than one
          page?";Title)
If(PP="y") PP:="Y"  EndIf
If(PP<>"Y")
     GetString(Page;Length=3;"Enter page number";Title)
     Type("p. ")
     Type(Page)
     Type(".")
     Else
     GetString(Start;Length=3;"Enter starting page
              number";Title)
     GetString(End;Length=3;"Enter ending page
              number";Title)
     Type("pp. ")
     Type(Start)
     Type("-")
     Type(End)
     Type(".")
EndIf
```

FIGURE B.1:

*Macro for creating
footnotes (continued)*

OUTLINING WITH WORDPERFECT

Creating an outline is often a required part of producing academic documents. WordPerfect for Windows simplifies the process with its automatic outlining feature.

With automatic outlining, WordPerfect inserts the level numbers and formats the entries for you. In addition, topics and their associated subtopics are treated as a unit, called a *family.* You can move or copy a family to other locations in the outline, and WordPerfect will automatically adjust the numbers in the entire outline.

The default outline format uses the traditional levels of I., A., 1., a., (1), and (a). To create an outline in this style, select Tools ➤ Outline ➤ Outline On, then press ↵ to enter the first outline number. Each time you press ↵, WordPerfect will insert the next number for that level in sequence: II, III. IV. and so on.

To insert the next level of the outline, press Tab after pressing ↵. Each time you press Tab, the number for the next lower level will appear. Press Shift-Tab to insert the next highest level. If you insert or delete entries within an outline, WordPerfect will automatically adjust the numbers following the insertion point. To stop outlining, select Tools ➤ Outline ➤ Outline Off.

An outline family includes the outline entry in which the insertion point is placed and all subordinate, or lower, levels. For example, if you place the insertion point in level 1, the family will include all outline entries up to the next equal or higher level, whichever occurs first. You can manipulate an entire family without selecting all its entries.

To delete a family, place the insertion point within the highest level of the family and select Tools ➤ Outline ➤ Delete Family, then Yes.

To move or copy a family, place the insertion point within it and select Tools ➤ Outline ➤ Move Family or Copy Family. Place the insertion point where you want the family to appear, and then press ↵.

You can change the outline-numbering system by selecting Tools ➤ Outline ➤ Define (Alt-Shift-F5). This displays the dialog box shown in Figure B.2. You can select from the four predefined formats—Paragraph, Outline, Legal, and Bullets—or create your own. When you select a format, the levels and their assignments will appear in the large list box.

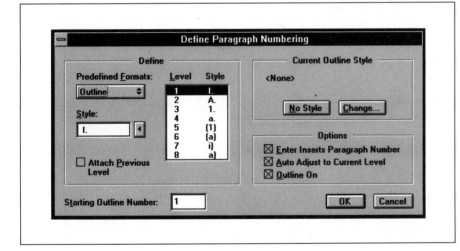

FIGURE B.2:

Define Paragraph Numbering dialog box

To create your own style, select User Defined in the Predefined Format list box, select a level in the list box, and then pull down the Style list box. The options are digits (numbers), uppercase and lowercase letters, uppercase and lowercase roman numerals, and uppercase and lowercase roman digits. To insert a bullet or another special character, select the Style text box, and then press Ctrl-W to display the WordPerfect Characters dialog box. Select the character desired, and then select Insert.

The Define Paragraph Numbering dialog box also includes the following options:

◆ **Attach Previous Level:** Use this option to combine level numbers, such as I.A.1 and I.A.2.

◆ **Enter Inserts Paragraph Number:** Turn off this option if you do not want a new level number to appear when you press ↵. With this featured turned off, you insert a level number by using the Tools ➤ Outline ➤ Paragraph Number command.

◆ **Auto Adjust to Current Level:** If you turn off this option, when you press ↵, WordPerfect enters the next consecutive number but at the same level as the last entry. For example, if you just entered an entry at level 1, the number 2 will appear when you press ↵. To move back to the next highest level, press Shift-Tab.

◆ **Outline On:** When this option is selected (the default), the outlining function is turned on when you exit the dialog box.

◆ **Starting Outline Number:** Enter the starting number that you want to use for the next outline entry. The number will also indicate the level. Use this option if you are creating an outline in sections.

USING OUTLINE STYLES

In WordPerfect 5.1 for DOS, outline styles are created and selected just like other styles. In WordPerfect for Windows, you access outline styles through the Define Paragraph Numbering dialog box.

An outline style combines an outline definition and a style, similar to the styles described in Chapter 2. By defining an outline style, you can set the level numbers as well as the character formats, indentations, and spacing of each level. You can also enter text that you want to appear at each instance of that level.

Select Tools ➤ Outline ➤ Define (Alt-Shift-F5) ➤ Change to display the Outline Styles dialog box. This box, which is identical to the Styles dialog box, lists three predefined outline styles: Document, Right Par, and Technical. Select Create to display the dialog box shown in Figure B.3.

Enter a style name in the Name text box and, optionally, a description in the Description text box. As with other styles, you can select either an open or paired style type. If you select a paired type, you must select the action of the ↵ key.

Next, define the formatting codes for each level you want to use in the outline style. Select the level in the Level list box, then Edit. The Style Editor

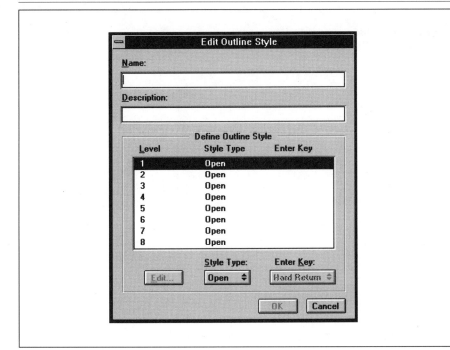

*Edit Outline Style
dialog box*

window will appear, with the Editing pane above and the Reveal Codes pane below. Enter the format codes and text that you want to appear at that level, and then select Close. Define each of the outline levels, then select OK to return to the Outline Styles dialog box. Save the stylesheet, then choose Select to return to the Define Paragraph Numbering dialog box.

DESIGNING TESTS

By combining outlines with merge commands, you can create multiple-choice and true-or-false tests, complete with answer keys. For example, the secondary file shown in Figure B.4 includes a record for each test question. Note that the fields include the question, four choices, and the answer.

The primary file for printing the test is shown in Figure B.5. To enter the paragraph number, follow these steps:

1. Select Layout ➤ Document ➤ Initial Codes.

2. Select Tools ➤ Outline ➤ Define (Alt-Shift-F5).

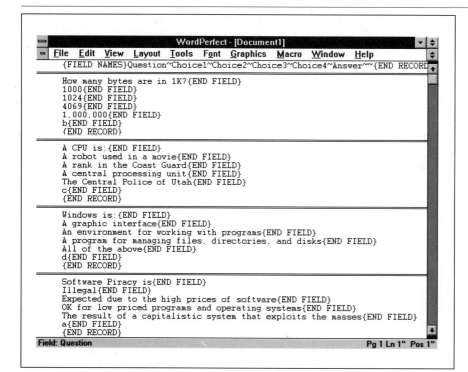

Secondary file for creating tests

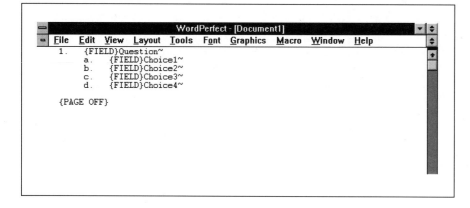

Primary file for merging tests

3. Pull down the Predefined Format list box and select Paragraph. Select OK, then Close to return to the document window.

4. Press ⏎ to insert the first number, and then enter the remainder of the primary merge file.

When you merge the files, the questions will be numbered consecutively.

To create an answer key, use a primary file with these two lines:

```
1. {FIELD}answer~
{PAGE OFF}
```

Insert the number as initial codes using the outline feature, as described for the test merge file.

If you want to vary the test from class to class, sort the secondary file on some randomly selected character in one of the fields, then generate a new test and answer key.

APPENDIX C

Using the WordPerfect for Windows Interim Release

The new release of WordPerfect builds on the powerful features found in the original version. For example, this release lets you move and copy text from one location to another using the *drag-and-drop* method. To move text, select it, point to it with the mouse, and then drag the pointer to the new location. To copy text, hold down the Ctrl key while using the drag-and-drop method. The new release also supports more fully the TrueType fonts available in Windows 3.1.

This appendix outlines the additional features and changes that relate to the tips and tricks discussed in the book.

CONTROLLING THE SCREEN DISPLAY

The ruler now contains a Zoom button (100%), which changes the magnification of the displayed image. (It affects only how the document appears on the screen; it does not affect the printed document.) Select the Zoom button, and then choose the magnification from the drop-down menu: 50%, 75%, 100% (the default), 150%, 200%, or Page Width. The Page Width option displays the full width of the text on screen.

The Display Settings dialog box also includes a Zoom button, which lets you set the displayed magnification from 50% to 400%. Another option added to this dialog box allows you to change the size of the Reveal Codes window from 1% to 99% of the workspace.

USING DEFAULT STYLES

Three additional default styles are available in the Styles dialog box:

◆ Heading 1

◆ Heading 2

◆ Bullet List

USING THE ENVELOPE MACRO

The Envelope macro is entirely different from the one available in the initial release of WordPerfect for Windows. When you run the new version of the Envelope macro, it looks for the inside address of the document and displays the dialog box shown in Figure C.1.

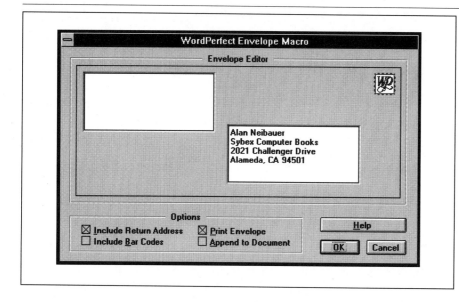

FIGURE C.1:

Envelope Editor dialog box

The macro assumes that the address is in a series of lines ending with carriage returns, at the beginning of the document. It also assumes that the date is on a single line, with a blank line above and below, at the beginning of the document. If there is an address in the document but it is not at the beginning, select it before running the macro.

SELECTING ENVELOPE OPTIONS

The Envelope Editor dialog box also includes the following options:

◆ **Include Return Address:** To include your return address, enter it in the text box in the upper-left corner and make sure the Include Return Address check box is selected. WordPerfect will retain the inside address.

◆ **Include Bar Codes:** If you select this option, the macro will create and print a bar code above the address. The bar code will be based on the zip code in the address.

◆ **Print Envelope:** Select this option to have the envelope print after you select OK in the dialog box.

◆ **Append to Document:** Select this option to add the envelope in its own page at the end of the document.

After you select options from the Envelope Editor dialog box and select OK, the envelope will be formatted according to the Envelope form size. If the form does not exist in your printer definition, a series of dialog boxes will lead you through the process of creating and adding the form. The procedure is similar to the one described in Chapter 3, but the dialog boxes differ slightly.

EDITING THE ENVELOPE MACRO

The section of the Envelope macro described in Chapter 8 has been changed. The size of the envelope is controlled by the Envelope form in the printer definition. The margins are defined in the section of the macro called Label (PlaceIt@), which contains these instructions:

```
If(CheckBox1=1)
    PageMargins
    (
    Top:0.5";
    Bottom:0.5";
    Left:0.5";
```

```
    Right:0.5"
    )
    Type(ReturnAddress)
Endif
Advance(Where:ToLine!;Amount:2.0")
PageMargins
(
Left:4.5";
Right:0.5"
)
```

If necessary, change the margins for the return address and mailing address, and then save the edited macro.

PERFORMING MATH IN TABLES

Five mathematical functions are available for performing spreadsheetlike operations on values within a table:

Ave(*range*)	Calculates the average of the values in the cells in the range.
Product(*range*)	Multiplies the values of the cells in the range.
Subtract(*range*)	Subtracts the cells in the range—the second value from the first, the third from that result, and so on.
Sum(*range*)	Adds the values of the cells in the range.
Quotient(*range*)	Divides the values of the cells in the range. It divides the value of the first cell by the second, then the result by the third cell's value, and so on.

The functions perform calculations on a range of table cells. The *range* can be specified as a block, as in A1:A4, or as a group of nonadjacent cells, such as A1, B5, C6.

USING BUTTON BARS

An additional Button Bar, called Features.wwb, is provided. It contains buttons for selecting Zoom settings, inserting bullets into the document, running the envelope macro, and displaying macro help information.

WRITING MACROS

The interim release provides more help on creating macros. To see macro Help information, click on the HlpMacros button in the Features.wwb Button Bar. Read the MACRO.DOC file for more information about writing macros. The interim release also includes a feature for inserting macro commands and new macro commands for creating custom dialog boxes.

INSERTING MACRO COMMANDS

The Macro Command Inserter is a new feature of the program. To insert a macro command, press Ctrl-M to display the dialog box shown in Figure C.2.

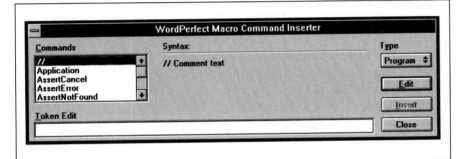

FIGURE C.2:

Macro Command Inserter dialog box

In the Type box, select the type of command you want to insert: a Programming command (Program) or a Product command (WP). Then select the command in the Commands list box. If you select a Product command that includes parameters, the parameters will appear in the Parameters list box. Select the parameter you want to set. If the parameter has optional items, they will appear in the Member list box, and you can select a value from the list. In the Token Edit text box, you can edit the macro command. When you are ready to insert the command, select Insert.

CREATING DIALOG BOXES

You can now create your own custom dialog boxes, complete with radio buttons, check boxes, list boxes, and hot spots. For example, the following macro displays a simple dialog box, with OK and Cancel buttons:

```
Application(WP;WPWP;Default)
DialogDefine(100;50;50;200;100;1+2;"My Own Dialog Box")
```

DialogDisplay(100;1)
DialogDestroy(100)

Selecting an option in the dialog box returns a value to the variable Macro-DialogResult. In the example above, if you select OK, the variable will contain 1; selecting Cancel will return the value 2.

The following commands are used for adding dialog boxes:

DialogAddCheckBox

DialogAddColorWheel

DialogAddComboBox

DialogAddCounter

DialogAddEditBox

DialogAddFilenameBox

DialogAddFrame

DialogAddGroupBox

DialogAddHLine

DialogAddVLine

DialogAddHotSpot

DialogAddIcon

DialogAddListBox

DialogAddListItem

DialogAddPopUpButton

DialogAddPushButton

DialogAddRadioButton

DialogAddScrollBar

DialogAddText

DialogAddViewer

These commands are described in the MACRO.DOC file in the WPWIN directory.

SORTING DATABASE RECORDS

In a WordPerfect for Windows database, the sort order is now case sensitive, with lowercase characters before uppercase.

The Sort dialog box now includes an Add Key button, which you choose to place a new key at the bottom of the list. When you are using the Add Key button, enter your keys in the order you want them to be used, not in reverse order (as is necessary when using the Insert Key button).

INDEX

FREE BROCHURE!

Complete this form today, and we'll send you a full-color brochure of Sybex bestsellers.

Please supply the name of the Sybex book purchased.

_____

How would you rate it?

_____ Excellent   _____ Very Good   _____ Average   _____ Poor

Why did you select this particular book?

_____ Recommended to me by a friend

_____ Recommended to me by store personnel

_____ Saw an advertisement in _____

_____ Author's reputation

_____ Saw in Sybex catalog

_____ Required textbook

_____ Sybex reputation

_____ Read book review in _____

_____ In-store display

_____ Other _____

Where did you buy it?

_____ Bookstore

_____ Computer Store or Software Store

_____ Catalog (name: _____)

_____ Direct from Sybex

_____ Other: _____

Did you buy this book with your personal funds?

_____ Yes   _____ No

About how many computer books do you buy each year?

_____ 1-3   _____ 3-5   _____ 5-7   _____ 7-9   _____ 10+

About how many Sybex books do you own?

_____ 1-3   _____ 3-5   _____ 5-7   _____ 7-9   _____ 10+

Please indicate your level of experience with the software covered in this book:

_____ Beginner   _____ Intermediate   _____ Advanced

Which types of software packages do you use regularly?

_____ Accounting	_____ Databases	_____ Networks
_____ Amiga	_____ Desktop Publishing	_____ Operating Systems
_____ Apple/Mac	_____ File Utilities	_____ Spreadsheets
_____ CAD	_____ Money Management	_____ Word Processing
_____ Communications	_____ Languages	_____ Other _____

(please specify)

Which of the following best describes your job title?

_____ Administrative/Secretarial   _____ President/CEO

_____ Director   _____ Manager/Supervisor

_____ Engineer/Technician   _____ Other _____
(please specify)

Comments on the weaknesses/strengths of this book: _____

_____

_____

_____

_____

Name _____

Street _____

City/State/Zip _____

Phone _____

PLEASE FOLD, SEAL, AND MAIL TO SYBEX

SYBEX, INC.
Department M
2021 CHALLENGER DR.
ALAMEDA, CALIFORNIA USA
94501

SYBEX

SEAL

WORDPERFECT FOR WINDOWS
MENUS AND SUBMENUS

TOOLS MENU

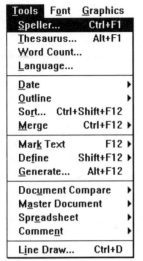

Tools menu:
Tools	Font	Graphics
Speller...		Ctrl+F1
Thesaurus...		Alt+F1
Word Count...		
Language...		
Date		▶
Outline		▶
Sort...	Ctrl+Shift+F12	
Merge	Ctrl+F12	▶
Mark Text		F12 ▶
Define	Shift+F12	▶
Generate...		Alt+F12
Document Compare		▶
Master Document		▶
Spreadsheet		▶
Comment		▶
Line Draw...		Ctrl+D

Date submenu

Text	Ctrl+F5
Code	Ctrl+Shift+F5
Format...	

Outline submenu

Outline On	
Outline Off	
Move Family	
Copy Family	
Delete Family	
Paragraph Number...	Alt+F5
Define...	Alt+Shift+F5

Merge submenu

End Field	Alt+Enter
End Record	Alt+Shift+Enter
Field...	
Input...	
Page Off	
Next Record	
Merge Codes...	
Convert...	
Merge...	

Mark Text submenu

Index...
List...
Table of Contents...
Cross-Reference...
ToA Short Form...
ToA Full Form...
ToA Edit Full Form...

Define submenu

Index...
List...
Table of Contents...
Table of Authorities...

Document Compare submenu

Add Markings...
Remove Markings...

Master Document submenu

Subdocument...
Expand Master
Condense Master...

Comment submenu

Create...
Edit...
Convert to Text

Spreadsheet submenu

Import...
Create Link...
Edit Link...
Update All Links...
Link Options...

FONT MENU

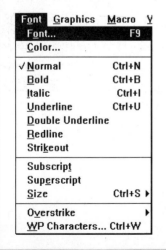

Font menu:
Font	Graphics	Macro	V
Font...			F9
Color...			
√ Normal			Ctrl+N
Bold			Ctrl+B
Italic			Ctrl+I
Underline			Ctrl+U
Double Underline			
Redline			
Strikeout			
Subscript			
Superscript			
Size			Ctrl+S ▶
Overstrike			▶
WP Characters...			Ctrl+W

Size submenu

Fine
Small
Large
Very Large
Extra Large

Overstrike submenu

Create...
Edit...